# DAILY THOUGHTS
# FOR DISCIPLES

# DAILY THOUGHTS
# FOR DISCIPLES

from
OSWALD CHAMBERS

ZONDERVAN
PUBLISHING HOUSE OF THE ZONDERVAN CORPORATION
GRAND RAPIDS, MICHIGAN 49506

Daily Thoughts for Disciples
Copyright © Oswald Chambers Publications Association 1976

Published by The Zondervan Corporation by special arrangement.

Second Zondervan edition  1977

**Library of Congress Cataloging in Publication Data**

Chambers, Oswald, 1874-1917.
  Daily thoughts for disciples.

  1.  Devotional calendars.    I.   Title.
BV4811.C45   1976        242'.2        76-41387
ISBN 0-551-05543-X

*Printed in the United States of America*

# FOREWORD

Some years ago, before Oswald Chambers' widow went to be with her Lord, I remember her remarking to me that the Oswald Chambers books were confined in their appeal to those who take their relationship to God seriously. Also, the books seemed to come into their own in times of crisis, individual as well as national and international.

It is therefore relevant that this new book of daily readings should appear now. At a time when things are being shaken, when men's hearts are failing them for fear, Christians need to know what 'staying power' means. As our eyes are upon Jesus, the Cause and Completer of our faith, we can remain steady and unmoved.

Oswald Chambers read Dr James Denney's *Jesus and the Gospel* a great deal and among many passages heavily underlined, was: 'The English equivalent of the words in Matthew 10:38 is that no one is worthy of Jesus who does not follow Him, as it were, with the rope round his neck—ready to die the most ignominious death rather than prove untrue.'

Oswald Chambers was a true disciple of Christ. He was passionately in love with and linked with the Person of our Lord. He depended upon his Lord for everything and absolutely. To him the Word of God was inviolably authoritative and his faith was without reserve in Him Who is the Lord.

As of Abel, so it may be said of Oswald Chambers, that '... he died, but by his faith he is speaking to us still' (Hebrews 11:4).

ERIC PEARSON
Oswald Chambers Publications Association

The letters at the end of each extract refer to titles of works by Oswald Chambers from which the extracts have been taken. Figures indicate page numbers. A list of full titles appears on page 243.

# DAILY THOUGHTS
# FOR DISCIPLES

## January 1

*And when they came down from the mountain...* Mark 9:9

We are not built for mountains and dawns and artistic affinities; they are for moments of inspiration, that is all. We are built for the valley, for the ordinary stuff of life, and this is where we have to prove our mettle. A false Christianity takes us up on the mount and we want to stay there. But what about the devil-possessed world? Oh, let it go to hell! We are having a great time up here.

The intellectualist or dreamer who by his dreams or isolation is not made fitter to deal with actual life, proves that his dreams are mere hysterical drivel. If his dreams only succeed in making him hold aloof from his fellow-men, a visionary who deals only with things belonging to the mountain-top, he is self-indulgent to a degree. No man has any right to be a spectator of his fellow-men; he ceases to be in touch with reality.

It is a great thing to be on the mount with God, and the mountains are meant for inspiration and meditation; but a man is taken there only in order that he may go down afterwards among the devil-possessed and lift them up...

If we cannot live in the demon-possessed valley, with the hold of God on us, lifting up those who are down by the power of the thing that is in us, our Christianity is only an abstraction.

SA 88, 91

## January 2

*When thou vowest a vow unto God, defer not to pay it: for he hath no pleasure in fools: pay that which thou vowest.* Ecclesiastes 5:4

At New Year time we hear much of vowing. Solomon's advice is 'Don't vow: because if you make a vow, even in ordinary matters, and do not fulfil it, you are the worse for it.' To make a promise may simply be a way of shirking responsibility. Never pile up promises before men, and certainly not before God. It is better to run the risk of being considered indecisive, better to be uncertain and not promise, than to promise and not fulfil. 'Better is it that thou shouldest not vow, than that thou shouldest vow and not pay.' Ecclesiastes 5:5

Modern ethical teaching bases everything on the power of the will, but we need to recognize also the perils of the will. The man who has achieved a moral victory by the sheer force of his will is less likely to

7

want to become a Christian than the man who has come to the moral frontier of his own need. It is the obstinate man who makes vows, and by the very fulfilment of his vow he may increase his inability to see things from Jesus Christ's standpoint. When a man is stirred, either by joy or sorrow, or by the seasons of the year, he is apt to make vows which are beyond the possibility of human power to keep.

Jesus Christ bases the entrance to His Kingdom not on a man's vowing and making decisions, but on the realization of his inability to decide. Decisions for Christ fail because the bedrock of Christianity is ignored. It is not our vows before God that tell, but coming to God exactly as we are, in all our weakness, and being held and kept by Him. Make no vows at this New Year time, but look to God and bank on the Reality of Jesus Christ.

GW 132

### January 3

_I was not disobedient to the heavenly vision._ Acts 26:19

Life is not as idle ore,
But iron dug from central gloom,
. . . . . . . . . . . . . . .
And batter'd by the shocks of doom
To shape and use.

Thank God for the sight of all you have never yet been. The vision is not an ecstasy or a dream, but a perfect understanding of what God wants, it is the Divine light making manifest the calling of God. You may call the vision an emotion or a desire, but it is something that absorbs you. Learn to thank God for making known His demands. You have had the vision, but you are not there yet by any means. You have seen what God wants you to be but what you are not yet. Are you prepared to have this 'iron dug from central gloom' battered into 'shape and use'? 'Battering' conveys the idea of a black-smith putting good metal into right useful shape. The batterings of God come in commonplace days and commonplace ways, God is using the anvil to bring us into the shape of the vision. The length of time it takes God to do it depends upon us. If we prefer to loll on the mount of transfiguration, to live on the memory of the vision, we are of no use to live with the ordinary stuff of which human life is made up. We have not to live always in ecstasy and conscious con-

8

templation of God, but to live in reliance on what we saw in the vision when we are in the midst of actualities. It is when we are going through the valley to prove whether we will be the 'choice' ones, that most of us turn tail; we are not prepared for the blows which must come if we are going to be turned into the shape of the vision.

SSY 26

### January 4

*A new commandment I give unto you, that ye love one another; as I have loved you, that ye also love one another.* John 13:34

There is no subject more intimately interesting to modern people than man's relationship to man; but men get impatient when they are told that the first requirement is that they should love God first and foremost. 'The first of all the commandments is...thou shalt love the Lord thy God with all thy heart, and with all thy soul, and with all thy mind, and with all thy strength: this is the first commandment.' In every crisis in our lives, is God first in our love? in every perplexity of conflicting duties, is He first in our leading? 'And the second is like, namely, this, Thou shalt love thy neighbour as thyself.' Remember the standard, *'as I have loved you'*. I wonder where the best of us are according to that standard? How many of us have turned away over and over again in disgust at men, and when we get alone with the Lord Jesus He speaks no word, but the memory of Him is quite sufficient to bring the rebuke—'as I have loved you'. It takes severe training to think habitually along the lines Jesus Christ has laid down, although we act on them impulsively at times.

How many of us are letting Jesus Christ take us into His school of thinking? The saint who is thoughtful is like a man fasting in the midst of universal intoxication. Men of the world hate a thoughtful saint. They can ridicule a living saint who does not think, but a thinking saint—I mean of course, one who lives rightly as well—is the annoyance, because the thinking saint has formed the Mind of Christ and re-echoes it. Let us from this time forth determine to bring into captivity every thought to the obedience of Christ.

BE 124

9

*Ye be witnesses unto yourselves, that ye are the children of them which killed the prophets.* Matthew 23:31

In the spiritual life we do not go from good to better, and from better to best; because there is only One to Whom we go, and that One is The Best, viz., God Himself. There can be no such thing as God's second best. We can perversely put ourselves out of God's order into His permissive will, but that is a different matter. In seeking the Best we soon find that our enemy is our good things, not our bad. The things that keep us back from God's best are not sin and imperfection, but the things that are right and good and noble from the natural standpoint. To discern that the natural virtues antagonize surrender to God is to bring our soul at once into the centre of our greatest battlefield. Very few of us debate with the sordid and the wrong, but we do debate with the good; and the higher up we go in the scale of the natural virtues, the more intense is the opposition to Jesus Christ, which is in inverse ratio to what one would naturally imagine.

NKW 47

*And he went down with them ... and was subject unto them.* Luke 2:51

An extraordinary exhibition of submissiveness! and 'the disciple is not above his master'. Think of it: thirty years at home with brothers and sisters who did not believe in Him! We fix on the three years which were extraordinary in Our Lord's life and forget altogether the earlier years at home, thirty years of absolute submission. Perhaps something of the same kind is happening to you, and you say – 'I don't know why I should have to submit to this.' Are you any better than Jesus Christ? 'As He is, so are we in this world.' The explanation of it all is our Lord's prayer — 'that they may be one, even as We are one'. If God is putting you through a spell of submission, and you seem to be losing your individuality and everything else, it is because Jesus is making you one with Him.

MU 48

10

*Abraham said, Behold now I have taken it upon me to speak unto the Lord ...* Genesis 18:27

Intercessory prayer is part of the sovereign purpose of God. If there were no saints praying for us, our lives would be infinitely balder than they are, consequently the responsibility of those who never intercede and who are withholding blessing from our lives is truly appalling. The subject of intercessory prayer is weakened by the neglect of the idea with which we ought to start. We take for granted that prayer is preparation for work, whereas prayer is *the* work, and we scarcely believe what the Bible reveals, viz. that through intercessory prayer God creates on the ground of the Redemption; it is His chosen way of working. We lean to our own understanding, or we bank on service and do away with prayer, and consequently by succeeding in the external we fail in the eternal, because in the eternal we succeed only by prevailing prayer ...

Jesus Christ carries on intercession for us in heaven; the Holy Ghost carries on intercession in us on earth; and we the saints have to carry on intercession for all men.

DPR 59, 60

*Ye shall ask what ye will.* John 15:7

A great many people do not pray because they do not feel any sense of need. The sign that the Holy Ghost is in us is that we realize, not that we are full, but that we are empty, there is a sense of absolute need. We come across people who try us, circumstances that are difficult, conditions that are perplexing, and all these things awaken a dumb sense of need, which is a sign that the Holy Ghost is there. If we are ever free from the sense of need, it is not because the Holy Ghost has satisfied us, but because we have been satisfied with as much as we have. 'A man's reach should exceed his grasp.' A sense of need is one of the greatest benedictions because it keeps our life rightly related to Jesus Christ ...

When we learn to pray in the Holy Ghost, we find there are some things for which we cannot pray, there is a sense of restraint. Never push and say, 'I know it is God's will and I am going to stick to it.' Beware, remember what is recorded of the children of Israel: 'He gave them their request; but sent leanness into their soul' (Psalm

106:15). Let the Spirit of God teach you what He is driving at and learn not to grieve Him. If we are abiding in Jesus Christ we shall ask what He wants us to ask, whether we are conscious of doing so or not.

IYA 60

... *believeth all things.* 1 Corinthians 13:7

It is a great thing to be a believer, but easy to misunderstand what the New Testament means by it. It is not that we believe Jesus Christ can *do* things, or that we believe in a plan of salvation; it is that we believe *Him*; whatever happens we will hang on to the fact that He is true. If we say, 'I am going to believe He will put things right', we shall lose our confidence when we see things go wrong. We are in danger of putting the cart before the horse and saying a man must believe certain things before he can be a Christian; whereas his beliefs are the result of his being a Christian, not the cause. Our Lord's word 'believe' does not refer to an intellectual act, but to a moral act; with our Lord to believe means to commit. 'Commit yourself to Me', and it takes a man all he is worth to believe in Jesus Christ.

The Great Life is to believe that Jesus Christ is not a fraud. The biggest fear a man has is never fear for himself, but fear that his Hero won't get through; that He won't be able to explain things satisfactorily; for instance, why there should be war and disease. The problems of life get hold of a man and make it difficult for him to know whether in the face of these things he really is confident in Jesus Christ. The attitude of a believer must be, 'Things do look black, but I believe Him; and when the whole thing is told I am confident my belief will be justified and God will be revealed as a God of love and justice.' It does not mean that we won't have problems, but it does mean that our problems will never come in between us and our faith in Him. 'Lord, I don't understand this, but I am certain that there will be an explanation, and in the meantime I put it on one side.' Our faith is in a Person Who is not deceived in anything He says or in the way He looks at things. Christianity is personal, passionate devotion to Jesus Christ as God manifest in the flesh.

AUG 114

**January 10**

*That ye may be blameless and harmless, the sons of God, without rebuke, in the midst of a crooked and perverse generation, among whom ye shine as lights in the world.* Philippians 2:15

Is it possible to be blameless in our social life? The apostle Paul says it is, and if we were asked whether we believed God could make us blameless, we would all say 'Yes'. Well, has He done it? If God has not sanctified us and made us blameless, there is only one reason why He has not—we do not want Him to. 'This is the will of God, even your sanctification.' We have not to urge God to do it, it is His will; is it our will? Sanctification is the work of the supernatural power of God ...

Beware of praising Jesus Christ whilst all the time you cunningly refuse to let the Spirit of God work His salvation efficaciously in your life. Remember, the battle is in the will; whenever we say 'I can't', or whenever we are indifferent, it means 'I won't'. It is better to let Jesus Christ uncover the obstinacy. If there is one point where we say 'I won't' then we shall never know His salvation. From the moment that God uncovers a point of obstinacy in us and we refuse to let Him deal with it, we begin to be sceptical, to sneer and watch for defects in the lives of others. But when once we yield to Him entirely, He makes us blameless in our personal life, in our practical life, and in our profound life. It is not done by piety, it is wrought in us by the sovereign grace of God, and we have not the slightest desire to trust in ourselves in any degree, but in Him alone.

NP 141, 143

**January 11**

*Ye are they which have continued with me in my temptations.* Luke 22:28

We are apt to imagine that our Lord was only tempted once and that then His temptations were over. His temptations went on from the first moment of His conscious life to the last, because His holiness was not the holiness of Almighty God, but the holiness of man, which can only progress by means of the things that go against it (see Hebrews 2:18, 4:15). Are we going with Jesus in His temptations? It is true that He is with us in our temptations, but are we with Him in His? Many of us cease to go with Jesus from the moment we have an experience of what He can do. Like Peter, we have all

13

had moments when Jesus has had to say to us, 'What, could ye not watch with me one hour?'

The temptations of our Lord in the days of His flesh are the kind of temptations He is subjected to in the temple of our body. Watch when God shifts your circumstances and see whether you are going with Jesus or siding with the world, the flesh and the devil. We wear His badge, but are we going with Him? 'Upon this many of his disciples went back and walked no more with him.'

The temptation may be to do some big startling thing in order to prove that we really are the children of God. Satan said to Jesus, 'If thou be the Son of God, cast thyself down from hence,' and to us he says, 'If you are saved and sanctified and true to God, everyone you know should be saved too.' If that were true, Jesus Christ is wrong in His revelation of God. If by our salvation and right relationship to God, we can be the means of turning our world upside down, what has Jesus Christ been doing all these years? The temptation is to claim that God does something that will prove who we are and what He has done for us. It is a temptation of the devil, and can only be detected as a temptation by the Spirit of God.

NP 152

**January 12**

*Likewise the Spirit also helpeth our infirmities.* Romans 8:26

To ask how we are to get our prayers answered is a different point of view from the New Testament. According to the New Testament, prayer is God's answer to our poverty, not a power we exercise to obtain an answer. We have the idea that prayer is only an exercise of our spiritual life. 'Pray without ceasing.' We read that the disciples said to our Lord, 'Lord, teach us to pray.' The disciples were good men and well-versed in Jewish praying, yet when they came in contact with Jesus Christ, instead of realizing they could pray well, they came to the conclusion they did not know how to pray at all, and our Lord instructed them in the initial stages of prayer. Most of us can probably remember a time when we were religious, before we were born again of the Spirit of God, when we could pray fairly well; but after we were born again we became conscious of what Paul mentions here, our utter infirmity—'I do not know how to pray.' We become conscious not only of the power God has given us by His Spirit, but of our own utter infirmity. We

14

hinder our life of devotion when we lose the distinction in thinking between these two. Reliance on the Holy Spirit for prayer is what Paul is bringing out in this verse. It is an unrealized point, we state it glibly enough, but Paul touches the thing we need to remember, he uncovers the truth of our infirmity. The whole source of our strength is receiving, recognizing and relying on the Holy Spirit.

IYA 100

### January 13

*Except ye be converted, and become as little children* ... Matthew 18:3

I have continually to convert the natural life into submission to the Spirit of God in me and not say—I will never do anything natural again; that is fanatical. When by the providence of God my body is brought into new conditions, I have to see that my natural life is converted to the dictates of the Spirit of God in me. Because it has been done once is not proof that it will be done again. 'Except ye be converted, and become as little children ...' is true for all the days of the saintly life, we have continually to turn to God. The attitude of continuous conversion is the only right attitude towards the natural life, and it is the one thing we object to. Either we say the natural is wrong and try to kill it, or else we say that the natural is all there is, and that everything natural and impulsive is right. Neither attitude is right. The hindrance in spiritual life is that we will not be continuously converted, there are 'wedges' of obstinacy where our pride spits at the throne of God and says—'I shan't; I am going to be boss.' We cannot remain boss by the sheer power of will; sooner or later our wills must yield allegiance to some force greater than their own, either God or the devil.

NKW 51

### January 14

*For God giveth to a man that is good in his sight wisdom, and knowledge, and joy: but to the sinner he giveth travail, to gather and to heap up, that he may give to him that is good before God. This also is vanity and vexation of spirit.* Ecclesiastes 2:26

There is a difference between God's order and God's permissive will. We say that God will see us through if we trust Him—'I prayed for my boy, and he was spared in answer to my prayer.' Does that

15

mean that the man who was killed was not prayed for, or that prayers for him were not answered? It is wrong to say that in the one case the man was delivered by prayer but not in the other. It is a misunderstanding of what Jesus Christ reveals. Prayer alters a man on the inside, alters his mind and his attitude to things. The point of praying is not that we get things from God, but that we learn by prayer to detect the difference between God's order and God's permissive will. God's order is—no pain, no sickness, no devil, no war, no sin: His permissive will is all these things. What a man needs to do is to get hold of God's order in the kingdom on the inside, and then he will begin to see how to handle the riddle of the universe on the outside.

The problem of the man who deals with practical things is not the problem of the universe, but the problem within his own breast. When I can see where the beast in me will end and where the wise man in me will end; when I have discovered that the only thing that will last is a personal relationship to God; then it will be time for me to solve the problems round about me. When once a man begins to know 'the plague of his own heart', it knocks the metaphysics out of him. It is in the actual circumstances of my life that I have to find out whether the wisdom of worshipping God can steer me.

SHH 19

January 15

*Whatsoever ye shall ask in my name* ... John 16:23

Never make the blunder of trying to forecast the way God is going to answer your prayer. When God made a tremendous promise to Abraham, he thought out the best way of helping God fulfil His promise and did the wisest thing he knew according to flesh and blood common-sense reasoning. But for thirteen years God never spoke to him until every possibility of his relying on his own intelligent understanding was at an end. Then God came to him and said, 'I am God Almighty'—El Shaddai—'walk before me, and be thou perfect.' Over and over again God has to teach us how to stand and endure, watching actively and wondering. It is always a wonder when God answers prayer. We hear people say, 'We must not say it is wonderful that God answers prayer'; but it is wonderful. It is so wonderful that a great many people believe it impossible. Listen!—'Whatsoever ye shall ask in my name, that will I do.' Isn't

16

that wonderful? It is so wonderful that I do not suppose more than half of us really believe it. 'Every one that asketh receiveth.' Isn't that wonderful? It is so wonderful that many of us have never even asked God to give us the Holy Spirit because we don't believe He will. 'If two of you shall agree on earth as touching anything that they shall ask, it shall be done for them of my father which is in heaven.' Isn't that wonderful? It is tremendously wonderful. 'The effectual fervent prayer of a righteous man availeth much.' Isn't that wonderful?

IYA 39

*He knew what was in man.* John 2:25

There is a sentimental notion that makes us make ourselves out worse than we think we are, because we have a lurking suspicion that if we make ourselves out amazingly bad, someone will say, 'Oh no, you are not as bad as that'; but Jesus says we are worse. Our Lord never trusted any man, 'for he knew what was in man'; but He was not a cynic for He had the profoundest confidence in what He could do for every man, consequently He was never in a moral or intellectual panic, as we are, because we will put our confidence in man and in the things that Jesus put no confidence in. Paul says, 'Don't glory in men; don't say, I am of Paul, or I am of Apollos, and don't think of yourself more highly than you ought to think, but think according to the measure of faith, that is, according to what the grace of God has done in you.' Never trust (in the fundamental meaning of the word) any other saving Jesus Christ. That will mean you will never be unkind to anybody on the face of the earth, whether it be a degraded criminal or an upright moral man, because you have learned that the only thing to depend on in a man is what God has done in him. When you come to work for Jesus Christ, always ask yourself, 'Do I believe Jesus Christ can do anything for that case?' Am I as confident in His power as He is in His own? If you deal with people without any faith in Jesus Christ it will crush the very life out of you. If we believe in Jesus Christ, we can face every problem the world holds.

IIG 66

17

*Ye did not choose me, but I chose you.* John 15:16

There is so much talk about our decision for Christ, our determination to be Christians, our decisions for this and for that. When we come to the New Testament we find that the other aspect, God's choosing of us, is the one that is brought out the oftenest. 'Ye did not choose me, but I chose you ...' We are not taken up into conscious agreement with God's purpose, we are taken up into His purpose without any consciousness on our part at all; we have no conception of what God is aiming at, and it gets more and more vague as we go on. At the beginning of our Christian life we have our own particular notions as to what God's purpose is—we are meant to go here, or there; or, God has called us to do this or that piece of work. We go and do the thing and still we find the big compelling of God remains. The majority of the work we do is so much scaffolding to further the purpose of the big compelling of God. 'He took unto him the twelve.' He takes us all the time; there is more than we have got at, something we have not seen.

PH 177

The call of God embarrasses us because of two things—it presents us with sealed orders, and urges us to a vast venture. When God calls us He does not tell us along the line of our natural senses what to expect; God's call is a command that *asks* us, that means there is always a possibility of refusal on our part. Faith never knows where it is being led, it knows and loves the One Who is leading. It is a life of *faith*, not of intelligence and reason, but a life of knowing Who is making me 'go'.

NKW 12

*And Peter answered and said to Jesus, Master, it is good for us to be here; and let us make three tabernacles; one for thee, and one for Moses, and one for Elias.* Mark 9:5

When God gives us a time of exaltation it is always exceptional. It has its meaning in our life with God, but we must beware lest spiritual selfishness wants to make it the only time. The sphere of exaltation is not meant to teach us anything. We are apt to think that everything that happens to us is to be turned into useful teach-

18

ing; it is to be turned into something better than teaching, viz. into character. We shall find that the spheres God brings us into are not meant to teach us something but to *make* us something. There is a great danger in asking, 'What is the use of it?' There is no *use* in it at all. If you want a life of usefulness, don't be a Christian after our Lord's stamp; you will be much more useful if you are not. The cry for the standard of usefulness knocks the spiritual Christian right out, he dare not touch it if he is going to remain true to his Master. Take the life of our Lord: for three years all He did was to walk about saying things and healing sick people—a useless life, judged from every standard of success and of enterprise. If our Lord and His disciples had lived in our day, they would have been put down as a most unuseful crowd. In spiritual matters we can never calculate on the line of—'What is the use of it?' 'What is the use of being at a Bible Training College? of learning Psychology and Ethics? *Do* something.' Great danger lies along that line. 'The good is ever the enemy of the best.' The mountain-top experiences are rare moments, but they are meant for something in the purposes of God. It was not until Peter came to write his Epistles that he realized the full purpose of his having been on the Mount of Transfiguration.

MU 52

### January 19

*They shall run and not be weary.* Isaiah 40:31

Whenever there is the experience of fag or weariness or degradation, you may be certain you have done one of two things—either you have disregarded a law of nature, or you have deliberately got out of touch with God. There is no such thing as weariness in God's work. If you are in tune with the joy of God, the more you spend out in God's service, the more the recuperation goes on, and when once the warning note of weariness is given, it is a sign that something has gone wrong. If only we would heed the warning, we would find it is God's wonderfully gentle way of saying—'Not that way; that must be left alone; this must be given up.' Spiritual fatigue comes from the unconscious frittering away of God's time. When you feel weary or are exhausted, don't ask for hot milk, but get back to God. The secret of weariness and nervous disease in the natural world is the lack of a dominating interest, and the same is true in spiritual life. Much of what is called Christian work is veneered spiritual disease; it is Christian activity that counts—dominating

19

life from God, and every moment is filled with an energy that is not our own, a super-abounding life that nothing can stand before.

NKW 37

**January 20**

*Ye call me Master and Lord: and ye say well; for so I am. If I then, your Lord and Master, have washed your feet, ye also ought to wash one another's feet.* John 13:13–14

We have to recognize that we are one half mechanical and one half mysterious; to live in either domain and ignore the other is to be a fool or a fanatic. The great supernatural work of God's grace is in the incalculable part of our nature; we have to work out in the mechanical realm what God works in in the mysterious realm. People accept creeds, but they will not accept the holy standards of Jesus Christ's teaching. To build on the fundamental work of God's grace and ignore the fact that we have to work it out in a mechanical life produces humbugs, those who make a divorce between the mysterious life and the practical life. In John 13 the mysterious and the mechanical are closely welded together.

You can't wash anybody's feet mysteriously; it is a purely mechanical, matter-of-fact job; you can't do it by giving him devotional books or by praying for him; you can only wash any-body's feet by doing something mechanical. Our Lord did not tell the disciples *how* they were to do it: He simply says—'Do it.' He is not questioning whether or not they can do it; He is saying that they must do what the mastery of His ruling shows them they should do.

BE 56

**January 21**

*And we know that to them that love God ...* Romans 8:28

Do you remember how Paul never wearied of saying, 'Don't you know that your body is the temple of the Holy Ghost'? Recall what Jesus Christ said about the historic temple which is the symbol of the body; He ruthlessly turned out those that sold and bought in the temple, and said, 'It is written, my house shall be called the house of prayer; but ye have made it a den of thieves.' Let us apply that to ourselves. We have to remember that our conscious life, though only a tiny bit of our personality, is to be regarded by us as a shrine of the Holy Ghost. The Holy Ghost will look after the unconscious part we do not know, we must see we guard the conscious part, for which we are responsible, as a shrine of the Holy Ghost. If we recognize this as we should, we shall be careful to keep our body undefiled for Him.

IYA 104

**January 22**

*Consecrate yourselves this day to the Lord.* Exodus 32:29
We are never told to consecrate our gifts to God, but we are told to dedicate ourselves.

The joy of anything, from a blade of grass upwards, is to fulfil its created purpose. '... that we should be to the praise of His glory' (Ephesians 1:12). We are not here to win souls, to do good to others, that is the natural outcome, but it is not our aim, and this is where so many of us us cease to be followers. We will follow God as long as He makes us a blessing to others, but when He does not we will not follow. Suppose Our Lord had measured His life by whether or not He was a blessing to others! Why, He was a 'stone of stumbling' to thousands, actually to His own neighbours, to His own nation, because through Him they blasphemed the Holy Ghost, and in His own country 'He did not many mighty works there because of their unbelief (Matthew 13:58). If Our Lord had measured His life by its actual results, He would have been full of misery.

MU 63

**January 23**

*In the day of prosperity be joyful, but in the day of adversity consider: God also hath set the one over against the other, to the end that man should find nothing after him.* Ecclesiastes 7:14
The test of elemental honesty is the way a man behaves himself in grief and in joy. The natural elemental man expresses his joy or sorrow straight off. Today in our schools boys are taught stoicism; it produces an admirable type of lad externally, but not so admirable internally. When we are rightly related to God we must let things have their way with us and not pretend things are not as they are. It is difficult not to simulate sorrow or gladness, but to remain natural and steadfastly true to God as things come. Don't deal only

21

with the section that is sad or with the section that is joyful, deal with them together. When we accept God's purpose for us in Christ Jesus, we know that 'all things work together for good'.

Stoicism has the effect of making a man hysterical and sentimental, it produces a denseness spiritually. When you are joyful, *be* joyful; when you are sad, *be* sad. If God has given you a sweet cup, don't make it bitter; and if He has given you a bitter cup, don't try and make it sweet; take things as they come. One of the last lessons we learn is not to be an amateur providence—'I shall not allow that person to suffer.' Suffering, and the inevitable result of suffering, is the only way some of us can learn, and if we are shielded God will ultimately take the one who interferes by the scruff of the neck and remove him. The fingers that caress a child may also hurt its flesh; it is the power of love that makes them hurt.

SHH 95

## January 24

*He that findeth his life shall lose it; and he that loseth his life for my sake shall find it.* Matthew 10:39

We have to recognize that our personal life is meant for Jesus Christ. The modern jargon is for self-realization—'I must save my life': Jesus Christ says, 'whosoever shall lose his life for my sake shall find it.' The cross is the deliberate recognition of what our personal self is for, viz., to be given to Jesus, and we take up that cross daily and prove we are no longer our own. Whenever the call is given for abandon to Jesus Christ, people say it is offensive and out of taste. The counterfeit of abandon is that misleading phrase 'Christian service'. I will spend myself for God, I will do anything and everything but the one thing He asks me to do, viz., give up my right to myself to Him. 'But surely Christian service is a right thing?' Immediately we begin to say that, we are off the track. It is the right *Person*, the Lord Jesus Christ, not the right thing: don't stop short of the Lord Himself—'*for my sake*'. The great dominating recognition is that my personal self belongs to Jesus. When I receive the Holy Spirit, I receive not a possible oneness with Jesus Christ, but a real intense oneness with Him. The point is, will I surrender my individual life entirely to Him? It will mean giving up not only bad things, but things which are right and good (cf. Matthew 5:29–30). If you have to calculate what you are willing

22

to give up for Jesus Christ, never say that you love Him. Jesus Christ asks us to give up the best we have got to Him, our right to ourselves.

SHL 85–6

January 25

*... till Christ be formed in you.* Galatians 4:19

Beware of refining away the radical aspect of our Lord's teaching by saying that God puts something in to counteract the wrong disposition—that is a compromise. Jesus never teaches us to curb and suppress the wrong disposition; He gives us a totally new disposition, He alters the mainspring of action. Our Lord's teaching can be interpreted only by the new Spirit which He puts in; it can never be taken as a series of rules and regulations.

A man cannot imitate the disposition of Jesus Christ: it is either there, or it is not. When the Son of God is formed in me, He is formed in my human nature, and I have to put on the new man in accordance with His life and obey Him; then His disposition will work out all the time. We make character out of our disposition. Character is what we make, disposition is what we are born with; and when we are born again we are given a new disposition. A man must make his own character, but he cannot make his disposition; that is a gift. Our natural disposition is gifted to us by heredity; by regeneration God gives us the disposition of His Son.

SSM 29

January 26

*Keep yourselves in the love of God.* Jude 21

When God saves and sanctifies a man his personality is raised to its highest pitch of freedom, he is free now to sin if he wants to; before, he is not free, sin is impelling and urging him; when he is delivered from sin he is free not to sin, or free to sin if he chooses. The doctrine of sinless perfection and consequent freedom from temptation runs on the line that because I am sanctified, I cannot now do wrong. If that is so, you cease to be a man. If God puts us in such a condition that we could not disobey, our obedience would be of no value to Him. But blessed be His Name, when by His redemption the love of God is shed abroad in our hearts, He gives us something to do to manifest it. Just as human nature is put to the test in the actual circumstances of life, so the love of God in us is put to the test. 'Keep yourselves in the love of God,' says Jude, that is keep your soul open not only to the fact that God loves you, but that He is *in* you, in you sufficiently to manifest His perfect love in every condition in which you can find yourself as you rely on Him.

CHI 89

*Not everyone that saith unto me, Lord, Lord, shall enter into the kingdom of heaven but he that doeth the will of my Father which is in heaven.* Matthew 7:21

Human nature is fond of labels, but a label may be the counterfeit of confession. It is so easy to be branded with labels, much easier in certain stages to wear a ribbon or a badge than to confess. Jesus never used the word *testify*; He used a much more searching word—*confess*. 'Whosoever therefore shall confess me before men ...' The test of goodness is confession by doing the will of God. 'If you do not confess me before men,' says Jesus, 'neither will your heavenly Father confess you.' Immediately we confess, we must have a badge, if we do not put one on, other people will. Our Lord is warning that it is possible to wear the label without having the goods; possible for a man to wear the badge of being His disciple when he is not. Labels are all right, but if we mistake the label for the goods we get confused. If the disciple is to discern between the man with the label and the man with the goods, he must have the spirit of discernment, viz., the Holy Spirit. We start out with the honest belief that the label and the goods must go together, they should do, but Jesus warns that sometimes they get severed, and we find cases where God honours His work although those who preach it are not living a right life. In judging the preacher, He says, judge him by his fruit.

SSM 105

*For if ye live after the flesh, ye shall die: but if ye through the Spirit do mortify the deeds of the body, ye shall live.* Romans 8:13

Sensuality is not sin, it is the way my body works in connection

24

with external circumstances whereby I begin to satisfy myself. Sensuality will work in a man who is delivered from sin by Jesus Christ as well as in a man who is not. I do not care what your experience may be as a Christian, you may be trapped by sensuality at any time. Paul says, 'Mortify the deeds of the body'; mortify means to destroy by neglect. One of the first big moral lessons a man has to learn is that he cannot destroy *sin* by neglect; sin has to be handled by the Redemption of Jesus Christ, it cannot be handled by me. Heredity is a bigger problem than I can cope with; but if I will receive the gift of the Holy Spirit on the basis of Christ's Redemption, He enables me to work out that Redemption in my experience. With regard to sensuality, that is my business; I have to mortify it, and if I don't, it will never be mortified. If I take any part of my natural life and use it to satisfy myself, that is sensuality. A Christian has to learn that his body is not his own. 'What? know ye not that your body is the temple of the Holy Ghost ... and ye are not your own?' Watch that you learn to mortify.

SA 70

January 29

*Except a man be born again, he cannot see the kingdom of God.* John 3:3

New birth is not the working of a natural law. The introduction of anything into this world is cataclysmic: before a tree can grow it must be planted; before a human being can evolve he must be born— a distinct and emphatic crisis. Every child born into the world involves a cataclysm to someone, the mother has practically to go through death. The same thing is true spiritually. Being 'born from above' is not a simple easy process; we cannot glide into the Kingdom of God. Common sense reasoning says we ought to be able to merge into the life of God, but according to the Bible, and in actual experience, that is not the order. The basis of things is not rational, it is tragic, and what Jesus Christ came to do was to put human life on the basis of Redemption whereby any man can receive the heredity of the Son of God and be lifted into the domain where He lives.

The historic Jesus represents the personal union of God and man. He lived on the human plane for thirty-three years and during that time He presented what God's normal Man was like. When we are

25

regenerated we enter into the Kingdom of God, we begin to grow, and the goal is certain—'... we know that, when he shall appear, *we shall be like him*: for we shall see him as he is.' But before I can begin to see what Jesus Christ stands for I have to enter into another domain—'Except a man be born again, *he cannot enter into the kingdom of God*.' I enter into the life of God by its entering into me, that is, I deliberately undertake to become the home of the life of the Son of God, 'Bethlehem'. I do not draw my life from myself, I draw it from the One who is the Source of life.

BE 45

January 30

*... and not one of them said that aught of the things which he possessed was his own; but they had all things common.* Acts 4:32
*... and let us consider one another to provoke unto love and good works; not forsaking the assembling of ourselves together* ... Hebrews 10:24–5.

These two passages serve to indicate the main characteristic of Christianity, viz., the 'together' aspect; false religions inculcate an isolated holy life. Try and develop a holy life in private, and you find it cannot be done. Individuals can only live the true life when they are dependent on one another. After the Resurrection our Lord would not allow Mary to hold a spiritual experience for herself, she must get into contact with the disciples and convey a message to them—'Touch me not ... but go unto my brethren, and say to them, I ascend unto my Father and your Father, and my God and your God.' After Peter's denial the isolation of misery would inevitably have seized on him and made him want to retire in the mood of 'I can never forgive myself', had not our Lord forestalled this by giving him something positive to do—'... and when thou art converted, strengthen thy brethren'. Immediately you try to develop holiness alone and fix your eyes on your own whiteness, you lose the whole meaning of Christianity. The Holy Spirit makes a man fix his eyes on his Lord and on intense activity for others. In the early Middle Ages people had the idea that Christianity meant living a holy life apart from the world and its sociability, apart from its work and citizenship. That type of holiness is foreign to the New Testament; it cannot be reconciled with the records of the

26

life of Jesus. The people of His day called Him 'the friend of publicans and sinners' because He spent so much time with them.

BE 29

*Go ye therefore and make disciples.* Matthew 28:19

The call to discipleship comes as mysteriously as being born from above; once a man hears it, it profoundly alters everything. It is like the call of the sea, the call of the mountains, not everyone hears these calls, only those who have the nature of the sea or the mountains—and then only if they pay attention to the call. To hear the call of God or the call to discipleship necessitates education in understanding and discernment. Never be afraid of the thing that is vague, the biggest things in life are vague as far as expression goes, but they are realities.

'Go ye therefore, and make disciples of all the nations'—not 'Go out and save souls', but 'Go and *make disciples*'. It is comparatively easy to proclaim salvation from sin, but Jesus comes and says, 'What about you—if *you* would be My disciple, deny yourself, take up that cross daily, and follow Me.' It has nothing to do with eternal salvation, it has everything to do with our temporal value to God, and most of us do not care anything about our temporal worth to God, all we are concerned about is being saved from hell and put right for heaven. There is something infinitely grander than that, and Jesus Christ gives us a marvellous chance of giving up our right to ourselves to Him in order that we might become the devoted bondslaves of the One who saves us so supernaturally.

HGM 142

*And he said unto them, Let us go over unto the other side of the lake; and they launched forth.* Luke 8:22

'If you obey Jesus you will have a life of joy and delight.' Well, it is not true. Jesus said to the disciples—'Let us go to the other side of the lake', and they were plunged into the biggest storm they had ever known. You say, 'If I had not obeyed Jesus I should not have got into this complication.' Exactly. The problems in our walk with God are to be accounted for along this line, and the temptation

27

is to say, 'God could never have told me to go there, if He had done so this would not have happened.' We discover then whether we are going to trust God's integrity or listen to our own expressed scepticism. Scepticism of the tongue is only transitional; real scepticism is wrung out from the man who knows he did not get where he is on his own account—'I was not seeking my own, I came deliberately because I believe Jesus told me to, and now there is the darkness and the deep and the desolation.' HGM 90

Darkness is not synonymous with sin; if there is darkness spiritually it is much more likely to be the shade of God's hand than darkness on account of sin; it may be the threshold of a new revelation coming through a big break in personal experience. Before the dawn there is desolation; but wait, the dawn will merge into glorious day—'... the light of dawn, that shineth more and more unto the perfect day'. If you are experiencing the darkness of desolation on individual lines, go through with it, and you will find yourself face to face with Jesus Christ as never before. 'I am come that they might have life'—life in which there is no death—'and that they might have it more abundantly.'

HGM 57

**February 2**

*Arm ye yourselves also with the same mind.* 1 Peter 4:1

Some people have on an armour of innocence, like Tennyson's knight whose 'strength was as the strength of ten because his heart was pure'; others have on an armour of love. Paul says, 'Put on the whole armour of God.' Don't rely on anything less than that, clothe yourself with your relationship to God, maintain it. If you do not arm yourself with the armour of God, you are open to interferences in your hidden personal life from supernatural powers which you cannot control; but buckle on the armour, bring yourself into real living contact with God, and you are garrisoned not only in the conscious realm but in the depths of your personality beneath the conscious realm. 'Praying always,' says Paul. Every time we pray our horizon is altered, our attitude to things is altered, not sometimes but every time, and the amazing thing is that we don't pray more. Prayer is a complete emancipation, it keeps us on the spiritual plane. When you are at one with another mind there is a telepathic influence all the time, and when born from above the communion

28

is between God and yourself; 'Keep that going,' says Peter. 'Arm ye yourselves also with the same mind.'

Are you neglecting prayer? No matter what else is neglected, switch back at once, if you don't you will be a dangerous influence to the people round about you. Watch the snare of self-pity—'Why should I go through this?' Be careful, you are a danger spot. I feel as if Jesus Christ were staggered with surprise at some of us, amazed at the things we say to Him, astonished at our attitude to Him, at the sulks we get into, because we have forgotten to arm ourselves with the same mind.

PH 214

**February 3**

*Therefore all things whatsoever ye would that men should do to you, do ye even so to them.* Matthew 7:12

Our Lord's use of this maxim is positive, not negative. *Do* to others whatsoever ye would that they should do to you—a very different thing from not doing to others what you do not want them to do to you. What would we like other people to do to us? 'Well,' says Jesus, 'do that to them; don't wait for them to do it to you.' The Holy Ghost will kindle your imagination to picture many things you would like others to do to you, and that is His way of telling you what to do to them—'I would like people to give me credit for the generous motives I have.' Well, give them credit for having generous motives. 'I would like people never to pass harsh judgments on me.' Well, don't pass harsh judgments on them. 'I would like other people to pray for me.' Well, pray for them. The measure of our growth in grace is our attitude towards other people. 'Thou shalt love thy neighbour as thyself,' says Jesus. Satan comes in as an angel of light and says, 'But you must not think about yourself.' The Holy Spirit will make you think about yourself, because that is His way of educating you so that you may be able to deal with others. He makes you picture what you would like other people to do to you, and then He says, 'Now go and do those things to them.' This verse is our Lord's standard for practical ethical conduct.

SSM 90

*Then was Jesus led up of the Spirit into the wilderness to be tempted of the devil.* Matthew 4:1

For thirty years Jesus had remained unknown, then He was baptized and had a wonderful manifestation of the Father's approval, and the next thing we read is that He is 'led up of the Spirit into the wilderness to be tempted of the devil'. The same thing puzzles us in our own spiritual experience; we have been born from above, or have had the wonderful experience of the baptism of the Holy Ghost—surely we are fit now to do something for God; and God deliberately puts us on the shelf, amongst the dust and the cobwebs, in an utterly unaccountable way.

The agony Jesus went through in the Temptation was surely because He had the vision of the long way and saw the suffering it would entail on men through all the ages if He took His Father's way. He knew it in a way we cannot conceive. His sensitiveness is beyond anything we can imagine. If He had not been true to His Father's way, His own home would not have been upset, His own nation would not have blasphemed the Holy Ghost. The way to approach Gethsemane is to try to understand the Temptation.

When we obey Jesus Christ it is never a question of what it costs us—it does not cost us anything, it is a delight—but of what it costs those whom we love, and there is always the danger of yielding to the temptation of the 'short cut'. Am I prepared to let my obedience to God cost other people something? Jesus deliberately took the long trail, and He says 'the disciple is not above his Master'. 'Because thou hast kept the word of my patience ...' We want to hurry things up by revivals. Over and over again we take the devil's advice and say, 'It must be done quickly—the need is the call; men must be saved.' An understanding of the inwardness of our Lord's temptation will throw light on the progress of Christian history as well as on personal experience.

PH 100

*And God is able to make all grace abound toward you.* 2 Corinthians 9:8

Our Lord emptied Himself and had nothing all the days of His earthly life, consequently He was free for God to lavish His gifts

30

through Him to others. Think of the rushes with which we come in front of our Heavenly Father; whenever we see an occasion we rush in and say, 'I can do this, you need not trouble God.' I wonder if we are learning determinedly to possess nothing? It is possessing things that makes us so conceited—'Oh yes, I can give prayer for you; I can give this and that for you.' We have to get to the place about which Jesus talked to the rich young ruler where we are so absolutely empty and poor that we have nothing, and God knows we have nothing, then He can do through us what He likes. Would that we would quickly get rid of all we have, give it away till there is nothing left, then there is a chance for God to pour through in rivers for other people.

IWP 79

### February 6

*Hear ye then the parable of the sower...* Matthew 13:18

It is the plough that prepares the ground for sowing the seed. The hard way through the field is the same soil as the good ground, but it is of no use for growing corn because it has never been ploughed. Apply that to your own soul and to the souls of men. There are lives that are absolutely stupid towards God, they are simply a way for the traffic of their own concerns. We are responsible for the kind of ground we are. No man on earth has any right to be a highroad; every man has the chance of allowing the plough to run through his life. Sorrow or bereavement or conviction of sin, anything that upsets the even, hard way of the life and produces concern, will act as the plough. A man's concern about his eternal welfare witnesses that the plough has begun to go through his self-complacency. The words of our Lord, 'Think not that I came to cast peace on the earth: I came not to cast peace, but a sword', are a description of what happens when the Gospel is preached—upset, conviction, concern and confusion.

SHL 112

### February 7

*All these evil things come from within, and defile the man.* Mark 7:23

Solomon was the wisest and the wealthiest of kings, yet he says that 'the plague of his own heart' knocked him out (see 1 Kings 8:38). This is the first lesson every one of us has to learn. To begin with we

31

are not prepared to accept Jesus Christ's diagnosis of the human heart, we prefer to trust our own ignorant innocence. Jesus Christ says, 'Out of the heart proceed fornication, adultery, murder, lasciviousness, thieving, lying,' etc. (Mark 7:21-23). No man has ever believed that. We have not the remotest conception that what Jesus says about the human heart is true until we come up against something further on in our lives. We are apt to be indignant and say—'I don't believe those things are in my heart', and we refuse the diagnosis of the only Master there is of the human heart. We need never know the plague of our own heart and the terrible possibilities in human life if we will hand ourselves over to Jesus Christ; but if we stand on our own right and wisdom at any second an eruption may occur in our personal lives, and we may discover to our unutterable horror that we can be murderers, etc. This is one of the most ghastly and humiliating and devastating truths in the whole of human experience...

Education cannot deal with the plague of the heart, all our vows cannot touch it; the only Being Who can deal with it is God through a personal relationship to Him, by receiving His Spirit after accepting the diagnosis of Jesus Christ.

SHH 104, 105


February 8

*And Abraham stretched forth his hand, and took the knife to slay his son.* Genesis 22:10

Sacrifice in the Bible means that we give to God the best we have; it is the finest form of worship. Sacrifice is not giving up things, but giving to God with joy the best we have. We have dragged down the idea of surrender and of sacrifice, we have taken the life out of the words and made them mean something sad and weary and despicable; in the Bible they mean the very opposite. To go out in surrender to God means the surrendering of the miserable sense of my own un-importance: Am I willing to surrender that mean little sense for the great big idea God has for me? Am I willing to surrender the fact that I am an ignorant, useless, worthless, too-old person? There is more hindrance to God's work because people cling to a sense of unworthiness than because of conceit. '*Who am I?*' Instantly the trend of the mind is to say—'Oh well, I have not had any education'; 'I did not begin soon enough.' Am I willing to surrender the whole thing, and go out in surrender to God? to

32

go out of the carnal mind into the spiritual?—'fools for Christ's sake'?

Abraham surrendered himself entirely to the supernatural God. Have you got hold of a supernatural God? not, do you know what God is going to do? You cannot know, but you have faith in Him, and therefore He can do what He likes.

NP 148

*Thou therefore endure hardness, as a good soldier of Jesus Christ.* 2 Timothy 2:3

The first requirement of the worker is discipline voluntarily entered into. It is easy to be passionate, easy to be thrilled by spiritual influences, but it takes a heart in love with Jesus Christ to put the feet in His footprints, and to square the life to a steady 'going up to Jerusalem' with Him. Discipline is the one thing the modern Christian knows nothing of, we won't stand discipline nowadays. God has given me an experience of His life and grace, therefore I am a law unto myself.

The discipline of a worker is not in order to develop his own life, but for the purposes of his Commander. The reason there is so much failure is because we forget that we are here for that one thing, loyalty to Jesus Christ; otherwise we have no business to have taken the vows of God upon us. If a soldier is not prepared to be killed, he has no business to have enlisted as a soldier. The only way to keep true to God is by a steady persistent refusal to be interested in Christian work and to be interested alone in Jesus Christ.

A disciplined life means three things—a supreme aim incorporated into the life itself; an external law binding on the life from its Commander; and absolute loyalty to God and His word as the ingrained attitude of heart and mind. There must be no insubordination; every impulse, every emotion, every illumination must be rigorously handled and checked if it is not in accordance with God and His word.

Our Lord Himself is the example of a disciplined life. He lived a holy life by sacrificing Himself to His Father; His words and His thinking were holy because He submitted His intelligence to His Father's word, and He worked the works of God because He steadily submitted His will to His Father's will; and as is the Master, so is the disciple.

AUG 64

33

*But, inasmuch as ye are partakers of Christ's sufferings, rejoice.*
1 Peter 4:13

If we are going to be used by God, He will take us through a multitude of experiences that are not meant for us at all, but meant to make us useful in His hands. There are things we go through which are unexplainable on any other line, and the nearer we get to God the more inexplicable the way seems. It is only on looking back and by getting an explanation from God's Word that we understand His dealings with us.

PH 34

Not only does God waste His saints according to the judgments of men, He seems to bruise them most mercilessly. You say, 'But it could never be God's will to bruise me': if it pleased the Lord to bruise His own Son, why should He not bruise you? To choose suffering is a disease; but to choose God's will even though it means suffering is to suffer as Jesus did—'according to the will of God'.

In the Bible it is never the idealizing of the sufferer that is brought out, but the glorifying of God. God always serves Himself out of the saint's personal experience of suffering.

SHL 121

*I count all things but loss for the excellency of the knowledge of Christ Jesus my Lord.* Philippians 3:8

The first thing the Spirit of God does in us is to efface the things we rely upon naturally. Paul argues this out in Philippians 3, he catalogues who he is and the things in which he might have confidence; 'but,' he says, 'I deliberately renounce all these things that I may gain Christ.' The continual demand to consecrate our gifts to God is the devil's counterfeit for sanctification. We have a way of saying—'What a wonderful power that man or woman would be in God's service.' Reasoning on man's broken virtues makes us fix on the wrong thing. The only way any man or woman can ever be of service to God is when he or she is willing to renounce all their natural excellencies and determine to be weak in Him—'I am here for one thing only, for Jesus Christ to manifest Himself in me.' That is to be the steadfast habit of a Christian's life. Whenever we think we are of use to God, we hinder Him. We have to form the habit of letting God carry on His work through us without let or hindrance as He did through Jesus, and He will use us in ways He dare not let us see. We have to efface every other thought but that of Jesus Christ. It is not done once for all; we have to be always doing it. If once you have seen that Jesus Christ is All in all, make the habit of letting Him be All in all. It will mean that you not only have implicit faith that He is All in all, but that you go through the trial of your faith and prove that He is. After sanctification God delights to put us into places where He can make us wealthy. Jesus Christ counts as service not what we do for Him, but what we are to Him, and the inner secret of that is identity with Him in person. '*That I may know Him.*'

MFL 106

*For he is an holy God . . . he will not forgive your transgressions or your sins.* Joshua 24:19

Have you ever been convicted of sin by conscience through the Spirit of God? If you have, you know this—that God dare not forgive you and be God. There is a lot of sentimental talk about God forgiving because He is love: God is so holy that He cannot forgive. God can only destroy for ever the thing that is unlike Himself. The Atonement does not mean that God forgives a sinner and allows him to go on sinning and receiving forgiveness; it means that God saves the sinner and turns him into a saint, i.e. destroys the sinner out of him, and through his conscience he realizes that by the Atonement God has done what He never could have done apart from it. When people testify you can always tell whether they have been convicted by the Spirit of God or whether their equilibrium has been disturbed by doing wrong things. When a man is convicted of sin by the Spirit of God through his conscience, his relationship to other people is absolute child's play. If when you were convicted of sin, you had been told to go and lick the dust off the boots of your greatest enemy, you would have done it willingly. Your relationship to men is the last thing that bothers you. It is your relationship to God that bothers you. I am completely out of the love of God, out of the holiness of God, and I tremble with terror when I think of God drawing near.

PS 65

## February 13

*If any man suffer as a Christian, let him not be ashamed.* 1 Peter 4:16

To 'suffer as a Christian' is not to be marked peculiar because of your views, or because you will not bend to conventionality; these things are not Christian, but ordinary human traits from which all men suffer irrespective of creed or religion or no religion. To 'suffer as a Christian' is to suffer because there is an essential difference between you and the world which rouses the contempt of the world, and the disgust and hatred of the spirit that is in the world. To 'suffer as a Christian' is to have no answer when the world's satire is turned on you, as it was turned on Jesus Christ when He hung upon the cross, when they turned His words into jest and jeer; they will do the same to you. He gave no answer, neither can you.

'... but if a man suffer as a Christian, let him not be ashamed.' It was in the throes of this blinding, amazing problem that Peter staggered. Peter meant to go with his Lord to death, and he did go; but never at any moment did he imagine that he would have to go without Him—that he would see Jesus taken by the power of the world, 'as a lamb that is led to the slaughter', and have no answer, no word to explain—that froze him to the soul. That is what it means to 'suffer as a Christian'—to hear men taunt Him, see them tear His words to pieces, and feel you cannot answer; to smart under their merciless, pitying sarcasm because you belong to that contemptible sect of 'Christians'... But when you have been 'comforted by His rod and His staff', you count it all joy to go through this God-glorifying suffering.

DS 70

## February 14

*I indeed baptize you with water unto repentance...he shall baptize you with the Holy Ghost, and with fire.* Matthew 3:11

I want to ask a very personal question—How much do you want to be delivered from? You say, 'I want to be delivered from wrong-doing'—then you don't need to come to Jesus Christ. 'I want to walk in the right way according to the judgment of men'—then you don't need Jesus Christ. But some heart cries out—'I want, God knows I want, that Jesus Christ should do in me all He said He would do.' How many of us 'want' like that? God grant that this 'want' may increase until it swamps every other desire of heart and life. Oh, the patience, the gentleness, the longing of the Lord Jesus

36

after lives, and yet men are turning this way and that, and even saints who once knew Him are turning aside, their eyes are fixed on other things, on the blessings that come from the baptism with the Holy Ghost and have forgotten the Baptizer Himself. Do you know what this mighty baptism will mean? It will mean being taken right out of every other setting in life but God's. Are you willing for that? It will mean that sin in you is put to death, not counteracted, but killed right out by identification with the death of Jesus; it will mean a blazing personal holiness like His. Are you willing for that? Face Jesus Himself; other lights are fading since He grew bright. You are getting tired of life as it is, tired of yourself as you are, getting sour with regard to the setting of your life; lift your eyes for one moment to Jesus Christ. Do you want, more than you want your food, more than you want your sleep, more than you want anything under heaven, or in heaven, that Jesus Christ might so identify you with Himself that you are His first and last and for ever? God grant that the great longing desire of your heart may begin to awaken as it has never done, not only the desire for the forgiveness of sins, but for identification with Jesus Himself until you say, 'I live; yet not I, but Christ liveth in me.'

GW 22

**February 15**

*I indeed baptize you with water unto repentance...he shall baptize you with the Holy Ghost, and with fire.* Matthew 3:11

Another thing about this mighty baptism– it takes you out of your individual life and fits you into God's purpose. Are some of you realizing the awful loneliness of being alive? You cannot mix in with the worldly crowd you used to, and there is a great hunger and longing after you know not what. Look to the Lord Jesus and say, 'My God, I want to be so identified with the Lord Jesus that I am pure with His purity, empowered with His power, indwelt with His life.' Do you know what will happen? God will take your lonely, isolated, individual life and fit it into a marvellous oneness, into the mystical Body of Christ. Oh, the isolated, lonely, Christian lives! What is needed is this mighty baptism with the Holy Ghost and with fire. 'I have been seeking for it, fasting for it,' you say; listen, 'Come unto me,' says Jesus. He is the Baptizer with the Holy Ghost, and with fire.

Have you seen Jesus as 'the Lamb of God, which taketh away the

37

sin of the world'? What is the first step to take? Come to Him just as you are and ask Him to give you the Holy Spirit. He begins to awaken in you the tremendous 'want', overwhelming, all-absorbing, passionate in its impelling rush, to be baptized with the Holy Ghost and with fire. If you have never received the Holy Spirit, why not receive Him now? Ask God for His Spirit on the authority of Jesus, and He will lead you, as you obey Him, straight to the place where you will be identified with the death of Jesus.

GW 23

**February 16**

*I indeed baptize you with water unto repentance... he shall baptize you with the Holy Ghost, and with fire.* Matthew 3:11

Where are we in regard to the personal experience of the baptism of the Holy Ghost? If Jesus Christ had said to us, 'All you need to do is to be as holy as you can, overcome sin as far as you can, and I will overlook the rest', no intelligent man under heaven would accept such a salvation. But He says—'Be ye perfect'; 'Love your enemies'; 'Be so pure that lust is an impossibility'. Instantly every heart calls back, 'My God, who is sufficient for these things?' Oceans of penitential tears, mountains of good works, all powers and energy sink down till they are under the feet of the Lord Jesus, and, incarnate in John the Baptist, they all point to Him—'Behold the Lamb of God, which taketh away the sin of the world!' If Jesus Christ cannot deliver from sin, if He cannot adjust us perfectly to God as He says He can, if He cannot fill us with the Holy Ghost until there is nothing that can ever appeal again in sin or the world or the flesh, then He has misled us. But blessed be the Name of God, He can! He can so purify, so indwell, so merge with Himself, that only the things that appeal to Him appeal to you, to all other appeals there is the sentence of death, you have nothing to answer. When you come amongst those whose morality and uprightness crown them the lord of their own lives, there is no affinity with you, and they leave you alone.

GW 23

**February 17**

*Put on the whole armour of God... and, having done all, to stand.* Ephesians 6:11–13

Paul is writing from prison; he knows all about the Roman soldier

38

whose armour he is describing, for he was chained to one of them. 'I am an ambassador in a chain,' he says.

These verses are not a picture of how to fight, but of how not to fight. If you have not put on the armour, you will have to fight; but 'having put on the whole armour of God, then *stand*', says Paul. There are times when God's servants are sent out to attack, to storm the citadel, but the counsel given here is as to how we are to hold the position which has been gained. We need to learn this conservation of energy, 'having done all, to stand', manifesting the full power of God.

'For we wrestle not against flesh and blood'—if we do, we are 'out of it'; our warfare is against 'the spiritual hosts of wickedness' which the world does not see. We are apt to forget that the enemy is unseen and that he is supernatural (cf. Daniel 10:12–13). 'Don't make any mistake,' says Paul, 'you are not wrestling against flesh and blood, you are wrestling against tremendous powers you will never be able to withstand unless you put on the whole armour of God. When you see men doing terrible things, remember you are not wrestling against them, they are the cat's-paw of the rulers of the darkness of this world.' We are to be taken up with a much more difficult wrestling, viz., the wrestling against the spiritual hosts of wickedness in the heavenly places which prevent us from seeing God . . .

'Praying always . . . for all saints.' It is not always a time of triumph; there are not only times of taking strongholds by storm, but times when spiritual darkness falls, when the great powers in the heavenlies are at work, when no one understands the wiles of Satan but God; at such times we have to stand steadily shoulder to shoulder for God. How often the Spirit of God emphasizes the 'together-ness' of the saints!

GW 98

February 18

*. . . and she brake the cruse, and poured it over his head.* Mark 14:3

It was an act no one else saw any occasion for, they said it was 'a waste'. It was not an extraordinary occasion, and yet Mary broke the box of ointment and spilt the whole thing. It was not a useful thing, but an act of extravagant devotion, and Jesus commended her and said wherever His gospel was preached, this also should be spoken of for a memorial of her.

God spilt the life of His Son that the world might be saved. Am

39

I prepared to spill my life out for Him? Our Lord is carried beyond Himself with delight when He sees any of us doing what Mary did, extravagantly wasting our substance for Him; not set for this or that economy, but being abandoned to Him.

In the Bible there is always a oneness between the spiritual and the material. It takes the incarnation of the Holy Ghost in a man's body to make him what Jesus Christ wants him to be. Unless the blessings of God can deal with our bodies and make them the temples of the Holy Ghost, then the religion of Jesus Christ is in the clouds. If I cannot exhibit the sentiment of the Holy Ghost in the sordid actualities of life and in doing menial things from the highest motive, I am not learning to pour out unto the Lord.

'He that believeth on me... out of him shall flow...'—not, he shall gain, but hundreds of others shall be continually refreshed. It is time now to break the life, to cease craving for satisfaction, and to spill the thing out. The Lord is asking for thousands of us to do it for Him.

PH 130

*Wherein ye greatly rejoice, though now for a little while, if need be, ye have been put to grief in manifold temptations.* 1 Peter 1:6

If you know a man who has a good spiritual banking account, borrow from him for all you are worth, because he will give you all you want and never look to be paid back. Here is the reason a saint goes through the things he does go through—God wants to know if He can make him good 'bread' to feed other people with. The man who has gone through the crucible is going to be a tremendous support to hundreds of others...

If you have a trial of faith, endure it till you get through. If you have been through trials of faith in the past, God is bringing across your path immature souls, and you have no business to despise them but rather to help them through—be to them something that has to be 'sucked'. 'He perceived that virtue had gone out of him', and you will feel the same thing: there are people who spiritually and morally have to suck the vitals out of you, and if you don't keep up the supply from the life of Jesus Christ, you will be like an exhausted volcano before long. You must keep that up and let them nourish themselves from you until they are able to stand on their own feet and take direct life from Him.

PH 204, 206

40

*It is written, Man shall not live by bread alone, but by every word that proceedeth out of the mouth of God.* Matthew 4:4

Our natural reactions are not wrong, although they may be used to express the wrong disposition. God never contradicts our natural reactions; He wants them to be made spiritual. When we are saved God does not alter the construction of our bodily life, but He does expect us to manifest in our bodily life the alteration He has made. We express ourselves naturally through our bodies, and we express the supernatural life of God in the same way, but it can only be done by the sacrifice of the natural. How many of us are spiritual in eating and drinking and sleeping? Those acts were spiritual in our Lord; His relationship to the Father was such that all His natural life was obedient to Him, and when He saw that His Father's will was for Him not to obey a natural reaction, He instantly obeyed His Father (see Matthew 4:1–4).

If our Lord had been fanatical He would have said—'I have been so long without food, I will never eat again.' That would have been to obey a principle instead of God. When God is educating us along the line of turning the natural into the spiritual, we are apt to become fanatical. Because by God's grace things have been done which are miraculous, we become devoted to the miracle and forget God, then when difficulties come we say it is the antagonism of the devil. The fact is we are grossly ignorant of the way God has made us. All that we need is a little of what we understand by pluck in the natural world put into the spiritual. Don't let your body get on top and say there is nothing after all in what God said. Stand up to the difficulty, and all that you ever believed about the transforming grace of God will be proved in your bodily life.

MFL 68

*Is not this the carpenter's son? is not his mother called Mary? and his brethren, James, and Joses, and Simon, and Judas? And his sisters, are they not all with us? Whence then hath this man all these things?* Matthew 13:55–56. (See also Mark 3:21; Luke 2:51; John 7:5)

These were the intimates our Lord grew up with in His own historic life. We say, 'Oh, but the Lord must have had a sweet and delightful home life.' But we are wrong: He had an exceedingly difficult home life. Jesus Christ's intimates were brothers and sisters

41

who did not believe in Him, and He says that the disciple is not above his Master (Luke 6:40). The next time you feel inclined to grouse over uncongenial companions, remember that Jesus Christ had a devil in His company for three years.

Our Lord preached His first public sermon in the place where He was brought up, where He was most intimately known, and they smashed up His service and tried to kill Him. 'Oh, but,' we say, 'I expected that when I was saved and sanctified, my father and mother and brothers and sisters would be made right, but instead they seem to be all wrong.' If the mother of our Lord misunderstood Him, and His brethren did not believe in Him, the same things will happen to His life in us, and we must not think it strange concerning the misunderstandings of others. The life of the Son of God in us is brought into the same kind of circumstances that the historic life of Jesus Christ was brought into, and what was true of Him will be true also of His life in us.

PR 44

### February 22

*Present your bodies a living sacrifice.* Romans 12:1

If we do not resolutely cast out the natural, the supernatural can never become natural in us. There are some Christians in whom the supernatural and the natural seem one and the same, and you say— Well, they are not one with me, I find the natural at 'loggerheads' with the spiritual. The reason is that the other life has gone through the fanatical stage of cutting off the right arm, gone through the discipline of maiming the natural, completely casting it out, and God has brought it back into its right relationship with the spiritual on top, and the spiritual manifests itself in a life which knows no division into sacred and secular. There is no royal road there, each one has it entirely in his own hands; it is not a question of praying but of performing . . .

'Present your bodies a living sacrifice'—go to the funeral of your own independence. It is not a question of giving up sin, but of giving up my right to myself, my natural independence and self-assertiveness. Immediately I do, the natural cries out and goes through terrific suffering. There are things in me which must go through death or they will abide alone and ruin the personal life (cf. John 12:24). But if I sternly put them through death, God will bring them back into the right inheritance. Jesus says 'If any man will be my disciple, let him

42

deny himself', i.e., deny his right to himself, and a man has to realize Who Jesus Christ is before he will do it. It is the things that are right and noble and good from the natural standpoint that keep us back from God's best. To discern that the natural virtues antagonize surrender to God, is to begin to see where the battle lies. It is going to cost the natural everything, not something.

NKW 104

**February 23**

*And Jesus called a little child unto him...and said... Except ye... become as little children...* Matthew 18:2-3

A healthy man does not know what health is: a sick man knows what health is, because he has lost it; and a saint rightly related to God does not know what the will of God is because he *is* the will of God. A disobedient soul knows what the will of God is because he has disobeyed. The illustration Jesus gives to His disciples of a saintly life is a little child. Jesus did not put up a child as an ideal, but to show them that ambition has no place whatever in the disposition of a Christian. The life of a child is unconscious in its fullness of life, and the source of its life is implicit love. To be made children over again causes pain because we have to reconstruct our mental ways of looking at things after God has dealt with our heart experience. Some of us retain our old ways of looking at things, and the deliverance is painful. Paul urges that we allow the pain—'Let this mind be in you, which was also in Christ Jesus'; 'bringing into captivity every thought to the obedience of Christ' It is hard to do it. In the beginning we are so anxious—'Lord, give me a message for this meeting', until we learn that if we live in the centre of God's will, He will give us messages when He likes and withhold them when He likes. We try to help God help Himself to us; we have to get out of the way and God will help Himself to our lives in every detail. Have we learned to form the mind of Christ by the pain of deliverance till we know we are drawing on Him for everything?

IWP 46

**February 24**

*O Lord, thou hast searched me, and known me...* Psalm 139:1

The 139th Psalm ought to be the personal experience of every Christian. My own introspection, or exploration of myself, will lead

43

me astray, but when I realize not only that God knows me, but that He is the only One who does, I see the vital importance of intercessory introspection. Every man is too big for himself, thank God for everyone who realizes it and, like the Psalmist, hands himself over to be searched out by God. We only know ourselves as God searches us. 'God knows me' is different from 'God is omniscient'; the latter is a mere theological statement; the former is a child of God's most precious possession—'O Lord, thou hast searched *me*, and known *me*.'

... The Psalmist implies—'Thou art the God of the early mornings, the God of the late at nights; the God of the mountain peaks, the God of the sea; but my God, my soul has further horizons than the early mornings, deeper darkness than the nights of the earth, higher peaks than any mountain, greater depths than any sea—Thou who art the God of all these, be my God. I cannot search to the heights or to the depths; there are motives I cannot trace, dreams I cannot get at; my God, search me out and explore me, and let me know that thou hast.' Look back over your past history with God and you will see that this is the place He has been bringing you to— 'God knows me, and I know He does.' You can't shift the man who knows that; there is the sanity of almighty God about him. It is an interpretation of what Jesus Christ said—'The very hairs of your head are all numbered. Fear not therefore...'

BE 85, 86

February 25

*And thine ears shall hear a word behind thee saying, This is the way, walk ye in it; when ye turn to the right hand, and when ye turn to the left.* Isaiah 30:21

The surest test of maturity is the power to look back without blinking anything. When we look back we get either hopelessly despairing or hopelessly conceited. The difference between the natural backward look and the spiritual backward look is in what we forget. Forgetting in the natural domain is the outcome of vanity —the only things I intend to remember are those in which I figure as being a very fine person! Forgetting in the spiritual domain is the gift of God. The Spirit of God never allows us to forget what we have been, but He does make us forget what we have attained to, which is quite unnatural. The surest sign that you are growing in mature appreciation of your salvation is that as you look back you

44

never think now of the things you used to bank on before. Think of the difference between your first realization of God's forgiveness, and your realization of what it cost God to forgive you; the hilarity in the one case has been merged into holiness, you have become intensely devoted to God who forgave you.

CHI 86

## February 26

*Submit yourself to every ordinance of man for the Lord's sake.*
1 Peter 2:13
Peter's statements in these verses are remarkable, and they are statements the modern Christian does not like. He is outlining what is to be the conduct of saints in relation to the moral institutions based on the government of man by man. No matter, he says, what may be the condition of the community to which you belong, behave yourself as a saint in it. Many people are righteous in connection with human institutions. Paul continually dealt with insubordination in spiritual people. Degeneration in the Christian life comes in because of this refusal to recognize the insistence God places on obedience to human institutions. Take the institution of home life. Home is God's institution, and He says, 'Honour thy father and thy mother'; are we fulfilling our duty to our parents as laid down in God's Book? Guard well the central institutions ordained by God, and there will be fewer problems in civilized life. We have to maintain spiritual reality wherever we are placed by the engineering of our circumstances by God; as servants we are to be subject to our masters, to the froward master as well as to the good and gentle.

BE 23

## February 27

*Bring forth therefore fruits meet for repentance.* Matthew 3:8
The experimental aspect of Redemption is repentance; the only proof that a man is born from above is that he brings forth 'fruits meet for repentance'. That is the one characteristic of New Testament regeneration, and it hits desperately hard because the Holy Spirit brings conviction on the most humiliating lines. Many a powerless, fruitless Christian life is the result of a refusal to obey in some insignificant thing—'first go'. It is extraordinary what we are brought up against when the Holy Spirit is at work in us, and the thing that

45

fights longest against His demands is my prideful claim to my right to myself. The only sign of regeneration in practical experience is that we begin to make our life in accordance with the demands of God. Jesus Christ did not only come to present what God's normal man should be, He came to make the way for everyone of us to get there, and the gateway is His Cross. I cannot begin by imitating Jesus Christ, but only by being born into His Kingdom; then when I have been regenerated and have received the heredity of the Son of God, I find that His teaching belongs to that heredity, not to my human nature.

All this means great deliberation on our part. God does not expect us to understand these things in order to be saved, salvation is of God's free grace; but He does expect us to do our bit in appreciation of His 'so great salvation'.

CHI 23

*Work out your own salvation.* Philippians 2:12

Our Lord warns that the devout life of a disciple is not a dream, but a decided discipline which calls for the use of all our powers. No amount of determination can give me the new life of God, that is a gift; where the determination comes in is in letting that new life work itself out according to Christ's standard. We are always in danger of confounding what we can do with what we cannot do. We cannot save ourselves, or sanctify ourselves, or give ourselves the Holy Spirit; only God can do that. Confusion continually occurs when we try to do what God alone can do, and try to persuade ourselves that God will do what we alone can do. We imagine that God is going to make us walk in the light; God will not; it is we who must walk in the light. God gives us the power to do it, but we have to see that we use the power. God puts the power and the life into us and fills us with His Spirit, but we have to work it out. 'Work out your own salvation,' says Paul, not, 'work for your salvation', but *'work it out'*; and as we do, we realize that the noble life of a disciple is gloriously difficult and the difficulty of it rouses us up to overcome, not faint and cave in. It is always necessary to make an effort to be noble.

SSM 94

*Why beholdest thou the mote that is in thy brother's eye, but considerest not the beam that is in thine own eye?* Matthew 7:3

We are all shrewd in pointing out the mote in our brother's eye. It puts us in a superior position, we are finer spiritual characters than they. Where do we find that characteristic? In the Lord Jesus? Never!...

We cannot get away from the penetration of Jesus Christ. If I see the mote in my brother's eye, it is because I have a beam in my own. It is a most home-coming statement. If I have let God remove the beam from my own outlook by His mighty grace, I will carry with me the implicit sunlight confidence that what God has done for me He can easily do for you, because you have only a splinter, I had a log of wood! This is the confidence God's salvation gives us, we are so amazed at the way God has altered us that we can despair of no one.

SSM 81

*And it came to pass in those days, that he went out into a mountain to pray, and continued all night in prayer to God. And when it was day, he called unto him his disciples.* Luke 6:12–13

It is not a haphazard thing, but in the constitution of God, that there are certain times of the day when it not only seems easier, but it *is* easier, to meet God. If you have ever prayed in the dawn you will ask yourself why you were so foolish as not to do it always: it is difficult to get into communion with God in the midst of the hurly-burly of the day. George MacDonald said that if he did not open wide the door of his mind to God in the early morning he worked on the finite all the rest of the day—'stand on the finite, act upon the wrong'. It is not sentiment but an implicit reality that the conditions of dawn and communion with God go together. When the day of God appears there will be no night, always dawn and day. There is nothing of the nature of strain in God's Day, it is all free and beautiful and fine. 'And there shall be night no more' ...

We all know when we are at our best intellectually, and if instead of giving that time to God we give it to our own development, we not only rob God, but rob ourselves of the possibility of His life thriving in us. We heard it said that we shall suffer if we do not

47

pray; I question it, What will suffer if we do not pray is the life of God in us; but when we do pray and devote the dawns to God His nature in us develops, there is less self-realization and more Christ-realization.

HGM 87, 88

### March 2

*Jesus . . . leadeth them up into a high mountain apart by themselves: and he was transfigured before them.* Mark 9:2

We all have what are called 'brilliant moments'. We are not always dull, not always contented with eating and drinking. There are times when we are unlike our usual selves, both in the way of depression and of brilliance, when one moment stands out from every other, and we suddenly see the way which we should go. And there is the counterpart in spiritual experience of those times in the natural life. There are tides of the spirit, immortal moments, moments of amazing clearness of vision, and it is by these moments and by what we see then, that we are to be judged. 'While ye have the light, believe on the light,' said Jesus—do not believe what you see when you are not in the light. God is going to judge us by the times when we have been in living communion with Him, not by what we feel like today. God judges us entirely by what we have seen. We are not judged by the fact that we live up to the light of our conscience; we are judged by the Light, Jesus Christ. 'I am the light of the world'; and if we do not know Jesus Christ, we are to blame. The only reason we do not know Him is because we have not bothered our heads about Him. Honestly, does it matter to us whether Jesus lived and died, or did anything at all? 'But there are so many humbugs.' There is no counterfeit without the reality. Is Jesus Christ a fraud? We are to be judged by Him. 'This is the condemnation, that light is come into the world, and men loved the darkness rather than the light.' We are not judged by the light we have, but by the light we have refused to accept. God holds us responsible for what we will not look at. A man is never the same after he has seen Jesus. We are judged by our immortal moments, the moments in which we have seen the light of God.

PH 119

48

**March 3**

*Come unto me.* Matthew 11:28

We make covenants with ourselves, or with our experiences, or with our transactions—I came out to the penitent form; or, I surrendered to God. That is a covenant of self-idolatry, an attempt to consecrate our earnest consecration to God. It is never a question of covenanting to keep our vows before God, but of our relationship to God Who makes the covenant with us. In the matter of salvation it is God's honour that is at stake, not our honour. Few of us have faith in God, the whole thing is a solemn vow with our religious selves. We promise that we will do what God wants; we vow that we will remain true to Him, and we solemnly mark a text to this effect; but no human being can do it. We have to steadily refuse to promise anything and give ourselves over to God's promise, flinging ourselves entirely on to Him, which is the only possible act of the faith that comes as God's gift. It is a personal relation to God's faith—'between me and thee'. 'Come unto me,' said Jesus. The thing that keeps us from coming is religious self-idolatry.

NKW 63

**March 4**

*...the love of God is shed abroad in our hearts by the Holy Ghost which is given unto us.* Romans 5:5

This does not mean that when we receive the Holy Spirit He enables us to have the capacity for loving God, but that He sheds abroad in our hearts *the love of God*, a much more fundamental and marvellous thing. It is pathetic the number of people who are piously trying to make their poor human hearts love God! The Holy Spirit sheds abroad in my heart, not the power to love God, but the very nature of God; and the nature of God coming into me makes me part of God's consciousness, not God part of my consciousness. I am unconscious of God because I have been taken up into His consciousness. Paul puts it in Galatians 2:20 (a verse with which we are perfectly familiar, but which none of us will ever fathom, no matter how long we live, or how much we experience of God's grace): 'I am crucified with Christ; nevertheless I live; yet not I, but Christ liveth in me.' ...

In the Sermon on the Mount Jesus Christ says, in effect, that when as His disciples we have been initiated into the kind of life He lives, we are based on the knowledge that God is our heavenly Father and

49

that He is love. Then there comes the wonderful working out of this knowledge in our lives; it is not that we *won't* worry, but that we have come to the place where we *cannot* worry, because the Holy Spirit has shed abroad the love of God in our hearts, and we find that we can never think of anything our heavenly Father will forget. Although great clouds and perplexities may come, as they did in the case of Job, and of the Apostle Paul, and in the case of every saint, yet they never touch 'the secret place of the Most High'. 'Therefore will not we fear, though the earth be removed, and though the mountains be carried into the midst of the sea.' The Spirit of God has so centred us in God and everything is so rightly adjusted that we do not fear.

BP 218

### March 5

*... for he himself knew what was in man.* John 2:25

Our Lord seemed to go so easily and calmly amongst all kinds of men—when He met a man who could sink to the level of Judas He never turned cynical, never lost heart or got discouraged; and when He met a loyal loving heart like John's He was not unduly elated, He never overpraised him. When we meet extra goodness we feel amazingly hopeful about everybody, and when we meet extra badness we feel exactly the opposite; but Jesus 'knew what was in man'. He knew exactly what human beings were like and what they needed; and He saw in them something no one else ever saw—hope for the most degraded. Jesus had a tremendous hopefulness about man.

CHI 96

In Matthew 15, our Lord tells His disciples what the human heart is like—'Out of the heart proceed...' and then follows the ugly catalogue. We say, 'I never felt any of those things in my heart', and we prefer to trust our innocent ignorance rather than Jesus Christ's penetration. Either Jesus Christ must be the supreme Authority on the human heart, or He is not worth listening to. If I make conscious innocence the test, I am likely to come to a place where I will find with a shuddering awakening that what Jesus said is true, and I will be appalled at the possibility of evil in me. If I have never been a blackguard, the reason is a mixture of cowardice and the protection of civilized life; but when I am undressed before God I find that

Jesus Christ is right in His diagnosis. As long as I remain under the refuge of innocence, I am living in a fool's paradise.

SSM 27

**March 6**

*And he, when he is come, will convict the world in respect of sin ... because they believe not on me.* John 16:8, 9

Note what causes you the deepest concern before God. Does social evil produce a deeper concern than the fact that people do not believe on Jesus Christ? It was not social evil that brought Jesus Christ down from heaven, it was the great primal sin of independence of God that brought God's Son to Calvary. Sin is not measured by a law or by a social standard, but by a Person. The Holy Spirit is unmistakable in His working: 'and he, when he is come, will convict the world in respect of sin... *because they believe not on me.*' That is the very essence of sin. The Holy Spirit brings moral conviction on that line, and on no other. A man does not need the Holy Spirit to tell him that external sins are wrong, ordinary culture and education will do that; but it does take the Holy Spirit to convict us of sin as our Lord defined it—'*because they believe not on me*'. Sin is not measured by a standard of moral rectitude and uprightness, but by my relationship to Jesus Christ. The point is, am I morally convinced that the only sin there is in the sight of the Holy Ghost, is disbelief in Jesus?

TGR 107

**March 7**

*I have set watchmen upon thy walls, O Jerusalem; they shall never hold their peace day nor night; ye that are the Lord's remembrancers, take ye no rest, and give him no rest, till he establish, and till he make Jerusalem a praise in the earth.* Isaiah 62:6–7

Do I know anything experimentally about this aspect of things? Have I ever spent one minute before God in intercessory importunity over the sins of other people? If we take this statement of the prophet and turn the searchlight on ourselves, we will be covered with shame and confusion because of our miserably selfish, self-centred Christianity.

How many of us have ever entered into this Ministry of the Interior

51

where we become identified with our Lord and with the Holy Spirit in intercession? It is a threefold intercession: at the Throne of God, Jesus Christ; within the saint, the Holy Ghost; outside the saint, common-sense circumstances and common-sense people, and as these are brought before God in prayer the Holy Spirit gets a chance to make intercession according to the will of God. That is the meaning of personal sanctification, and that is why the barriers of personal testimony must be broken away and effaced by the realization of why we are sanctified—not to be fussy workers for God, but to be His servants, and this is the work, vicarious intercession.

One of the first lessons we learn in the Ministry of the Interior is to talk things out before God in soliloquy—tell God what you know He knows in order that you may get to know it as He does. All the harshness will go and the suffering sadness of God's Spirit will take its place, and gradually you will be brought into sympathy with His point of view.

When God puts a weight on you for intercession for souls don't shirk it by talking to them. It is much easier to talk to them than to talk to God about them—much easier to talk to them than to take it before God and let the weight crush the life out of you until gradually and patiently God lifts the life out of the mire. That is where very few of us go.

GW 20

### March 8

*Ye believe in God, believe also in me.* John 14:1

We begin our religious life by believing our beliefs, we accept what we are taught without questioning; but when we come up against things we begin to be critical, and find out that the beliefs, however right, are not right for us because we have not bought them by suffering. What we take for granted is never ours until we have bought it by pain. A thing is worth just what it costs. When we go through the suffering of experience we seem to lose everything, but bit by bit we get it back.

It is absurd to tell a man he must believe this and that; in the meantime he can't! Scepticism is produced by telling men what to believe. We are in danger of putting the cart before the horse and saying a man must believe certain things before he can be a Christian; his beliefs are the effect of his being a Christian, not the cause of it. Our Lord's word 'believe' does not refer to an intellectual act, but to a moral act. With Him 'to believe' means 'to commit'. 'Commit yourself to me,' He says, and it takes a man all he is worth to believe in Jesus Christ. The man who has been through a crisis is more likely to commit himself to a Person, he sees more clearly; before the crisis comes we are certain, because we are shallow.

AUG 78

*Consider the lilies, how they grow.* Luke 12:27

Have you ever noticed the kind of pictures God gives to the saints? There are always pictures of creation, never pictures of men. God speaks of the unfailing stars and the upholding of the 'worm Jacob'. He talks about the marvels of creation, and makes His people forget the rush of business ideas that stamp the kingdoms of this world. The Spirit of God says—'Do not take your pattern and print from those; the God who holds you is the God who made the world— take your pattern from Him.'

Our Lord always took His illustrations from His Father's handi-work. In illustrating the spiritual life, our tendency is to catch the tricks of the world, to watch the energy of the business man, and to apply these methods to God's work. Jesus Christ tells us to take the lessons of our lives from the things men never look at—'Consider the lilies'; 'Behold the fowls of the air'. How often do we look at clouds, or grass, at sparrows, or flowers? Why, we have no time to look at them, we are in the rush of things—it is absurd to sit dreaming about sparrows and trees and clouds! Thank God, when He raises us to the heavenly places, He manifests in us the very mind that was in Christ Jesus, unhasting and unresting, calm, steady and strong.

OBH 33

*My heart consulted in me.* Nehemiah 5:7

Meditation means getting to the middle of a thing; not being like a pebble in a brook letting the water of thought go over us; that is reverie, not meditation. Meditation is an intense spiritual activity, it means bringing every bit of the mind into harness and concentrat-ing its powers; it includes both deliberation and reflection.

Deliberation means being able to weigh well what we think, conscious all the time that we are deliberating and meditating. 'My heart consulted in me' (Nehemiah 5:7, marg.)—that is exactly the meaning of meditation, also—'But Mary kept all these things, pondering them in her heart' (Luke 2:19, RV marg.).

A great many delightful people mistake meditation for prayer; meditation often accompanies prayer, but it is not prayer, it is simply the power of the natural heart to get to the middle of things. Prayer is asking, whereby God puts processes to work and creates things which are not in existence until we ask. Prayer is definite talk to God, around which God puts an atmosphere, and we get answers back. Meditation has a reflex action; men without an ounce of the Spirit of God in them can meditate, but that is not prayer. This fundamental distinction is frequently obscured. Mary 'pondered' these things in her heart, i.e., she meditated on them, got right to the centre of the revelations about her Son, but as far as we know, she did not utter a word to anyone. But read St John's Gospel, and a wonder will occur to you. St Augustine has called John's Gospel 'the Heart of Jesus Christ'. Recall what Jesus said to His mother about John: 'Woman, behold, thy son!' and to John about Mary, 'Behold, thy mother! And from that hour the disciple took her unto his own home.' It is surely quite legitimate to think that Mary's meditations found marvellous expression to John under the guidance of the Spirit of God, and found a place in his Gospel and Epistles.

BP 112

**March 11**

*And God said ... Let it not be grievous in thy sight.* Genesis 21:12

The dilemmas of our personal life with God are few if we obey and many if we are wilful. Spiritually the dilemma arises from the disinclination for discipline; every time I refuse to discipline my natural self, I become less and less of a person and more and more of an independent, impertinent individual. Individuality is the characteristic of the natural man; personality is the characteristic of the spiritual man. That is why our Lord can never be defined in terms of individuality, but only in terms of personality. Individuality is the characteristic of the child, it is the husk of the personal life. It is all 'elbows', it separates and isolates; personality can merge and be

54

blended. The shell of individuality is God's created covering for the protection of the personal life, but individuality must go in order that the personal life may be brought out into fellowship with God—'that they may be one, even as We are one'.

NKW 101

If we have never been hurt by a statement of Jesus, it is questionable whether we have ever really heard Him speak. Jesus Christ has no tenderness whatever towards anything that is ultimately going to ruin a man for the service of God. If the Spirit of God brings to our mind a word of the Lord that hurts, we may be perfectly certain there is something He wants to hurt to death.

SSY 50

### March 12

*As the Father taught me, I speak these things.* John 8:28 (RV)

The secret of our Lord's holy speech was that He habitually submitted His intelligence to His Father. Whenever problems pressed on the human side, as they did in the temptation, our Lord had within Himself the Divine remembrance that every problem had been solved in counsel with His Father before He became Incarnate (cf. Revelation 13:8), and that therefore the one thing for Him was to do the will of His Father, and to do it in His Father's way. Satan tried to hasten Him, tried to make Him face the problems as a Man and do God's will in His own way: 'The Son can do nothing of himself, but what he seeth the Father doing' (John 5:19, RV).

Are we intellectually insubordinate, spiritually stiffnecked, dictating to God in pious phraseology what we intend to let Him make us, hunting through the Bible to back up our pet theories? Or have we learned the secret of submitting our intelligence and our reasoning to Jesus Christ's word and will as He submitted His mind to His Father?

The danger with us is that we will only submit our minds to New Testament teaching where the light of our experience shines. 'If we walk in the light'— as our experience is in the light? No, 'if we walk in the light *as he is in the light* ...' We have to keep in the light that God is in, not in the rays of the light of our experience. There are phases of God's truth that cannot be experienced, and as long

55

as we stay in the narrow grooves of our experience we shall never become God-like, but specialists of certain doctrines—Christian oddities. We have to be specialists in devotion to Jesus Christ and in nothing else. If we want to know Jesus Christ's idea of a saint and to find out what holiness means, we must not only read pamphlets about sanctification, we must face ourselves with Jesus Christ, and as we do so He will make us face ourselves with God.

MFL 109

**March 13**

*The young man saith unto him, All these things have I kept from my youth up: what lack I yet?* Matthew 19:20

In listening to some evangelical addresses the practical conclusion one is driven to is that we have to be great sinners before we can be saved; and the majority of men are not great sinners. The rich young man was an upright, sterling, religious man; it would be absurd to talk to him about sin, he was not in the place where he could understand what it meant. There are hundreds of clean-living, upright men who are not convicted of sin, I mean sin in the light of the commandments Jesus mentioned. We need to revise the place we put conviction of sin in and the place the Spirit of God puts it in. There is no mention of sin in the apprehension of Saul of Tarsus, yet no one understood sin more fundamentally than the Apostle Paul. If we reverse God's order and refuse to put the recognition of who Jesus is first, we present a lame type of Christianity which excludes for ever the kind of man represented by this rich young ruler. The most staggering thing about Jesus Christ is that He makes human destiny depend not on goodness or badness, not on things done or not done, but on who we say He is.

IWP 116

**March 14**

*... ourselves your servants for Christ's sake.* 2 Corinthians 4:5

We make the mistake of imagining that service for others springs from love of others; the fundamental fact is that supreme love for our Lord alone gives us the motive power of service to any extent for others—'ourselves your servants for Jesus' sake'. That means I have to identify myself with God's interests in other people, and

God is interested in some extraordinary people, viz., in you and in me, and He is just as interested in the person you dislike as He is in you. I don't know what your natural heart was like before God saved you, but I know what mine was like. I was misunderstood and misrepresented; everybody else was wrong and I was right. Then when God came and gave me a spring-cleaning, dealt with my sin, and filled me with the Holy Spirit, I began to find an extraordinary alteration in myself. I still think the great marvel of the experience of salvation is not the alteration others see in you, but the alteration you find in yourself. When you come across certain people and things and remember what you used to be like in connection with them, and realize what you are now by the grace of God, you are filled with astonishment and joy; where there used to be a well of resentment and bitterness, there is now a well of sweetness.

CHI 90

**March 15**

*What I tell you in the darkness, speak ye in the light; and what ye hear in the ear, proclaim upon the housetops.* Matthew 10:27

'What I tell you in the darkness ...' Let it be understood that the darkness our Lord speaks of is not darkness caused by sin or disobedience, but rather darkness caused from excess of light. There are times in the life of every disciple when things are not clear or easy, when it is not possible to know what to do or say. Such times of darkness come as a discipline to the character and as the means of fuller knowledge of the Lord. Such darkness is a time for listening, not for speaking. This aspect of darkness as a necessary side to fellowship with God is not unusual in the Bible (see Isaiah 5:30; 50:10; 1 Peter 1:6–7). The Lord shares the darkness with His disciple— 'What I tell you in the darkness' ... He is there. He knows all about it. The sense of mystery must always be, for mystery means being guided by obedience to Someone Who knows more than I do. On the Mount of Transfiguration this darkness from excess of light is brought out—'They feared as they entered into the cloud', but in the cloud 'they saw no one any more, save Jesus only with themselves.'

PH 10

57

*I will give thee the treasures of darkness.* Isaiah 45:3

We would never have suspected that treasures were hidden there, and in order to get them we have to go through things that involve us in perplexity. There is nothing more wearying to the eye than perpetual sunshine, and the same is true spiritually. The valley of the shadow gives us time to reflect, and we learn to praise God for the valley because in it our soul was restored in its communion with God. God gives us a new revelation of His kindness in the valley of the shadow. What are the days and the experiences that have furthered us most? The days of green pastures, of absolute ease? No, they have their value; but the days that have furthered us most in character are the days of stress and cloud, the days when we could not see our way but had to stand still and wait; and as we waited, the comforting and sustaining and restoring of God came in a way we never imagined possible before.

PH 84

*Whosoever shall come after me, let him deny himself, and take up his cross, and follow me. For whosoever will save his life shall lose it; but whosoever shall lose his life for my sake and the gospel's, the same shall save it.* Mark 8:34–5

Jesus says if a man gains himself, he loses himself; and if he loses himself for His sake, he gains himself.

Beware of introducing the idea of time; the instant the Spirit of God touches your spirit, it is manifested in the body. Do not get the idea of a three-storied building with a vague, mysterious, ethereal upper story called spirit, a middle story called soul, and a lower story called body. We are personality, which shows itself in three phases—spirit, soul, and body. Never think that what energizes the spirit takes time before it gets into the soul and body, it shows itself instantly, from the crown of the head to the soles of the feet.

Jesus says that men are capable of missing the supreme good and His point of view is not acceptable to us because we do not believe we are capable of missing it. We are far removed from Jesus Christ's point of view today, we take the natural rationalistic line, and His teaching is no good whatever unless we believe the main gist of His

58

gospel, viz., that we have to have something planted into us by supernatural grace. Jesus Christ's point of view is that a man may miss the chief good; we like to believe we will end all right somehow, but Jesus says we won't. If my feet are going in one direction, I cannot advance one step in the opposite direction unless I turn right round.

HG 62

**March 18**

*The waters wear the stones: thou washest away the things which grow out of the dust of the earth; and thou destroyest the hope of man.* Job 14:19

In physical nature there is something akin to habit. Flowing water hollows out for itself a channel which grows broader and deeper, and after having ceased to flow for a time, it will resume again the path traced before. It is never as easy to fold a piece of paper the first time as after, for after the first time it folds naturally. The process of habit runs all through physical nature, and our brain is physical. When once we understand the bodily machine with which we have to work out what God works in, we find that our body becomes the greatest ally of our spiritual life. The difference between a sentimental Christian and a sanctified saint is just here. The sanctified saint is one who has disciplined the body into perfect obedience to the dictates of the Spirit of God, consequently his body does with the greatest of ease whatever God wants him to do. The sentimental type of Christian is the sighing, tear-flowing, beginning-over-again Christian who always has to go to prayer meetings, always has to be stirred up, or to be soothed and put in bandages, because he has never formed the habit of obedience to the Spirit of God. Our spiritual life does not grow *in spite of* the body, but *because* of the body. 'Of the earth, earthy—is man's glory, not his shame; and it is in the 'earth, earthy' that the full regenerating work of Jesus Christ has its ultimate reach.

MFL 39

**March 19**

*If thou be the Son of God, command that these stones become bread.* Matthew 4:3

It is this temptation which has betaken the Christian Church

59

today. We worship Man, and God is looked upon as a blessing machine for humanity. We find it in the most spiritual movements of all. For instance, watch how subtly the missionary call has changed. It is not now the watchword of the Moravian call, which saw behind every suffering heathen the Face of Christ: the need has come to be the call. It is not that Jesus Christ said 'Go', but that the heathen will not be saved if we do not go. It is a subtle change that is sagacious, but not spiritual. The need is never the call: the need is the opportunity. Jesus Christ's first obedience was to the will of His Father—'Lo, in the volume of the Book it is written of me, I delight to do thy will', and, 'As the Father hath sent me, even so send I you.' The saint has to remain loyal to God in the midst of the machinery of successful civilization, in the midst of worldly prosperity, and in the face of crushing defeat ...

The insinuation of putting men's needs first, success first, has entered into the very domain of evangelism, and has substituted 'the passion for souls' for 'the passion for Christ', and we experience shame when we realize how completely we have muddled the whole thing by not maintaining steadfast loyalty to Jesus Christ.

SHL 95–7

March 20

*Every one that asketh receiveth.* Matthew 7:8

It appears as if God were sometimes most unnatural; we ask Him to bless our lives and bring benedictions, and what immediately follows turns everything into actual ruin. The reason is that before God can make the heart into a garden of the Lord, He has to plough it, and that will take away a great deal of natural beauty. If we interpret God's designs by our desires, we will say He gave us a scorpion when we asked an egg, and a serpent when we asked a fish, and a stone when we asked for bread. But our Lord indicates that such thinking and speaking is too hasty, it is not born of faith or reliance on God. 'Everyone that asketh receiveth.'

DPR 48

'In everything give thanks,' says Paul, not—Give thanks *for* everything, but give thanks that in everything that transpires there abides the real Presence of God. God is more real than the actual things—'therefore will we not fear, though the earth be removed'. We think that our actual life is profound until something happens—a war or a bereavement, and we are flung clean abroad, then through the agony of the mystery of life we cry out to God and there comes the voice of Jesus—'Come unto Me.'

PH 135

*I have heard of thee by the hearing of the ear; but now mine eye seeth thee. Wherefore I abhor myself, and repent in dust and ashes.*
Job 42:5–6

Because a man has altered his life it does not necessarily mean that he has repented. A man may have lived a bad life and suddenly stopped being bad, not because he has repented, but because he is like an exhausted volcano. The fact that he has become good is no sign of his having become a Christian. The bedrock of Christianity is repentance. The apostle Paul never forgot what he had been; when he speaks of 'forgetting those things which are behind', he is referring to what he has attained to; the Holy Spirit never allowed him to forget what he had been (see 1 Corinthians 15:9, Ephesians 3:8, 1 Timothy 1:13–15). Repentance means that I estimate exactly what I am in God's sight and I am sorry for it, and on the basis of the Redemption I become the opposite. The only repentant man is the holy man, i.e., the one who becomes the opposite of what he was because something has entered into him. Any man who knows himself knows that he cannot be holy, therefore if he does become holy, it is because God has 'shipped' something into him; he is now 'presenced with Divinity', and can begin to bring forth 'fruits meet for repentance' ...

'Now mine eye seeth thee,' said Job, 'wherefore I abhor myself' ('I loathe my words' RV marg.) 'and repent in dust and ashes.' When I enthrone Jesus Christ I say the thing that is violently opposed to the old rule. I deny my old ways as entirely as Peter denied his Lord.

Jesus Christ's claim is that He can put a new disposition, His own disposition, Holy Spirit, into any man, and it will be manifested in all that he does. But the disposition of the Son of God can only enter my life by the way of repentance.

BFB 103

## March 22

*Though our outward man perish, yet the inward man is renewed day by day.* 2 Corinthians 4:16

Paul faces the possibility of old age, of decay, and of death, with no rebellion and no sadness. Paul never hid from himself the effect which his work had upon him, he knew it was killing him, and, like his Master, he was old before his time; but there was no whining and no retiring from the work. Paul was not a fool, he did not waste his energy ridiculously, neither did he ignore the fact that it was his genuine apostolic work and nothing else that was wearing him out. Michelangelo said a wonderful thing—'the more the marble wears, the better the image grows', and it is an illustration of this very truth. Every wasting of nerve and brain in work for God brings a corresponding uplift and strengthening to spiritual muscle and fibre.

MIC 81

## March 23

*Moreover if thy brother shall trespass against thee, go and tell him his fault between thee and him alone: if he shall hear thee, thou hast gained thy brother.* Matthew 18:15

It would be an immoral thing to forgive a man who did not say he was sorry. If a man sins against you and you go to him and point out that he has done wrong—if he hears you, then you can forgive him; but if he is obstinate you can do nothing; you cannot say 'I forgive you', you must bring him to a sense of justice. Jesus Christ said, 'I say unto you, Love your enemies', but He also said the most appallingly stern things that were ever uttered, e.g. '... neither will your Father forgive your trespasses.' I cannot forgive my enemies and remain just unless they cease to be my enemies and give proof of their sorrow, which must be expressed in repentance. I have to remain steadfastly true to God's justice. There are times when it would be easier to say, 'Oh well, it does not matter, I forgive you', but Jesus insists that the uttermost farthing must be paid. The love of God is based on justice and holiness, and I must forgive on the same basis.

HGM 104

*Jesus said unto them, Come ye after me.* Mark 1:17
We have come to the conclusion nowadays that a man must be a conscious sinner before Jesus Christ can do anything for him. The early disciples were not attracted to Jesus because they wanted to be saved from sin; they had no conception that they needed saving. They were attracted to Him by a dominating sincerity, by sentiments other than those which we say make men come to Jesus. There was nothing theological in their following, no consciousness of passing from death unto life, no knowledge of what Jesus meant when He talked about His Cross.... They did not follow Jesus because they wanted to be saved, but because they could not help following. Three years later when again Jesus said, 'Follow me,' it was a different matter; many things had happened during these years. The first 'Follow me' meant an external following; now it was to be a following in internal martyrdom (see John 21:18–19).

MC 102

*Blessed be the God and Father of our Lord Jesus Christ, who hath blessed us with all spiritual blessings in heavenly places in Christ.* Ephesians 1:3
The sanctified saint has to alter the horizon of other people's lives, and he does it by showing that they can be lifted on to a higher plane by the grace of God, viz., into the heavenly places in Christ Jesus. If you look at the horizon from the sea shore you will not see much of the sea, but climb higher up the cliff, and as you rise higher the horizon keeps level with your eye and you see more in between. Paul is seated in the heavenly places and he can see the whole world mapped out in God's plan. He is looking ahead like a watchman, and his words convey the calm, triumphant contemplation of a conqueror. Some of us get distracted because we have not this world-wide outlook, we see only the little bit inside our own 'bandbox'. The apostle Paul has burst his bandbox, he has been lifted up on to a new plane in Christ Jesus and he sees now from His standpoint. The preacher and the worker must learn to look at life as a whole.

MIC 86

Always keep in contact with those books and those people that enlarge your horizon and make it possible for you to stretch yourself mentally. The Spirit of God is always the spirit of liberty; the spirit that is not of God is the spirit of bondage, the spirit of oppression and depression. The Spirit of God convicts vividly and tensely, but He is always the Spirit of liberty. God Who made the birds never made bird-cages; it is men who make bird-cages, and after a while we become cramped and can do nothing but chirp and stand on one leg. When we get out into God's great free life, we discover that that is the way God means us to live 'the glorious liberty of the children of God'.

MFL 92

### March 26

*Be still, and know that I am God.* Psalm 46:10

It is only when our lives are hid with Christ in God that we learn how to be silent unto God, not silent about Him, but silent with the strong restful certainty that all is well, behind everything stands God, and the strength of the soul is that it knows it. There are no panics intellectual or moral. What a lot of panicky sparrows we are, the majority of us. We chatter and tweet under God's eaves until we cannot hear His voice at all—until we learn the wonderful life and music of the Lord Jesus telling us that our heavenly Father is the God of the sparrows, and by the marvellous transformation of grace He can turn the sparrows into His nightingales that can sing through every night of sorrow. A sparrow cannot sing through a night of sorrow, and no soul can sing through a night of sorrow unless it has learned to be silent unto God—one look, one thought about my Father in heaven, and it is all right.

IWP 91

### March 27

*Ye are the salt of the earth.* Matthew 5:13

Some modern teachers seem to think our Lord said 'Ye are the *sugar* of the earth', meaning that gentleness and winsomeness without curative-ness is the ideal of the Christian. It is a disadvantage to be salt. Think of the action of salt on a wound, and you will realize this. If you get salt into a wound, it hurts, and when God's children are amongst those who are 'raw' towards God, their presence hurts. The man who is wrong with God is like an open wound, and when 'salt' gets in it causes annoyance and distress and he is spiteful and bitter. The disciples of Jesus in the present dispensation preserve society from corruption; the 'salt' causes excessive irritation which spells persecution for the saint.

SSM 19

The Spirit of God will not work for the cure of some souls without you, and God is going to hold to the account of some of us the souls that have gone uncured, unhealed, untouched by Jesus Christ because we have refused to keep our souls open towards Him, and when the sensual, selfish, wrong lives came around we were not ready to present the Lord Jesus Christ to them by the power of the Holy Spirit.

WG 28

### March 28

*Blessed are they which do hunger and thirst after righteousness: for they shall be filled.* Matthew 5:6

*Blessed are they which are persecuted for righteousness' sake: for theirs is the kingdom of heaven.* Matthew 5:10

The majority of us know nothing whatever about the righteousness that is gifted to us in Jesus Christ, we are still trying to bring human nature up to a pitch it cannot reach because there is something wrong with human nature. The old Puritanism which we are apt to ridicule did the same service for men that Pharisaism did for Saul, and that Roman Catholicism did for Luther; but nowadays we have no 'iron' in us anywhere; we have no idea of righteousness, we do not care whether we are righteous or not. We have not only lost Jesus Christ's idea of righteousness, but we laugh at the Bible idea of righteousness; our god is the conventional righteousness of the society to which we belong.

The claim that our Lord was original is hopelessly wrong, He most emphatically took care not to be; He states that He came to fulfil what was already here but undiscerned. 'Think not that I am come to destroy the law, or the prophets: I am come not to destroy, but to fulfil.' That is why it is so absurd to put our Lord as a Teacher first, He is not first a Teacher, He is a Saviour first. He did not come

65

to give us a new code of morals: He came to enable us to keep a moral code we had not been able to fulfil. Jesus did not teach new things; He taught 'as one having authority'—with power to make men into accordance with what He taught. Jesus Christ came *to make us holy*, not to tell us to be holy: He came to do for us what we could not do for ourselves.

HG 56

**March 29**

*In all things approving ourselves as the ministers of God.* 2 Corinthians 6:4

One of the greatest proofs that you are drawing on the grace of God is that you can be humiliated without manifesting the slightest trace of anything but His grace in you.

2 Corinthians 6, verses 4–10, are Paul's spiritual diary, they describe the outward hardships which proved the hot-bed for the graces of the Spirit—the working together of outward hardships and inward grace. You have been asking the Lord to give you the graces of the Spirit and then some set of circumstances has come and given you a sharp twinge, and you say—'Well, I have asked God to bring out in me the graces of the Spirit, but every time the devil seems to get the better of me.' What you are calling 'the devil' is the very thing God is using to manifest the graces of the Spirit in you.

MIC 96

**March 30**

*Jesus of Nazareth, a man approved of God among you ... Him ye have taken and by wicked hands have crucified and slain.* Acts 2:22-3

The basis of Christ's character appeals to us all. One of the dangers of denominational teaching is that we are told that before we can be Christians we must believe that Jesus Christ is the Son of God, and that the Bible is the Word of God from Genesis to Revelation. Creeds are the effect of our belief, not the cause of it. I do not have to believe all that before I can be a Christian; but after I have become a Christian I begin to try and expound to myself Who Jesus Christ is, and to do that I must first of all take into consideration the New Testament explanation. 'Blessed art thou, Simon Bar-jona, for flesh

66

and blood hath not revealed it unto thee, but my Father which is in heaven.' The *character* of Jesus Christ was lived on an ordinary plane, and exhibits one side only. To ten men who talk about the character of Jesus there is only one who will talk about His Cross. 'I like the story of Jesus Christ's life, I like the things He said. The Sermon on the Mount is beautiful, and I like to read of the things Jesus did; but immediately you begin to talk about the Cross, about forgiveness of sins, about being born from above, it is out of it.' The New Testament reveals that Jesus Christ is God manifest in the flesh, not a Being with two personalities; He is Son of God (the exact expression of Almighty God) and Son of Man (the presentation of God's normal man). As Son of God He reveals what God is like (John 14:9); as Son of Man He mirrors what the human race will be like on the basis of Redemption—a perfect oneness between God and man (Ephesians 4:13). But when we come to the *Cross* of Jesus Christ, that is outside our domain. If Jesus Christ was only a martyr, the New Testament teaching is stupid.

SA 34

### March 31

*The law is spiritual: but I am carnal, sold under sin.* Romans 7:14

Talk about conviction of sin! I wonder how many of us have ever had one five minutes' conviction of sin. It is the rarest thing to know of a man or woman who has been convicted of sin. I am not sure but that if in a meeting one or two people came under the tremendous conviction of the Holy Ghost, the majority of us would not advocate they should be put in a lunatic asylum, instead of referring them to the Cross of Christ. We are unfamiliar nowadays with this tremendous conviction of sin, which Paul refers to as being 'sold under sin', but it is not a bit too strong to say that when once the Spirit of God convicts a man of sin, it is either suicide or the Cross of Christ, no man can stand such conviction long. We have any amount of conviction about pride and wrong dealing with one another, but when the Holy Ghost convicts He does not bother us on that line, He gives us the deep conviction that we are living in independence of God, of a death away from God, and we find all our virtues and goodness and religion has been based on a ruinous thing, viz., the boundless inheritance of covetousness. That is what the Fall means. Let it soak into your thinking, and you will understand the marvel of the salvation of Jesus Christ which means deliverance from covetousness, root and branch. Never lay the flattering unction to your soul that because you are not covetous for money or wordly possessions, you are not covetous for anything. The fuss and distress of owning anything is the last remnant of the disposition of sin. Jesus Christ possessed nothing for Himself (see 2 Corinthians 8:9). Right through the warp and woof of human nature is the ruin caused by the disposition of covetousness which entered into the human race through the Fall, and it is this disposition which the Holy Spirit convicts of.

IWP 25

### April 1

*And they come unto thee as the people cometh, and they sit before thee as my people, and they hear thy words, but do them not.* Ezekiel 33:31 (RV)

There are many today who like to hear the word of God spoken straightly and ruggedly; they listen to, and are delighted with, the stern truth about holiness, about the baptism of the Holy Ghost, and deliverance from sin; they say to one another, 'Come, I pray you, and hear what is the word that cometh forth from the Lord.' They take up a pose of religion, but they are not penitent; they change the truth God requires into a mere attitude. God not only requires us to have a right attitude to Him, He requires us to allow His truth to so react in us that we are actively related to Him. These people flocked to Ezekiel like disciples to a teacher, they looked exactly like God's children, the difference was not on the outside but on the inside, and it would take the penetration of God to see it; but it was all pose, they were not real. The real attitude of sin in the heart towards God is that of being without God; it is pride, the worship of myself, that is the great atheistic fact in human life.

I wonder if any of us are among the enchanted but unchanged crowd? We follow any man or woman who speaks the truth of God; in fact, we are so enchanted that we say, 'If you come and hear this man or woman, you will hear the word of God.' But has it ever altered us into an active, living relationship with God or is it altogether pose? If any of us have got the pose of the people of God but are not real, may God deal with us until He brings us into a right relationship to Himself through the Atonement of the Lord Jesus Christ.

GW 90

*I live; and yet no longer I, but Christ liveth in me.* Galatians 2:20
As long as we use the image of our experience, of our feelings, of our answers to prayer, we shall never begin to understand what the Apostle Paul means when he says, 'I live; and yet no longer I, but Christ liveth in me.' The whole exercise of man's essential reason is drawing on God as the source of life. The hindrance comes when we begin to keep sensuous images spiritually in our minds. Those of us who have never had visions or ecstasies ought to be very thankful. Visions, and any emotions at all, are the greatest snare to a spiritual life, because immediately we get them we are apt to build them round our reasoning, and our reasoning round them and go no further. Over and over again sanctified people stagnate, they do not go back and they do not go on, they stagnate, they become stiller and stiller, and muddier and muddier, spiritually not morally, until ultimately there comes a sort of scum over the spiritual life and you wonder what is the matter with them. They are still true to God, still true to their testimony of what God has done for them, but they have never exercised the great God-given reason that is in them and got beyond the images of their experience into the knowledge that 'God alone is life'—transcending all we call experience. It is because people will not take the labour to think that the snare gets hold of them, and remember, thinking is a tremendous labour (see 2 Corinthians 10:5).

IWP 74

*Whatsoever a man soweth, that shall he also reap.* Galatians 6:7
The words our Lord uttered in reference to Himself are true of every seed that is sown—'Except a corn of wheat fall into the ground and die, it abideth alone; but if it die, it bringeth forth much fruit.' All Christian work, if it is spiritual, must follow that law, because it is the only way God's fruit can be brought forth.
Be endlessly patient. There is nothing more impertinent than our crass infidelity in God. If He does not make us ploughers and sowers and reapers all at once, we lose faith in Him. Modern evangelism makes the mistake of thinking that a worker must plough his field, sow the seed, and reap the harvest in half an hour. Our Lord was

never in a hurry with the disciples, He kept on sowing the seed and paid no attention to whether they understood Him or not. He spoke the truth of God, and by His own life produced the right atmosphere for it to grow, and then left it alone, because He knew well that the seed had in it all the germinating power of God and would bring forth fruit after its kind once it was put in the right soil. We are never the same after listening to the truth; we may forget it, but we will meet it again. Sow the Word of God, and everyone who listens will get to God. If you sow vows, resolutions, aspirations, emotions, you will reap nothing but exhaustion '... and ye shall sow your seed in vain, for your enemies shall eat it' (Leviticus 26:16); but sow the Word of God, and as sure as God is God, it will bring forth fruit. ... A man may not grasp all that is said, but something in him is intuitively held by it. See that you sow the real seed of the Word of God, and then leave it alone.

SHL 114


**April 4**

*They that are whole need not a physician but they that are sick.* Luke 5:31

There is a type of suffering caused because we do not see the way out. A man may say that the basis of things is rational—'Get to the bottom of things and you will find it all simple and easy of explanation'—well, that simply is not true. The basis of things is not rational, but tragic, and when you enter the domain of suffering and sorrow you find that reason and logic are your guide amongst things as they are, but nothing more. Is it rational that I should be born with an heredity over which I have no control? Is it rational that nations that are nominally Christian should be at war? The basis of things is tragic, and the only way out is through the Redemption. Many a man in mental stress of weather is driven to utter what sounds like blasphemy, and yet he may be nearer God than in his complacent acceptance of beliefs that have never been tried. Never be afraid of the man who seems to you to talk blasphemously, he is up against problems you may never have met with; instead of being wrathful, be patient with him. The man to be afraid of is the one who is indifferent, what morality he has got is well within his own grasp, and Jesus Christ is of no account at all.

BE 93

70

*Ye are they which have continued with me in my temptations.* Luke 22:28

Jesus Christ looked upon His life as one of temptation; and He goes through the same kind of temptation in us as He went through in the days of His flesh. The essence of Christianity is that we give the Son of God a chance to live and move and have His being in us, and the meaning of all spiritual growth is that He has an increasing opportunity to manifest Himself in our mortal flesh. The temptations of Jesus are not those of a Man as man, but the temptations of God as Man. 'Wherefore it behoved Him in all things to be made like unto His brethren' (Hebrews 2:17). Jesus Christ's temptations and ours move in different spheres until we become His brethren by being born from above. 'For both He that sanctifieth and they that are sanctified are all of one: for which cause He is not ashamed to call them brethren' (Hebrews 2:11). By regeneration the Son of God is formed in me and He has the same setting in my life as He had when on earth. The honour of Jesus Christ is at stake in my bodily life; am I remaining loyal to Him in the temptations which beset His life in me?

PH 34

Put away the reverential blasphemy that what Jesus Christ feared in Gethsemane was death on the cross. There was no element of fear in His mind about it; He stated most emphatically that He came on purpose for the Cross (Matthew 16:21). His fear in Gethsemane was that He might not get through as Son of Man. Satan's onslaught was that although He would get through as Son of God, it would only be as an Isolated Figure; and this would mean that He could be no Saviour.

PR 85

*We preach Christ crucified.* 1 Corinthians 1:23

Never confuse the Cross of Christ with the benefits that flow from it. For all Paul's doctrine, his one great passion was the Cross of Christ, not salvation, nor sanctification, but the great truth that God so loved the world that He gave His only begotten Son; consequently you never find him artificial, or making a feeble statement. Every doctrine Paul taught had the blood and the power of God in it. There is an amazing force of spirit in all he said because the great passion behind was not that he wanted men to be holy, that was secondary, but that he had come to understand what God meant by the Cross of Christ. If we have the only idea of personal holiness, of being put in God's showroom, we shall never come anywhere near seeing what God wants; but when once we have come where Paul is and God is enabling us to understand what the Cross of Christ means, then nothing can ever turn us (Romans 8:35–9) ...

Most of our emphasis today is on what our Lord's death means to us: the thing that is of importance is that we understand what God means in the Cross. Paul did not understand the Cross in order that he might receive the life of God; but by understanding the Cross, he received the life. Study the Cross for no other sake than God's sake, and you will be holy without knowing it.

AUG 54, 56

April 7

*And he, bearing his cross, went forth ...* John 19:17

The Cross of Jesus is often wrongly taken as a type of the cross we have to carry. Jesus did not say, 'If any man will come after me, let him take up *my* cross', but, 'let him deny himself, and take up his cross, and follow me'. Our cross becomes our divinely appointed privilege by means of His Cross. We are never called upon to carry His Cross. We have so hallowed the Cross by twenty centuries of emotion and sentiment that it sounds a very beautiful and pathetic thing to talk about carrying our cross. But a wooden cross with iron nails in it is a clumsy thing to carry. The real cross was like that, and do we imagine that the external cross was more ugly than our actual one? Or that the thing that tore our Lord's hands and feet was not really so terrible as our imagination of it?

PR 100

The Cross of Jesus Christ stands unique and alone. His Cross is not our cross. Our cross is that we manifest before the world the fact that we are sanctified to do nothing but the will of God. By means of His Cross, our cross becomes our divinely appointed privilege. It is necessary to emphasize this because there is so much right feeling

72

and wrong teaching abroad on the subject. We are never called upon to carry Christ's Cross: His Cross is the centre of Time and Eternity; the answer to the enigmas of both.

DS 90

## April 8

*For hereunto were ye called: because Christ also suffered for us, leaving us an example, that ye should follow his steps.* 1 Peter 2:21
This is the essence of fellowship with His sufferings. 'He suffered for you.' Are you suffering on account of someone else, or for someone else? Are your agonizing prayers and suffering before the Lord on behalf of that 'distressing case' because it hurts you, discomforts you, makes you long for release? If so, you are not in fellowship with His suffering, nor anything like it. But if your soul, out of love for God, longs for others and bears with them in a voluntary, vicarious way, then you have a fellowship Divine indeed.

DS 90

The devotion of the saint is to 'fill up that which is behind of the afflictions of Christ for His body's sake' ... How can we fill up the sufferings that remain behind? 1 John 5:16 is an indication of one way, viz., that of intercession. Remember, no man has time to pray, he has to take time from other things that are valuable in order to understand how necessary time for prayer is. The things that act like thorns and stings in our personal lives will go instantly we pray; we won't feel the smart any more, because we have got God's point of view about them. Prayer means that we get into union with God's view of other people. Our devotion as saints is to identify ourselves with God's interests in other lives. God pays no attention to our personal affinities; He expects us to identify ourselves with *His* interests in others.

PR 96

## April 9

*And when Jesus had received the vinegar, he said, It is finished. and he bowed his head, and gave up the ghost.* John 19:30
Death is a great dread. It is easy to say that God is love until death has snatched away your dearest friend, then I defy you to say that

73

God is love unless God's grace has done a work in your soul. Death means extinction of life as we understand it; our dead are gone and have left an aching void behind them. They do not talk to us, we do not feel their touch, and when the bereaved heart cries out, nothing comes back but the hollow echo of its own cry. The heart is raw, no pious chatter, no scientific cant can touch it. It is the physical calamity of death *plus* the thing behind which no man can grasp, that makes death so terrible. We have so taken for granted the comfort that Jesus Christ brings in the hour of death that we forget the awful condition of men apart from that revelation. Do strip your mind and imagination of the idea that we have comfort about the departed apart from the Bible; we have not. Every attempt to comfort a bereaved soul apart from the revelation Jesus Christ brings is a vain speculation. We know nothing about the mystery of death apart from what Jesus Christ tells us; but blessed be the Name of God, what He tells us makes us more than conquerors, so that we can shout the victory through the darkest valley of the shadow that ever a human being can go through.

SHL 24

*For I determined not to know any thing among you, save Jesus Christ, and Him crucified.* 1 Corinthians 2:2

The death of Jesus is the only entrance into the life He lived. We cannot get into His life by admiring Him, or by saying what a beautiful life His was, so pure and holy. To dwell only on His life would drive us to despair. We enter into His life by means of His death. Until the Holy Spirit has had His way with us spiritually, the death of Jesus Christ is an insignificant thing, and we are amazed that the New Testament should make so much of it. The death of Jesus Christ is always a puzzle to unsaved human nature. Why should the Apostle Paul say, 'For I determined not to know any thing among you, save Jesus Christ, and Him crucified'? Because unless the death of Jesus has the meaning the Apostle Paul gave to it, viz., that it is the entrance into His life, the Resurrection has no meaning for us either. The life of Jesus is a wonderful example of a perfect human life, but what is the good of that to us? ...

We walk about imitating Jesus, but isn't it highly absurd! Before we have taken three steps, we come across lust, pride, envy, jealousy,

74

hatred, malice, anger—things that never were in Him, and we get disheartened and say there is nothing in it. If Jesus Christ came to *teach* the human race only, He had better have stayed away. But if we know Him first as Saviour by being born again, we know that He did not come to teach merely: He came to *make* us what He teaches we should be; He came to *make* us sons of God. He came to give us the right disposition, not to tell us that we ought not to have the wrong one; and the way into all these benedictions is by means of His death.

PR 79–80

### April 11

*Woman, why weepest thou?* John 20:15

Mary Magdalene was weeping at the sepulchre—what was she asking for? The dead body of Jesus. Of whom did she ask it? Of Jesus Himself, and she did not know Him! Did Jesus give her what she asked for? He gave her something infinitely grander than she had ever conceived—a risen, living impossible-to-die Lord. How many of us have been blind in our prayers? Look back and think of the prayers you thought had not been answered, but now you find God has answered them with a bigger manifestation than you ever dreamed. God has trusted you in the most intimate way He could trust you, with an absolute silence, not of despair but of pleasure, because He saw you could stand a much bigger revelation than you had at the time. Some prayers are followed by silence because they are wrong, others because they are bigger than we can understand. It will be a wonderful moment for some of us when we stand before God and find that the prayers we clamoured for in early days and imagined were never answered, have been answered in the most amazing way, and that God's silence has been the sign of the answer.

IYA 49

### April 12

*He saith unto him, Feed my sheep.* John 21:17

After the Resurrection, Jesus Christ did not invite the disciples to a time of communion on the Mount of Transfiguration, He said—'Feed my sheep.' When God gives a man work to do, it is seldom

75

work that seems at all proportionate to his natural ability. Paul, lion-hearted genius though he was, spent his time teaching the most ignorant people. The evidence that we are in love with God is that we identify ourselves with His interests in others, and other people are the exact expression of what we ourselves are; that is the humiliating thing! Jesus Christ came down to a most miserably insignificant people in order to redeem them. When He has lifted us into relationship with Himself, He expects us to identify ourselves with His interests in others.

PR 107

**April 13**

*Blessed are ye.* Matthew 5:11

The first time we read the Beatitudes they appear to be simple and beautiful and un-startling statements, and they go unobserved into the subconscious mind. We are so used to the sayings of Jesus that they slip over us unheeded, they sound sweet and pious and wonderfully simple, but they are in reality like spiritual torpedoes that burst and explode in the subconscious mind, and when the Holy Spirit brings them back to our conscious minds we realize what startling statements they are ...

The test of discipleship is obedience to the light when these truths are brought to the conscious mind. We do not hunt through the Bible for some precept to obey—Jesus Christ's teaching never leads to making ourselves moral prigs, but we live so in touch with God that the Holy Spirit can continually bring some word of His and apply it to the circumstances we are in. We are not brought to the test until the Holy Spirit brings the word back.

Neither is it a question of applying the Beatitudes literally, but of allowing the life of God to invade us by regeneration, and then soaking our minds in the teaching of Jesus Christ which slips down into the subconscious mind. By and by a set of circumstances will arise when one of Jesus Christ's statements emerges, and instantly we have to decide whether we will accept the tremendous spiritual revolution that will be produced if we do obey this precept of His. If we do obey it, our actual life will become different, and we shall find we have the power to obey if we will. That is the way the Holy Spirit works in the heart of a disciple.

SSM 14

*Pray ye therefore* . . . Matthew 9:38

Prayer is simple, prayer is supernatural, and to anyone not related to our Lord Jesus Christ, prayer is apt to look stupid. It does sound unreasonable to say that God will do things in answer to prayer, yet our Lord said that He would. Our Lord bases everything on prayer, then the key to all our work as Christians is, 'Pray ye therefore.'

When we pray for others the Spirit of God works in the unconscious domain of their being that we know nothing about, and the one we are praying for knows nothing about, but after the passing of time the conscious life of the one prayed for begins to show signs of unrest and disquiet. We may have spoken until we are worn out, but have never come anywhere near, and we have given up in despair. But if we have been praying, we find on meeting them one day that there is the beginning of a softening in an enquiry and a desire to know something. It is that kind of intercession that does most damage to Satan's kingdom. It is so slight, so feeble in its initial stages that if reason is not wedded to the light of the Holy Spirit, we will never obey it, and yet it is that kind of intercession that the New Testament places most emphasis on, though it has so little to show for it. It seems stupid to think that we can pray and all that will happen, but remember to whom we pray, we pray to a God who understands the unconscious depths of personality about which we know nothing, and He has told us to pray. The great Master of the human heart said, 'Greater works than these shall he do ... And whatsoever ye shall ask in my name, that will I do.'

IYA 93

*Who can understand his errors? cleanse thou me from secret faults.* Psalm 19:12

Is there some fault God has been checking you about and you have left it alone? Be careful lest it end in a dominant sin. The errors are silent, they creep in on us, and when we stand in the light of Jesus Christ we are amazed to find the conclusions we have come to. The reason is that we have deluded ourselves. This self-security keeps us entirely ignorant of what we really are, ignorant of the things that make the salvation of Jesus Christ necessary. When we say to ourselves—'Oh well, I am no worse than anyone else', that is the beginning; we shall soon produce blindness to our own defects and entrench ourselves around with a fictitious security. Jesus Christ has no chance whatever with the man who has the silent security of self-ignorance. When he hears anyone speak about deliverance from sin, he is untouched—'I have no need to be delivered'. Paul says, 'If our gospel be hid, it is hid to those in whom the god of this world hath blinded their minds'—blinded to everything Jesus Christ stands for, and a man is to blame for getting there.

SHL 56

### April 16

*Ye are my friends, if ye do whatsoever I command you.* John 15:14

God created man to be His friend. If we are the friends of Jesus we have deliberately and carefully to lay down our life for Him. It is difficult, and thank God it is! When once the relationship of being the friends of Jesus is understood, we shall be called upon to exhibit to everyone we meet the love He has shown to us. Watch the kind of people God brings across your path, you will find it is His way of picturing to you the kind of person you have been to Him.—'You are My child, the friend of My Son, now exhibit to that "hedgehoggy" person the love I exhibited to you when you were like that towards Me; exhibit to that mean, selfish person exactly the love I showed you when you were mean and selfish.' We shall find ample room to eat 'humble pie' all the days of our life. The thing that keeps us going is to recognize the humour of our heavenly Father in it all, and we shall meet the disagreeable person with a spiritual chuckle because we know what God is doing, He is giving us a mirror that we may see what we have been like towards Him; now we have the chance to prove ourselves His friends, and the other person will be amazed and say—'Why, the more I poke her, the sweeter she gets!' and will tumble in where we tumbled in, into the grace of God.

AHW 109

### April 17

*If thou seest the oppression of the poor, and violent perverting of judgment and justice in a province, marvel not at the matter: for he*

*that is higher than the highest regardeth; and there be higher than they.*
Ecclesiastes 5:8
All through the Bible the difference between God's order and God's permissive will is brought out. God's permissive will is the things that are now, whether they are right or wrong. If you are looking for justice, you will come to the conclusion that God is the devil; and if the providential order of things today were God's order, then that conclusion would be right. But if the order of things today is God's permissive will, that is quite another matter. God's order is no sin, no Satan, no wrong, no suffering, no pain, no death, no sickness and no limitation: God's providential will is every one of these things—sin, sickness, death, the devil, you and me, and things as they are. God's permissive will is the haphazard things that are on just now in which we have to fight and make character in, or else be damned by. We may kick and yell and say God is unjust, but we are all 'in the soup'. It is no use saying things are not as they are; it is no use being amazed at the providential order of tyranny, it is there. In personal life and in national life God's order is reached through pain, and never in any other way. Why it should be so is another matter, but that it is so is obvious. '... though he were a Son, yet learned he obedience by the things which he suffered.'

We have to get hold of God's order in the midst of His permissive will. God is bringing many 'sons' to glory. A son is one who has been through the fight and stood the test and come out sterlingly worthy. The Bible attitude to things is absolutely robust, there is not the tiniest whine about it; there is no possibility of lying like a limp jellyfish on God's providence, it is never allowed for a second. There is always a sting and a kick all through the Bible.

SHH 59

*... they saw no man any more, save Jesus only with themselves.*
Mark 9:8
It was not that they saw no one else, but they saw no one else without seeing Jesus. The identified meaning of life is that we see 'every man perfect in Christ Jesus'. We do not need a transfiguration experience to see meanness, because we are mean; we do not need a transfiguration experience to see sin, because we are sinners; but we do need a transfiguration experience to see Christ Jesus in the mean, in the sinner, in the all-but-lost, in the wrong and in the evil,

so that it can be true of the experience of every saint—'they saw no one any more, save Jesus only with themselves'. That is what contact with Jesus means. It is easy to see the specks and the wrong in others, because we see in others that of which we are guilty ourselves. 'Wherefore thou art without excuse, O man, whosoever thou art that judgest: for wherein thou judgest another, thou condemnest thyself; for thou that judgest dost practise the same things' (Romans 2:1). The greatest cure for spiritual conceit is for God to give us a dose of the 'plague of our own heart'.

What a wonderful thing it will be for us if we enter into the transfigured experience of life! There is never any snare in the man or woman who has seen Jesus. Have you anyone 'save Jesus only' in your cloud? If you have, then it will get darker. You must get to the place where there is 'no one any more, save Jesus only'.

PH 116

April 19

*Yea doubtless, and I count all things but loss for the excellency of the knowledge of Christ Jesus my Lord ...* Philippians 3:8

Paul goes on to state that he not only *estimated* the cost, he experienced it—'for whom I have suffered the loss of all things ... that I may win Christ, and be found in him, not having mine own righteousness...' Imagine anyone who has seen Jesus Christ transfigured saying he is sorry to find himself mean and ignoble! The more I whine about being a miserable sinner, the more I am hurting the Holy Spirit. It simply means I don't agree with God's judgment of me, I think after all I am rather desirable: God thought me so undesirable that He sent His Son to save me. To discover I am what God says I am ought to make me glad; if I am glad over anything I discover in myself, I am very short-sighted. The only point of rest is in the Lord Himself.

CHI 127

April 20

*With the mouth confession is made unto salvation.* Romans 10:10

In the Bible confession and testimony are put in a prominent place, and the test of a man's moral calibre is the 'say so'. I may try and make myself believe a hundred and one things, but they will never be mine until I 'say so'. If I say with my self what I believe and confess it with my mouth, I am lifted into the domain of that thing. This is always the price of spiritual emancipation …

'When ye pray, say, Our Father.' 'But I don't feel that God is my Father': Jesus said, 'Say it'—'*say*, Our Father', and you will suddenly discover that He is. The safeguard against moral imprisonment is prayer. Don't pray according to your moods, but resolutely launch out on God, say 'Our Father', and before you know where you are, you are in a larger room. The door into a moral or spiritual emancipation which you wish to enter is a word. Immediately you are prepared to abandon your reserve and say the word, the door opens and in rushes the Godward side of things and you are lifted on to another platform immediately. 'Speech maketh a full man.' If you want to encourage your own life in spiritual things, talk about them. Beware of the reserve that keeps to itself, that wants to develop spirituality alone; spirituality must be developed in the open. Shyness is often unmitigated conceit, an unconscious over-estimate of your own worth; you are not prepared to speak until you have a proper audience. If you talk in the wrong mood, you will remain in the wrong mood and put the 'bastard self' on the throne; but if you talk in the mood which comes from revelation, emancipation will be yours.

PH 209

### April 21

*Come unto me.* Matthew 11:28

The questions that matter in life are remarkably few, and they are all answered by these words 'Come unto me'. Not—'Do this' and 'Don't do that', but 'Come'…

Have you ever come to Jesus? Watch the stubbornness of your heart and mind, you will find you will do anything rather than the one simple, childlike thing— Come. Be stupid enough to come, and commit yourself to what Jesus says. The attitude of coming is that the will resolutely lets go of everything and deliberately commits the whole thing to Jesus. At the most unexpected moments there comes the whisper of the Lord—'Come unto me', and we are drawn to Him. Personal contact with Jesus alters everything. He meets our sins, our sorrows, and our difficulties with the one word—'Come'.

AHW 106

*Come after me.* Mark 1:17

If you do come after Jesus, you will realize that He pays no attention whatever to your natural affinities. One of the greatest hindrances to our coming to Jesus is the talk about temperament. I have never seen the Spirit of God pay any attention to a man's temperament, but over and over again I have seen people make their temperament and their natural affinities a barrier to coming to Jesus. We have to learn that our Lord does not heed our selective natural affinities. The idea that He does heed them has grown from the notion that we have to consecrate our gifts to God. We cannot consecrate what is not ours. The only thing I can give to God is 'my right to myself' (Romans 12:1). If I will give God that, He will make a holy experiment out of me, and God's experiments always succeed. The one mark of a disciple is moral originality. The Spirit of God is a well of water in the disciple, perennially fresh. When once the saint begins to realize that God engineers circumstances, there will be no more whine, but only a reckless abandon to Jesus. Never make a principle out of your own experience; let God be as original with other people as He is with you.

AHW 104

### April 22

*And the chapiters that were on top of the pillars were of lily work.* 1 Kings 7:19

The lily work added nothing to the strength of the building; many would notice the strength and the majesty of the whole building, but the inspiration of it all was in the detail, in the 'lily work'. In architecture it is not so much the massive strength that counts as the finely proportioned ornament, and that is never obtrusive. If we look at men and women who have been long at work for God and have been going through chastening, we notice that they have lost their individual harshness, lost a great deal of their apparent go-aheadness for God; but they have acquired something else, viz., the most exquisite 'lily work' in their lives, and this after all is the thing most like Jesus Christ. It is the quiet, undisturbable Divinity that is characteristic of Jesus, not aggressiveness, and the same is true of God's children.

MU 39

*And we know that all things work together for good to them that love God, to them who are the called according to his purpose.* Romans 8:28

The shrine of our conscious life is placed in a sacredness of circumstances engineered by God whereby He secures our effectual calling. That God engineers our circumstances for us if we accept His purpose in Christ Jesus is a thought of great practical moment.

Allow yourself to think for a little that you are to be a walking, living edition of the prayers of the Holy Spirit. No wonder God urges us to walk in the light! No wonder His Spirit prays in us and makes intercessions with groanings we cannot utter. We may feel burdened or we may not; we may consciously know nothing about it; the point is that God puts us into circumstances where He can answer the prayers of His Son and of the Holy Spirit. Remember the prayer of Jesus is 'that they may be one, even as we are one'. That is a oneness of personality in which individuality is completely transfigured; it is independence lost and identity revealed.

It is well to remember that it is the 'together' of circumstances that works for good. God changes our circumstances; sometimes they are bright, sometimes they are the opposite; but God makes them work together for our good, so that in each particular set of circumstances we are in, the Spirit of God has a better chance to pray the particular prayers that suit His designs, and the reason is only known to God, not to us.

DPR 55

*Be ye therefore followers of God.* Ephesians 5:1

The one striking thing about following is we must not find our own way, for when we take the initiative we cease to follow. In the natural world everything depends upon our taking the initiative, but if we are followers of God, we cannot take the initiative, we cannot choose our own work or say what we will do; we have not to find out at all, we have just to follow ...

In following Our Lord Jesus Christ we are not following His followers. When Paul said, 'who shall bring you into remembrance of my ways', he was careful to add, 'which be in Christ' (1 Corinthians

83

4:17). We are not called to follow in all the footsteps of the saints, but only in so far as they followed their Lord.

DF 61

Discipleship must always be a personal matter; we can never become disciples in crowds, or even in twos. It is so easy to talk about what 'we' mean to do—'we' are going to do marvellous things, and it ends in none of us doing anything. The great element of discipleship is the personal one.

IWP 104

### April 25

*That which hath been is named already, and it is known that it is man: neither may he contend with him that is mightier than he ... For who can tell a man what shall be after him under the sun?* Ecclesiastes 6:10, 12

In order to estimate man properly in the 'soup' he is in just now, we must remember what he was in the beginning. God created man in His own image, a son of God. Adam was to have control over the life in the air and on the earth and in the sea, on one condition— that he allowed God to rule him absolutely. Man was to develop the earth and his own life until he was transfigured. But instead there came the introduction of sin, man took the rule over himself, he became his own god, and thereby lost control over everything else. It is this that accounts for the condition of things as they are now.

If we are going to have a sympathetic understanding of the Bible, we must rid ourselves of the abominable conceit that we are the wisest people that have ever been on the earth; we must stop our patronage of Jesus Christ and of the Bible, and have a bigger respect for the fundamental conception of life as it is. At the basis of Hebrew wisdom first of all, is confidence in God; and second, a terrific sigh and sob over the human race as a magnificent ruin of what God designed it to be. Modern wisdom says that man is a magnificent promise of what he is going to be. If that point of view is right, then there is no need to talk about sin and Redemption, and the Bible is a cunningly devised fable. But the Bible point of view seems to cover most of the facts.

SHH 76

*He that followeth me shall not walk in darkness, but shall have the light of life.* John 8:12

Supposing you are walking over a moor at night, you know there is a path but it is too dark and obscure for you to see; then the moon struggles through the clouds and you see the path, a clear strip of white, straight across the hill; in a little while all is obscure again, but you have seen the path and you know the way to go. There are times in our experience when life is just like that. We do not see the path though we know it is there, then the light shines and we see it, and when darkness comes again we can step boldly. Sometimes the light is as the moonlight or the dawn, or it comes as a terrifying flash of lightning, when all of a sudden we see the way we should go. 'While ye have light, believe in the light, that ye may be the children of light' (John 12:36). Have we believed in the light we have had? Can we recall the time when the light of God in the Face of Jesus Christ was clearer to us than anything else has ever been, when we saw perfectly clearly and understood exactly what the Lord wanted? Did we believe in that light; and have we walked up to the light? Can we say, 'I was not disobedient unto the heavenly vision'? So many of us see the light, we see the way across the moor; by a sudden lightning flash of God's revealing grace we see the way to go, but we do not take it. We say, 'Oh, yes, I did receive the Spirit of God, and I thought that it would be like this and that, but it has not been.' The reason is that we did not believe in the light when it was given ...

If we have entered into the heavenly places in Christ Jesus, the light has shone, and, this is the marvellous thing, as we begin to do what we know the Lord would have us do, we find He does not enable us to do it, He simply puts through us all His power and the thing is done in His way. Thank God for everyone who has seen the light, who has understood how the Lord Jesus Christ clears away the darkness and brings the light by showing His own characteristics through us.

OBH 39

*I must work the works of him that sent me, while it is day: the night cometh, when no man can work.* John 9:4

Today we hold conferences and conventions and give reports and make our programmes. None of these things were in the life of Jesus, and yet every minute of His life He realized that He was fulfilling the purpose of His Father. How did He do it? By maintaining the one relationship, and it is that one relationship He insists on in His disciples, and it is the one we have lost in the rubbish of modern civilization. If we try and live the life Jesus Christ lived, modern civilization will fling us out like waste material; we are no good, we do not add anything to the hard cash of the times we live in, and the sooner we are flung out the better.

In St John's Gospel this aspect of our Lord's life is more elaborately worked out than anywhere else. It is indicated in the other Gospels (see Luke 2:49, 13:32; 12:50). Jesus knew He was here for His Father's purpose and He never allowed the cares of civilization to bother Him. He did nothing to add to the wealth of the civilization in which He lived, He earned nothing, modern civilization would not have tolerated Him for two minutes.

HG 71


April 28

*Be filled with the Spirit.* Ephesians 5:18

The sovereign emotions are guided and controlled by love, but bear in mind that love in its highest moral meaning is the preference of one person for another person. A Christian's love is personal, passionate devotion to Jesus Christ, and he learns to grip on the threshold of his mind as in a vice every sentiment awakened by wrong emotions. God holds the saints responsible for emotions they have not got and ought to have as well as for the emotions they have allowed which they ought not to have allowed. If we indulge in inordinate affection, anger, anxiety, God holds us responsible; but He also insists that we have to be passionately filled with the right emotions ...

If we have no emotional life, then we have disobeyed God. 'Be filled with the Spirit'; it is as impossible to be filled with the Spirit and be free from emotion as it is for a man to be filled with wine and not show it. The reason some of us are so amazingly dull and get sleeping-sickness is that we have never once thought of paying attention to the stirring up the Spirit of God gives the mind and our emotional nature. How many of us are terrified out of our wits lest we should be emotional! Jesus Christ demands the whole nature,

86

and He demands that part of our nature the devil uses most, viz., the emotional part.

BE 73-4

*That they might have my joy fulfilled in themselves.* John 17:13

All degrees of joy reside in the heart. How can a Christian be full of happiness (if happiness depends on the things that happen) when he is in a world where the devil is doing his best to twist souls away from God, where people are tortured physically, where some are downtrodden and do not get a chance? It would be the outcome of the most miserable selfishness to be happy under such conditions; but a joyful heart is never an insult, and joy is never touched by external conditions. Beware of preaching the gospel of temperament instead of the Gospel of God. Numbers of people today preach the gospel of temperament, the gospel of 'cheer up'. The word 'blessed' is sometimes translated 'happy', but it is a much deeper word; it includes all that we mean by joy in its full fruition. Happiness is the characteristic of a child, and God condemns us for taking happiness out of a child's life; but as men and women we should have done with happiness long ago, we should be facing the stern issues of life, knowing that the grace of God is sufficient for every problem the devil can present.

BP 115

*How much more shall the blood of Christ ... purge your conscience from dead works to serve the living God.* Hebrews 9:14

Has conscience the place in our salvation and sanctification that it ought to have? Hyper-conscientious people blind themselves to the realization of what the death of Jesus means by saying, 'No, I have wronged this person and I must put the thing right.' It springs from the panging remorse that we experience when we realize we have wronged another. 'All you say about the Cross may be true, but I have been so mean and so wrong that there are things I must put right first.' It sounds noble to talk like that, but it is the essence of the pride that put Jesus Christ to death. The only thing to do is to cast the whole thing aside: 'My God, this thing in me is worthy only of death, the awful death of crucifixion to the last strand of life. Lord, it is my sin, my wrong, not Jesus Christ, that ought to be on that Cross.' When we get there and abandon the whole thing, the blood of Christ cleanses our conscience and the freedom is ineffable and amazing ...

It is freedom not only from sin and the damage sin has done, but emancipation from the impairing left by sin, from all the distortions left in mind and imagination. Then when our conscience has been cleansed from dead works, Jesus Christ gives us the marvellously healing ministry of intercession as 'a clearing-house for conscience'. Not only is all sense of past guilt removed, but we are given the very secret heart of God for the purpose of vicarious intercession (see Romans 8:26–7).

PS 20

### May 1

*Whence then cometh wisdom? and where is the place of understanding? ... Behold, the fear of the Lord, that is wisdom: and to depart from evil is understanding.* Job 4:20, 28.

Neither logic nor science can explain the sublimities of Nature. Supposing a scientist with a diseased olfactory nerve says that there is no perfume in a rose, and to prove his statement he dissects the rose and tabulates every part, and then says, 'Where is the perfume? It is a fiction; I have demonstrated that there is none.' There is always one fact more that science cannot explain, and the best thing to do is not to deny it in order to preserve your sanity, but to say, as Job did, 'No, the one fact more which you cannot explain means that God must step in just there, or there is no explanation to be had.'

Every common-sense fact requires something for its explanation which common-sense cannot give. The facts of every day and night reveal things our own minds cannot explain. When a scientific man comes across a gap in his explanations, instead of saying, 'There is no gap here', let him recognize that there is a gap he cannot bridge, and that he must be reverent with what he cannot understand. The tendency is to deny that a fact has any existence because it cannot be fitted into any explanation as yet. That 'the exception proves the rule' is not true: the exception proves that the rule won't do; the rule is only useful in the greatest number of cases. When scientists treat a thesis as a fact they mean that it is based on the highest degree of probability. There are no 'infallible' findings, and the man who bows down to scientific findings may be as big a fool as the man who refuses to do so. The man who prays ceases to be a fool, while the man who refuses to pray nourishes a blind life within his own brain and he will find no way out that road. Job cries out that prayer is the only way out in all these matters.

BFB 79, 82

## May 2

*Be ye not unwise, but understanding what the will of the Lord is.* Ephesians 5:17

An artist is one who not only sees but is prepared to pay the price of acquiring the technical knowledge to express what he sees. An artistic person is one who has not enough art in him to make him work at the technique of art whereby he can express himself, he indulges in moods and tones and impressions; consequently there are more artistic people than there are artists. The same is true of poetry, there are many people with poetic notions, but very few poets. It is not enough for a man to feel the divine flame burning in him; unless he goes into the concentrated, slogging business of learning the technique of expression, his genius will be of no use to anyone. Apply these illustrations spiritually: if we have not enough of the life of God in us to overcome the difficulty of expressing it in our bodies, then we are living an impoverished spiritual life. Think of the illuminations the Spirit of God has given you; He expected you to bring your physical body which He made into obedience to the vision, and you never attempted to but let it drift, and when the crisis came and God looked for you to be His mouthpiece, you crumpled all to pieces. You had not formed the habit of apprehending; your physical machine was not under control. It is a terrible thing to sit down to anything.

Beware of being side-tracked by the idea that you can develop a spiritual life apart from physical accompaniments. It is a desperately dangerous thing to allow the spiritual vision to go ahead of physical obedience.

*Do some practical obeying.*

MFL 81

*The sleep of a labouring man is sweet, whether he eat little or much; but the abundance of the rich will not suffer him to sleep.* Ecclesiastes 5:12

The sleep of a labouring man is sweet, it recreates him. The Bible indicates that sleep is not meant only for the recuperation of a man's body, but that there is a tremendous furtherance of spiritual and moral life during sleep. According to the Bible, a great deal more than physical recuperation happens in the sleep of any man who has done his daily toil in actual work. 'He giveth *to* his beloved in sleep' (Psalm 127:2, RV, marg.). This is a phase that is cut out altogether, because we ignore the deeper issues.

'Whether he eat little or much.' Paul's counsel is that 'if any would not work, neither should he eat'. There are plenty of folks who eat but don't work, and they suffer for it. If we are physically healthy, the benefit of the food we eat corresponds to the work we do, and the same is true in mental, moral and spiritual health. The prayer Our Lord taught us is full of wisdom along this line, 'Give us this day our daily bread.' That does not mean that if we do not pray we shall not get it. The word 'give' has the sense of 'receiving'. When we become children of God we receive our daily bread from Him, the basis of blessing lies there, otherwise we take it as an animal with no discernment of God.

SHH 63

*It is good and comely for one to eat and to drink, and to enjoy the good of all his labour that he taketh under the sun all the days of his life, which God giveth him: for it is his portion.* Ecclesiastes 5:18

The Bible makes much of man's body. The teaching of Christianity on this point has been twisted by the influence of Plato's teaching, which says that a man can only further his moral and spiritual life by despising his body. The Bible teaches that the body is the temple of the Holy Ghost, it was moulded by God of the dust of the ground and is man's chief glory, not his shame. When God became Incarnate 'he took not on him the nature of angels', but was made 'in the likeness of men', and it is man's body that is yet to manifest the glory of God on earth. Material things are going to be translucent with the light of God.

Jesus Christ 'came eating and drinking', and from Genesis to Revelation eating and drinking, and labouring in the ordinary toil of life in the condition of things as they are, are the things in which man will find his right relationship to life and to God.

SHH 67

## May 5

*... for a man's life consisteth not in the abundance of the things which he possesseth.* Luke 12:15

The whole teaching of Jesus is opposed to the idea of civilization, viz., possessing things for myself—'This is mine.' The sense of property is connected, not with the lasting element of our personality, but with that which has to do with sin; it is the sense of property that makes me want to gratify myself. Jesus Christ had no sense of property, there was never any attempt to gratify Himself by possessing things for Himself—'the Son of man hath not where to lay his head'. What was His, He gave—'I lay down my life ... I lay it down of myself.' The thing that leads me wrong always and every time is what I am persuaded I possess. The thing that is mine is the thing I have with the power to give it. All that I want to possess without the power to give, is of the nature of sin. . . .

According to Jesus Christ a man's life does not consist in the abundance of the things he possesses—not only in the way of goods and chattels, but in the way of a good name, a virtuous character; these things are a man's inheritance, but not his *life*. When the Holy Spirit begins to try and break into the house of our possessions in order to grant us the real life of God, we look on Him as a robber, as a disturber of our peace, because when He comes He reveals the things which are not of God and must go; and they are the things which constituted our life before He came in, our golden affections were carefully nested in them. The thing that hurts shows where we live. If God hurts it is because we are not living rightly related to Him.

GW 29

## May 6

*Sell all that thou hast, and distribute unto the poor.* Matthew 19:21
There is a general principle here and a particular reference. We

91

are always in danger of taking the particular reference for the general principle and evading the general principle. The particular reference here is to selling material goods. The rich young ruler had deliberately to be destitute, deliberately to distribute, deliberately to discern where his treasure was, and devote himself to Jesus Christ. The principle underlying it is that I must detach myself from everything I possess. Many of us suppress our sense of property, we don't starve it, we suppress it. Undress yourself morally before God of everything that might be a possession until you are a mere conscious human being, and then give God that. That is where the battle is fought—in the domain of the will before God; it is not fought in external things at all. Is He sovereign Lord or is He not? Am I more devoted to my notion of what Jesus Christ wants than to Himself? If so, I am likely to hear one of His hard sayings that will produce sorrow in me. What Jesus says *is* hard, it is only easy when it comes to those who really are His disciples. Beware of allowing anything to soften a hard word of Jesus ...

I can be so rich in poverty, so rich in the consciousness that I am nobody, that I will never be a disciple of Jesus Christ; and I can be so rich in the consciousness that I am somebody that I will never be a disciple. Am I willing to be destitute of the sense that I am destitute? It is not giving up outside things, but making yourself destitute to yourself, and that is where the discouragement comes in.

GW 78

### May 7

*As sorrowful, yet always rejoicing; as poor, yet making many rich; as having nothing, and yet possessing all things.* 2 Corinthians 6:10

As we draw on the grace of God He increases voluntary poverty all along the line. Always give the best you have got every time; never think about who you are giving it to, let other people take it or leave it as they choose. Pour out the best you have, and always be poor. Never reserve anything; never be diplomatic and careful about the treasure God gives.

AUG 128

'Give to him that asketh thee.' Why do we always make this mean money? Our Lord makes no mention of money. The blood of most of us seems to run in gold. The reason we make it mean money

92

is because that is where our heart is. Peter said, 'Silver and gold have I none; but such as I have give I thee.' God grant we may understand that the spring of giving is not impulse nor inclination, but the inspiration of the Holy Spirit, I give because Jesus tells me to. . . .

The way Christians wriggle and twist and compromise over this verse springs from infidelity in the ruling providence of our Heavenly Father. We enthrone common-sense as God and say, 'It is absurd; if I give to every one that asks, every beggar in the place will be at my door.' Try it. I have yet to find the man who obeyed Jesus Christ's command and did not realize that God restrains those who beg.

SSM 46

## May 8

*Whatsoever thy hand findeth to do, do it with thy might: for there is no work nor device, nor knowledge, nor wisdom, in the grave, whither thou goest.* Ecclesiastes 9:10

The Bible nowhere teaches us to work for work's sake. That is one of the greatest bugbears of the anti-Christian movement in the heart of Christianity today. It is Work with a capital W in which the worship of Jesus Christ is lost sight of. People will sacrifice themselves endlessly for *the work*. Perspiration is mistaken for inspiration. Our guidance with regard to work is to remember that its value is in what it does for us. It is difficult not to let ulterior considerations come in—'What's the good of doing this, we are only here for a short time, why should we do it as if it were to last for ever?' Solomon's counsel is—'Whatsoever thy hand attaineth to do by thy strength *that do*' (RV, marg.). He is not recommending work for work's sake, but because through the drudgery of work the man himself is developed. When you deify work, you apostatize from Jesus Christ. In the private spiritual life of many a Christian it is work that has hindered concentration on God. When work is out of its real relation it becomes a means of evading concentration on God. Carlyle pointed out that the weariness and sickness of modern life is shown in the restlessness of work. When a man is not well he is always doing things, an eternal fidget. Intense activity may be the sign of physical weariness. When a man is healthy his work is so

93

much part of himself that you never know he is doing it; he does it with his might, and that makes no fuss. We lose by the way we do our work the very thing it is intended to bring us.

At the back of all is the one thing God is after, what a man is, not what he does, and Solomon keeps that in view all the time. It is what we are in our relation to things that counts not what we attain to in them. If you put attainment as the end you may reap a broken heart and find that all your outlay ends in disaster, death cuts it short, or disease, or ruin.

SHH 128

May 9

*I am the living bread which came down out of heaven: if any man eat of this bread, he shall live for ever: yea and the bread which I will give is my flesh, for the life of the world.* John 6:51

Good corn is not bread; if we are compelled to eat corn we will suffer for it. Corn must be ground and mixed and kneaded and baked, and baked sufficiently, before it is fit to be eaten. When the husk is away and the kernel garnered, we are apt to think that all is done; but the process has only just begun. A granary of corn is not bread; people cannot eat handfuls of corn and be nourished, something must be done to the corn first. Apply that illustration to the life of a sanctified saint. The afflictions after sanctification are not meant to purify us, but to make us broken bread in the hands of our Lord to nourish others. Many Christian workers are like Ephraim, 'a cake not turned'; they are faddists and cranks, and when they are given out for distribution they produce indigestion instead of giving nourishment.

SHL 111

Jesus Christ was made broken bread and poured out wine for us, and He expects us to be made broken bread and poured out wine in His hands for others. If we are not thoroughly baked, we will produce indigestion because we are dough instead of bread. We have to be made into good nutritious stuff for other people. The reason we are going through the things we are is that God wants to know whether He can make us good bread with which to feed others. The stuff of our lives, not simply of our talk, is to be the nutriment of those who know us.

MU 48

*Thou shalt love the Lord thy God with all thy heart, and with all thy soul, and with all thy mind. This is the first and great commandment.* Matthew 22:37–8

*If ye love me, keep my commandments.* John 14:15

Before we can love God we must have the Lover of God in us, viz., the Holy Spirit. When the Holy Spirit has shed abroad the love of God in our hearts, then that love requires cultivation. No love on earth will develop without being cultivated. We have to dedicate ourselves to love, which means identifying ourselves with God's interests in other people, and God is interested in some funny people, viz., in you and in me! We must beware of letting natural affinities hinder our walking in love. One of the most cruel ways of killing love is by disdain built on natural affinities. To be guided by our affinities is a natural tendency, but spiritually this tendency must be denied, and as we deny it we find that God gives us affinity with those for whom we have no natural affinity. Is there anyone in your life who would not be there if you were not a Christian? The love of God is not mere sentimentality; it is a most practical thing for the saint to love as God loves. The springs of love are in God, not in us. The love of God is only in us when it has been shed abroad in our hearts by the Holy Spirit, and the evidence that it is there is the spontaneous way in which it is manifested.

AIIW 117

*And the second is like unto it, Thou shalt love thy neighbour as thyself.* Matthew 22:39

Everything our Lord taught about the duty of man to man might be summed up in the one law of giving. It is as if He set Himself to contradict the natural counsel of the human heart, which is to acquire and keep. A child will say of a gift, 'Is it my own?' When a man is born again that instinct is replaced by another, the instinct of giving. The law of the life of a disciple is Give, Give, Give (e.g. Luke 6:38). As Christians our giving is to be proportionate to all we have received of the infinite giving of God. 'Freely ye have received, freely give.' Not how much we give, but what we do not give, is the test of our Christianity. When we speak of giving we nearly always think only of money. Money is the life-blood of most

95

of us. We have a remarkable trick—when we give money we don't give sympathy; and when we give sympathy we don't give money. The only way to get insight into the meaning for ourselves of what Jesus taught is by being indwelt by the Holy Spirit, because He enables us first of all to understand our Lord's life; unless we do that, we will exploit His teaching, take out of it only what we agree with. There is one aspect of giving we think little about, but which had a prominent place in our Lord's life, viz., that of social intercourse. He accepted hospitality on the right hand and on the left, from publicans and from the Pharisees, so much so that they said He was 'a gluttonous man, and a wine bibber, a friend of publicans and sinners!' He spent Himself with one lodestar all the time, to seek and to save that which was lost, and Paul says, 'I am become all things to all men, that I might by all means save some.' How few of us ever think of giving socially! We are so parsimonious that we won't spend a thing in conversation unless it is on a line that helps us!

CHI 77–8

### May 12

*Give a portion to seven, and also to eight; for thou knowest not what evil shall be upon the earth. If the clouds be full of rain, they empty themselves upon the earth: and if the tree fall toward the south or toward the north, in the places where the tree falleth, there it shall be.* Ecclesiastes 11:2

'Economy is doing without what you want just now in case a time may come when you will want what you don't want now.' It is possible to be so economical that you venture nothing. We have deified economy, placed insurance and economy on the throne, consequently we will do nothing on the line of adventure or extravagance. To use the word 'economy' in connection with God is to belittle and misunderstand Him. Where is the economy of God in His sunsets and sunrises, in the grass and flowers and trees? God has made a superabounding number of things that are of no *use* to anyone. How many of us bother our heads about the sunrises and sunsets? Yet they go on just the same. Lavish extravagance to an extraordinary degree is the characteristic of God, never economy. Grace is the overflowing favour of God. Imagine a man who is in love being economical! The characteristic of a man when he is awake is never that he is calculating and sensible.

Today we are so afraid of poverty that we never dream of doing anything that might involve us in being poor. We are out of the running of the mediaeval monks who took on the vow of poverty. Many of us are poor, but none of us chooses to be. These men chose to be poor, they believed it was the only way they could perfect their own inner life. Out attitude is that if we are extravagant a rainy day will come for which we have not laid up. You cannot lay up for a rainy day and justify it in the light of Jesus Christ's teaching. We are not Christians at heart, we don't believe in the wisdom of God, but only in our own. We go in for insurance and economy and speculation, everything that makes us secure in our own wisdom.

SHH 142

### May 13

*Your body is the temple of the Holy Ghost.* 1 Corinthians 6:19
Have I ever realized that the most wonderful thing in the world is the thing that is nearest to me, viz., my body? Who made it? Almighty God. Do I pay the remotest attention to my body as being the temple of the Holy Ghost? Remember our Lord lived in a body like ours. The next reality that I come in contact with by my body is other people's bodies. All our relationships in life, all the joys and all the miseries, all the hells and all the heavens, are based on bodies; and the reality of Jesus Christ's salvation brings us down to the Mother Earth we live on, and makes us see by the regenerating power of God's grace how amazingly precious are the ordinary things that are always with us. Master that, and you have mastered everything. We imagine that our bodies are a hindrance to our development, whereas it is only through our bodies that we develop. We cannot express a character without a body.

MFL 62

### May 14

*Your body is the temple of the Holy Ghost.* 1 Corinthians 6:19
The instinct of ownership is a right one, though the disposition expressed through it may be wrong. In a saint the idea of ownership is that we have the power to glorify God by good works (see Matthew 5:16). What we own is the honour of Jesus Christ. Have I ever

97

realized that His honour is at stake in my bodily life? 'What? know ye not that your body is the temple of the Holy Ghost which is in you ...?' Do I own my body for that one purpose? Do I own my brain to think God's thoughts after Him? We have to be intensely and personally God's.

The Spirit of God brings us into the realization of our ownership, and the instinct of ownership becomes a tremendous wealth in the life. 'All things are yours', and Paul prays that the eyes of our understanding may be enlightened that we may know what is ours in Christ Jesus.

No personality, from a tiny child to Almighty God, is without this sense of ownership. How wonderfully sprightly a dog looks when he is owned! How weary and hang-dog we become when we are convicted of sin; but when we experience God's salvation, we straighten up immediately, everything is altered, we can fling our heads back and look the world in the face because the Lord Jesus Christ is ours and we are His. A dominant ownership, such as the ownership of the Lord means that we own everything He owns. 'The meek shall inherit the earth.'

MFL 75

*Truly the light is sweet, and a pleasant thing it is for the eyes to behold the sun: Yea, if a man live many years, let him rejoice in them all; but let him remember the days of darkness, for they shall be many. All that cometh is vanity.* Ecclesiastes 11:7–8

Solomon is stating the practical attitude to things in the midst of the haphazard. You have to live this actual life, he says, with our confidence based on God, and see that you keep your day full of the joy and light of life; enjoy things as they come. When we have a particularly good time, we are apt to say, 'Oh well, it can't last long.' We expect the worst. When we have one trouble, we expect more. The Bible counsels us to rejoice—'yet let him remember the days of darkness'.

The Bible talks about drinking wine when we are glad (see Psalm 104:15); this is different from the modern view. It is bad to drink wine when you are in the dumps. Solomon is amazingly keen that a man should enjoy the pleasant things, remembering that that is why they are here. The universe is meant for enjoyment. '... God, who giveth us richly all things to enjoy.' 'Whatsoever ye do whether ye eat or drink, do all to the glory of God.' We argue on the rational line—Don't do this or that because it is wrong. Paul argues in this way: Don't do it, not because it is wrong, but because the man who follows you will stumble if he does it, therefore cut it out, never let him see you do it any more (cf. 1 Corinthians 8:9–13). Solomon's attitude is a safe and sane one, that when a man is rightly related to God he has to see that he enjoys his own life and that others do too.

SHH 145

**May 16**

*Take no thought for your life* ... Matthew 6:25

Immediately we look at these words of our Lord, we find them the most revolutionary of statements. We argue in exactly the opposite way, even the most spiritual of us—'I *must* live, I *must* make so much money, I *must* be clothed and fed.' That is how it begins; the great concern of the life is not God, but how we are going to fit ourselves to live. Jesus Christ says, 'Reverse the order, get rightly related to Me first, see that you maintain that as the great care of your life, and never put the concentration of your care on the other things.' It is a severe discipline to allow the Holy Spirit to bring us into harmony with the teaching of Jesus in these verses.

SSM 68

If after you have received the Holy Spirit, you try and put other things first instead of God, you will find confusion. The Holy Spirit presses through and says—'Where does God come in in this new relationship? in this mapped-out holiday? in these new books you are buying?' The Holy Spirit always presses that point until we learn to make concentration on God our first consideration. It is not only wrong to worry, it is real infidelity because it means we do not believe God can look after the little practical details of our lives, it is never anything else that worries us. Notice what Jesus said would choke the word He puts in—the devil? No, the cares of this world. That is how infidelity begins. It is 'the little foxes that spoil the vines', the little worries always. The great cure for infidelity is obedience to the Spirit of God.

SSM 72

99

## May 17

*Take no thought saying, What shall we eat? or What shall we drink? or, Wherewithal shall we be clothed?* Matthew 6:31

Today we enthrone insurance and economy, but it is striking to recall that the one thing Jesus Christ commended was extravagance. Our Lord only called one work 'good', and that was the act of Mary of Bethany when she broke the alabaster box of ointment. It was neither useful nor her duty, it sprang from her devotion to Jesus, and He said of it—'Wheresoever this gospel shall be preached throughout the whole world, this also that she hath done shall be spoken of for a memorial of her.'

The object of a man's life is not to hoard; he has to get enough for his brute life and no more; the best of his life is to be spent in confidence in God. Man is meant to utilize the earth and its products for food and the nourishment of his body, but he must not live in order to make his existence. If the children of Israel gathered more manna than they needed, it turned into dry rot, and that law still holds good.

SHH 73

## May 18

*When ye come into the land which I give you, then shall the land keep a sabbath unto the Lord ... in the seventh year shall be a sabbath of solemn rest for the land, a sabbath unto the Lord.* Leviticus 25:1–4

The twenty-fifth chapter of Leviticus is the great classic on the rights of the land. The establishment of men's rights on the earth is limited by the rights of the earth itself. If you keep taking from the land, never giving it any rest, in time it will stop giving to you. We talk about the rights of the land, and make it mean our right to grab as much from it as we can. In God's sight the land has rights just as human beings have, and many of the theories which are being advanced today go back to God's original prescription for the land. When God ordained 'a sabbath of solemn rest for the land', it was a reiteration of the instructions given to Adam in the Garden of Eden —'Be fruitful, and multiply, and replenish the earth, and subdue it' (Genesis 1:28). Man was intended to replenish the earth by looking after it, being its lord not its tyrant; sin has made man its tyrant (cf. Romans 8:19). The rights of the land will probably only be fully realized in the Millennium, because in this dispensation men ignore obedience to God's laws.

BE 24

## May 19

*I have uttered that I understood not; things too wonderful for me, which I knew not.* Job 42:3

Everything a man takes to be the key to a problem is apt to turn out another lock. For instance, the theory of evolution was supposed to be the key to the problem of the universe, but instead it has turned out a lock. Again, the atomic theory was thought to be the key; then it was discovered that the atom itself was composed of electrons, and each electron was found to be a universe of its own, and that theory too becomes a lock and not a key. Everything that man attempts as a simplification of life, other than a personal relationship to God, turns out to be a lock, and we should be alert to recognize when a thing turns from a key to a lock. The creed Job held, which pretended to be a key to the character of God, turned out to be a lock, and Job is realizing that the only key to life is not a statement of faith in God, nor an intellectual conception of God, but a personal relationship to Him. God Himself is the key to the riddle of the universe, and the basis of things is to be found only in Him. If a man leaves out God and takes any scientific explanation as the key, he only succeeds in finding another lock.

BFB 99

## May 20

*Except ye see signs and wonders, ye will not believe.* John 4:48

A miracle is a work done by one who has fuller knowledge and authority than we have. Things that were called miracles a hundred years ago are not thought of as miracles today because men have come to a fuller knowledge. The miracles of Jesus were an exhibition of the power of God, that is, they were simply mirrors of what God Almighty is doing gradually and everywhere and all the time; but every miracle Jesus performed had a tremendous lesson behind it. It was not merely an exhibition of the power of God, there was always a moral meaning behind for the individual. That is why God does not heal some people. We are apt to confine life to one phase only, the physical: there are three phases—physical, psychical and spiritual. Whenever Jesus touched the physical domain a miracle happened in the other phases as well. If a miracle is wrought by any other power in the physical it leaves no corresponding stamp of truth in the other domains of soul and spirit.

SHL 32

## May 21

*The Son of Man hath not where to lay His head.* Matthew 8:20
The poverty of our Lord and of His disciples is the exact expression of the nature of the religion of Jesus Christ—just man and God; man possessing nothing, professing nothing; yet when the Lord asks at some dawn, after a heart-breaking failure, 'Lovest thou me?' the soul confesses, 'Yea, Lord, thou knowest that I love thee.' And when that poverty is a disgust to the full-fed religious world, the disciple does not *profess*, but confesses, with aching hands and bleeding feet, 'I love Him', and goes 'outside the camp, bearing his reproach'.

We have grown literally afraid of being poor. We despise anyone who elects to be poor in order to simplify and save his inner life. If he does not join the general scramble, and pant with the money-making street, we deem him spiritless and lacking in ambition. We have lost the power of imagining what the ancient idealization of poverty could have meant—the liberation from material attachments, the unbribed soul, the manlier indifference, the paying our way by what we are or do, and not by what we have; the right to fling away our life at any moment irresponsibly, the more athletic trim, in short, the moral fighting shape.

DL 76, 77

## May 22

*Then the lust, when it hath conceived, beareth sin: and the sin, when it is full grown, bringeth forth death.* James 1:15 (RV).
How do we think about sin habitually, as Christians? If we have light views about sin we are not students in the school of Christ. The fact of sin is the secret of Jesus Christ's Cross; its removal is the secret of His risen and ascended life. Do we think along these lines? It is quite possible to be living in union with God through the Atonement and yet be traitors mentally....

If you read carefully the modern statements regarding sin you will be amazed to find how often we are much more in sympathy with them than with the Bible statements. We have to face the problem that our hearts may be right with God while our heads have a startling affinity with a great deal that is antagonistic to the Bible teaching. What we need, and what we get if we go on with God, is an intellectual re-birth as well as a heart re-birth.

The trouble with the modern statements regarding sin is that they make sin far too slight. Sin according to the modern view simply means selfishness, and preachers and teachers are as dead against selfishness as the New Testament is. Immediately we come to the Bible we find that sin is much deeper than that. According to the Bible, sin in its final analysis is not a defect but a defiance, a defiance that means death to the life of God in us. Sin is seen not only in selfishness, but in what men call unselfishness. It is possible to have such sympathy with our fellow-men as to be guilty of red-handed rebellion against God. Enthusiasm for humanity as it is, is quite a different thing from the enthusiasm for the saints which the Bible reveals, viz., enthusiasm for readjusted humanity.

BE 114-15

## May 23

*Marvel not that I said unto thee, ye must be born again.* John 3:7

The reason we do not see the need to be born from above is that we have a vast capacity for ignoring facts. People talk about the evolution of the race. The writers of today seem to be incapable of a profound understanding of history, they write glibly about the way the race is developing, where are their eyes and their reading of human life as it is? We are not evolving and developing in any sense to justify what is known as evolution. We have developed in certain domains but not in all. We are nowhere near the massive, profound intellectual grasp of the men who lived before Christ was born. What brain today can come near Plato or Socrates? And yet people say we are developing and getting better, and we are laying the flattering unction to our souls that we have left Jesus Christ and His ideas twenty centuries behind. No wonder Jesus said that if we stand by Him and take His point of view, men will hate us as they hated Him.

HG 64

*I am crucified with Christ: nevertheless I live; yet not I, but Christ liveth in me.* Galatians 2:20

To imagine that Jesus Christ came to save and sanctify *me* is heresy: He came to save and sanctify me *into Himself*, to be His absolute bondslave; so completely His bondslave that when He speaks there is no possibility of dispute. 'I reckon on you for extreme service, with no complaining on your part and no explanation on Mine.' We begin to debate and say, 'Why shouldn't I do this? I'm within my rights.' That idea is so foreign to our Lord's conception that He has made no provision for it. The passion of Christianity is that I deliberately sign away my own rights and become a bondslave of Jesus Christ. Any fool can insist on his rights, and any devil will see that he gets them; but the Sermon on the Mount means that the only right the saint will insist on is the right to give up his rights. That is the New Testament idea of sanctification, and that is why so few get anywhere near the baptism with the Holy Ghost. 'I want to be baptized with the Holy Ghost so that I may be of use'—then it is all up. We are baptized with the Holy Ghost not *for* anything at all, but entirely, as our Lord puts it, to be His witnesses, those with whom He can do exactly what He likes.

HGM 130

*And without shedding of blood is no remission of sins.* Hebrews 9:22

The first fundamental reference in this verse is unquestionably to our Lord's Atonement; and yet there is a direct reference to ourselves. Do we begin to know what the Bible means by 'the blood of Jesus Christ'? Blood and life are inseparable. In the Bible the experiences of salvation and sanctification are never separated as we separate them; they are separable in experience, but when God's Book speaks of being 'in Christ' it is always in terms of entire sanctification. We are apt to look upon the blood of Christ as a kind of magic-working thing, instead of an impartation of His very life. The whole purpose of being born again and being identified with the death of the Lord Jesus is that His blood may flow through our mortal body; then the tempers and the affections and the dispositions which were manifested in the life of the Lord will be manifested in us in some degree.... There are two sides to the Atonement—it is not only the

104

life of Christ *for* me but His life *in* me for my life; no Christ *for* me if I do not have Christ *in* me. All through there is to be this strenuous, glorious practising in our bodily life of the changes which God has wrought in our soul through His Spirit, and the only proof that we are in earnest is that we work out what God works in. As we apply this truth to ourselves, we shall find in practical experience that God does alter passions and nerves and tempers. God alters every physical thing in a human being so that these bodies can be used now as slaves to the new disposition. We can make our eyes, and ears, and every one of our bodily organs express as slaves the altered disposition of our soul.

BP 70

*And there appeared unto them Elias and Moses: and they were talking with Jesus.* Mark 9:4

Jesus was standing in the full blaze and glory of His pre-Incarnate glory while the two representatives of the Old Covenant talked with Him about the issue which He was about to accomplish at Jerusalem. Then He turned His back upon that glory, and came down from the Mount to be identified with fallen humanity, symbolized by the demon-possessed boy. Had He gone back into the glory which was His before the Incarnation having only reached the Mount of Transfiguration, He would have left the human race exactly where it was; His life would only have been a sublime ideal. There are many who look at the life of Jesus Christ as an ideal and nothing more—'His teachings are so fine, we do not need to have anything to do with the Atonement, or with those crude doctrines of the apostle Paul's about the Cross and personal apprehension; it is quite enough for us to have the Sermon on the Mount.' I should think it was! If Jesus Christ came to be an Example only, He is the greatest torturer of the human race. But our Lord did not come primarily to teach us and give us an example; He came to lift us into a totally new kingdom, and to impart a new life to which His teachings would apply.

PR 78

**May 27**

*I will restore to you the years that the locust hath eaten.* Joel 2:25

The greatest problems of conscience are not the wrong things we have done, but wrong relationships. We may have become born again, but what about those we have wronged? It is of no use to sit down and say, 'It is irreparable now, I cannot alter it.' Thank God He can alter it! We may try to repair the damage in our own way, by apologizing, by writing letters; but it is not a simple easy matter of something to apologize for. Behind the veil of human lives God begins to reveal the tragedies of hell. Or we may say, 'I have been atoned for, therefore I do not need to think about the past.' If we are conscientious the Holy Spirit will make us think about the past, and it is just here that the tyranny of nerves and the bondage of Satan comes in. The shores of life are strewn with ruined friendships, irreparable severances through our own blame or others, and when the Holy Spirit begins to reveal the tremendous twist, then comes the strange distress, 'How can we repair it?' Many a sensitive soul has been driven into insanity through anguish of mind because he has never realized what Jesus Christ came to do, and all the asylums in the world will never touch them in the way of healing; the only thing that will is the realization of what the death of Jesus means, viz., that the damage we have done may be repaired through the efficiency of His Cross. Jesus Christ has atoned for all, and He can make it good in us, not only as a gift but by a participation on our part. The miracle of the grace of God is that He can make the past as though it had never been; He can 'restore the years that the locust hath eaten, the cankerworm, and the caterpillar, and the palmerworm'.

PS 21

**May 28**

*God so loved the world...* John 3:16

The Bible says that 'God so loved the world, that he gave his only begotten Son...', and yet it says that if we are friends of the world we are enemies of God. 'Know ye not that the friendship of the world is enmity with God?' (James 4:4). The difference is that God loves the world so much that He goes all lengths to remove the wrong from it, and we must have the same kind of love. Any other kind of love for the world simply means that we take it as it is and are

106

perfectly delighted with it. The world is all right and we are very happy in it; sin and evil and the devil are so many Orientalisms. It is that sentiment which is the enemy of God. Do we love the world in this sense sufficiently to spend and be spent so that God can manifest His grace through us until the wrong and the evil are removed?

BP 121

## May 29

*Consider the lilies.* Matthew 6:28

When Jesus said 'Consider the lilies of the field, how they grow', He was referring to the new life in us. If we make His words apply to the natural life only, we make Him appear foolish. If we are born of God and are obeying Him, the unconscious life is forming in us just where we are. God knows exactly the kind of garden to put His lilies in, and they grow and take form unconsciously. What is it that deforms natural beauty? Overmuch cultivation; and overmuch denominational teaching will deform beauty in the spiritual world...

The new life must go on and take form unconsciously. God is looking after it, He knows exactly the kind of nourishment as well as the kind of disintegration that is necessary. Be careful that you do not bury the new life, or put it into circumstances where it cannot grow. A lily can only grow in the surroundings that suit it, and in the same way God engineers the circumstances that are best fitted for the development of the life of His Son in us.

PR 40

## May 30

*Whatsoever I speak therefore, even as the Father said unto me, so I speak.* John 12:50

Jesus Christ said He always spoke as His Father wished Him to. Did His Father write out the words and tell Him to learn them by heart? No, the mainspring of the heart of Jesus Christ was the mainspring of the heart of God the Father, consequently the words Jesus Christ spoke were the exact expression of God's thought. In our Lord the tongue was in its right place; He never spoke from His head, but always from His heart. 'If any man among you seem to be religious, and bridleth not his tongue...this man's religion is vain' (James

107

1:26), there is nothing in it. The tongue and the brain are under our control, not God's...

Sometimes Jesus Christ's speech sounded anything but nice to natural ears, e.g. Matthew 23. Some of the words He used, and some applications He made of His truth were terrible and rugged. Read our Lord's description of the heart: 'Out of the heart,' says Jesus, 'proceed...'—and then comes the ugly catalogue (Matthew 15:19). Upright men and women of the world simply do not believe this. Jesus Christ did not speak as a man there. He spoke as the Master of men, with an absolute knowledge of what the human heart is like. That is why He so continually pleads with us to hand the keeping of our hearts over to Him.

BP 126

### May 31

*Ye call me Master and Lord: and ye say well; for so I am.* John 13:13
Our Lord never takes measures to make us obey Him. Our obedience is the outcome of a oneness of spirit with Him through His Redemption.

Obedience to Jesus Christ is essential, but not compulsory; He never insists on being Master. We feel that if only He would insist, we should obey Him. But our Lord never enforces His 'thou shalt's' and 'thou shalt not's'; He never takes means to force us to do what He says; He never coerces. If we do not keep His commandments, He does not come and tell us we are wrong, we know it, we cannot get away from it. There is no ambiguity in our mind as to whether what He says is right. Our Lord never says 'you *must*', but if we are to be His disciples we know we must....

'Ye call me Master and Lord: and ye say well; for so I am'—But *is* He? 'Master' and 'Lord' have very little place in our spiritual vocabulary; we prefer the words 'Saviour' and 'Sanctifier' and 'Healer'. In other words, we know very little about love as Jesus revealed it. It is seen in the way we use the word 'obey'. Our use of the word implies the submission of an inferior to a superior; obedience in our Lord's use of the word is the relationship of equals, a son and father. '...though he was a Son, yet learned he obedience by the things which he suffered.' Our Lord was not a servant of God. He was His Son. The Son's obedience as Redeemer was *because He was* Son, not in order *to be* Son.

SSY 84

108

**June 1**

*And behold, I send forth the promise of my Father upon you.*
Luke 24:49

Do you say 'I am waiting for my Pentecost'? Who told you to wait? 'Oh, I am waiting as the disciples did in the upper room.' Not all the waiting on earth will ever gain you the baptism with the Holy Ghost. The baptism with the Holy Ghost is the infallible sign that Jesus has ascended to the right hand of God and has received of the Father the promise of the Holy Ghost. We too often divorce what the New Testament never divorces: the baptism with the Holy Ghost is not an experience apart from Christ, it is the evidence that He has ascended.

HGM 21

We are told by some that it is foolish to tell people to ask for the Holy Spirit because this is the dispensation of the Holy Spirit. Thank God it is! God's mighty Spirit is with all men, He impinges on their lives at all points and in unexpected ways, but the great need is to receive the Holy Spirit. There stands the promise for every one who will put it to the test: 'If ye then, being evil, know how to give good gifts to your children: how much more shall your heavenly Father give the Holy Spirit to them that ask Him?' The bedrock in Jesus Christ's kingdom is poverty, not possession; not decisions for Christ, but a sense of absolute futility 'I can't begin to do it.' That is the entrance; and it does take us a long while to believe we are poor. It is at the point of destitution that the bounty of God can be given.

HGM 17

**June 2**

*And when the day of Pentecost was now come . . . ('was being fulfilled',*
RV marg.). Acts 2:1

What an unspeakably wonderful day the Day of Pentecost was! There is only one Bethlehem, one Calvary, one Pentecost; these are the landmarks of Time and Eternity, everything and everyone is judged by them.

Beware of thinking of Pentecost in the light of personal experience only. The descent of the Holy Ghost can never be experimental, it is historical. The reception of the Holy Ghost into our hearts is experimental. Those who insist on the experimental line are in danger

109

of forgetting the revelation and of putting all the emphasis on experience, while those who emphasize the revelation are in danger of forgetting the practical experience. In the New Testament the two are one; the experimental must be based on and regulated by the revelation. We imagine that we have the monopoly of the teaching about the Holy Spirit when we deal with His work in individual lives, viz., His power to transform men on the inside—the most important phase to us, but in God's Book the tiniest phase of the work of the mighty Spirit of God.

HGM 20

## June 3

*It is God which worketh in you.* Philippians 2:13

We cannot give ourselves the Holy Spirit; the Holy Spirit is God Almighty's gift if we will simply become poor enough to ask for Him. 'If ye then, being evil, know how to give good gifts unto your children; how much more shall your heavenly Father give the Holy Spirit to them that ask him?' (Luke 9:13). But when the Holy Spirit has come in, there is something we can do and God cannot do, we can obey Him. If we do not obey Him, we shall grieve Him. 'And grieve not the Holy Spirit of God' (Ephesians 4:30). Over and over again we need to be reminded of Paul's counsel, 'Work out your own salvation with fear and trembling. For it is God that worketh in you both to will and to do of His good pleasure.' Thank God, it is gloriously and majestically true that the Holy Spirit can work in us the very nature of Jesus Christ if we will obey Him, until in and through our mortal flesh may be manifested works which will make men glorify our Father in heaven, and take knowledge of us that we have been with Jesus.

BP 220

## June 4

*If any man be in Christ, he is a new creature: old things are passed away.* 2 Corinthians 5:17

The way the Holy Spirit corrupts our natural virtues when He comes in is one of the most devastating experiences. He does not build up and transfigure what we possess in the way of virtue and

110

goodness by natural heredity; it is corrupted to death, until we learn that we

> '...dare not trust the sweetest frame,
> But wholly lean on Jesus' name.'

It is a deep instruction to watch how natural virtues break down. The Holy Spirit does not patch up our natural virtues, for the simple reason that no natural virtue can come anywhere near Jesus Christ's demands. God does not build up our natural virtues and transfigure them, He totally recreates us on the inside. 'And every virtue we possess is His alone.' As we bring every bit of our nature into harmony with the new life which God puts in, what will be exhibited in us will be the virtues that were characteristic of the Lord Jesus, not our natural virtues. The supernatural is made natural. The life that God plants in us develops its own virtues, not the virtues of Adam but of Jesus Christ, and Jesus Christ can never be described in terms of the natural virtues.

AHW 98

### June 5

*Till we all attain ... unto the measure of the stature of the fulness of Christ.* Ephesians 4:13

The personal Holy Spirit builds us up into the body of Christ. All that Jesus Christ came to do is made ours experimentally by the Holy Spirit, and all His gifts are for the good of the whole body, not for individual exaltation. Individuality must go in order that the personal life may be brought out into fellowship with God. By the baptism of the Holy Ghost we are delivered from the husk of independent individuality, our personality is awakened and brought into communion with God. We too often divorce what the New Testament never divorces. The baptism of the Holy Ghost is not an experience apart from Christ: it is the evidence of the ascended Christ. It is not the baptism of the Holy Ghost that changes men, but the power of the ascended Christ coming into men's lives by the Holy Ghost that changes them. 'Ye shall be witnesses unto me.' This great Pentecostal phrase puts the truth for us in unforgettable words. Witnesses not so much of what Jesus Christ can do, but *witnesses unto me*, a delight to the heart of Jesus, a satisfaction to Him wherever He places us.

MC 131

111

June 6

*For by one Spirit are we all baptized into one body...* 1 Corinthians 12:13

God is the Architect of the human body and He is also the Architect of the Body of Christ. There are two Bodies of Christ: the Historic Body and the Mystical Body. The historic Jesus was the habitation of the Holy Ghost (see Luke 3:22; John 1:32–3), and the Mystic Christ, i.e., the Body of Christ composed of those who have experienced regeneration and sanctification, is likewise the habitation of the Holy Ghost. When we are baptized with the Holy Ghost we are no longer isolated believers but part of the Mystical Body of Christ. Beware of attempting to live a holy life alone, it is impossible. Paul continually insists on the 'together' aspect — 'God hath quickened us *together*... and hath raised us up *together*, and made us sit *together*...' (Ephesians 2:4–6). The 'together' aspect is always the work of the Holy Ghost.

HGM 25

'Be filled with the Spirit,' says Paul. We have all seen the seashore when the tide is out, with all its separate pools, how are those pools to be made one? By digging channels between them? No, wait till the tide comes in, and where are the pools? Absolutely lost, merged in one tremendous floodtide. That is exactly what happens when Christians are indwelt by the Holy Spirit. Once let people be filled with the Holy Spirit and you have the ideal of what the New Testament means by the Church. The Church is a separated band of people who are united to God by the regenerating power of the Spirit, and the bedrock of membership in the Church is that we know who Jesus is by a personal revelation of Him.

CHI 49

June 7

*Listen, O isles, unto me; and hearken, ye people, from far; The Lord hath called me from the womb...and he hath made my mouth like a sharp sword.* Isaiah 49:1, 2

A saint is made by God, 'He made me'. Then do not tell God He is a bungling workman. We do that whenever we say 'I can't'. To say 'I can't' literally means we are too strong in ourselves to depend on God. 'I can't pray in public; I can't talk in the open air.'

112

Substitute 'I won't', and it will be nearer the truth. The thing that makes us say 'I can't' is that we forget that we must rely entirely on the creative purpose of God and on this characteristic of perfect finish for God.

Much of our difficulty comes because we choose our own work—'Oh well, this is what I am fitted for.' Remember that Jesus took a fisherman and turned him into a shepherd. That is symbolical of what He does all the time. The idea that we have to consecrate our gifts to God is a dangerous one. We cannot consecrate what is not ours (1 Corinthians 4:7). We have to consecrate ourselves, and leave our gifts alone. God does not ask us to do the thing that is easy to us naturally; He only asks us to do the thing we are perfectly fitted to do by grace, and the cross will always come along that line.

SSY 108

### June 8

*But thou, when thou prayest...* Matthew 6:6

'But it is so difficult to get time.' Of course it is, we have to make time, and that means effort, and effort makes us conscious of the need to re-organize our general ways. It will facilitate matters to remember, even if it humbles us, that we take time to eat our breakfast and our dinner, etc. Most of the difficulty in forming a special habit is that we will not discipline ourselves ...

You say you cannot get up early in the morning; well, a very good thing to do is to get up in order to prove that you cannot! This does not contradict at all the notion that we must not put earnestness in the place of God; it means that we have to understand that our bodily mechanism is made by God, and that when we are regenerated He does not give us another body, we have the same body, and therefore the way we use our wits in order to learn a secular thing is the way to learn any spiritual thing. 'But thou, when thou prayest ...' begin now.

DPR 30

### June 9

*The first (commandment) is ... thou shalt love the Lord thy God with all thy heart, and with all thy soul, and with all thy mind, and with all thy strength ('from all thy heart ...'* RV marg.). Mark 12:29–30

113

My relationship to God embraces every faculty, I am to love Him with *all* my heart, *all* my soul, *all* my mind, *all* my strength, every detail is instinct with devotion to Him; if it is not I am disjointed somewhere. Think what you do for someone you love! The most amazingly minute details are perfectly transfigured because your whole nature is embraced, not one faculty only. You don't love a person with your heart and leave the rest of your nature out, you love with your whole being, from the crown of the head to the sole of the foot. That is the attitude of the New Testament all through. In 1 Corinthians 15 the Apostle Paul has been speaking about the stupendous mystery of the resurrection, and suddenly, like a swinging lamp in a mine, he rushes it right straight down and says, 'Now concerning the collection...' The New Testament is continually doing it—'Jesus knowing... that the Father had given all things into His hands... began to wash the disciples' feet.' It takes God Incarnate to wash feet properly. It takes God Incarnate to do anything properly.

GW 9

### June 10

*He that hath ears to hear, let him hear.* Matthew 11:15

We hear only what we listen for. Have we listened to what Jesus has to say? Have we paid any attention to finding out what He did say? Most of us do not know what He said. If we have only a smattering of religion, we talk a lot about the devil; but what hinders us spiritually is not the devil nearly so much as inattention. We may *hear* the sayings of Jesus Christ, but our wills are left untouched, we never *do* them. The understanding of the Bible only comes from the indwelling of the Holy Spirit making the universe of the Bible real to us.

SSM 107

Much is written about our Lord speaking so simply that anyone could understand, and we forget that while it remains true that the common people heard him gladly, no one, not even His own disciples, understood Him until after the Resurrection and the coming of the Holy Spirit, the reason being that a pure heart is the essential requirement for being 'of the truth'. 'Blessed are the pure in heart: for they shall see God.'

GW 34

*Jesus said unto them, Verily, verily, I say unto you, Before Abraham was, I am.* John 8:58. (See also Matthew 18:3–5)

Spiritually we never grow old; through the passing of the years we grow so many years young. The characteristic of the spiritual life is its unageing youth, exactly the opposite of the natural life. 'I am ...the First and the Last.' The Ancient of Days represents the Eternal Childhood. God Almighty became the weakest thing in His own creation, a Baby. When He comes into us in new birth we can easily kill His life in us, or else we can see to it that His life is nourished according to the dictates of the Spirit of God so that we grow 'unto the measure of the stature of the fulness of Christ'. The mature saint is just like a little child, absolutely simple and joyful and gay. Go on living the life that God would have you live and you will grow younger instead of older. There is a marvellous rejuvenescence when once you let God have His way. If you are feeling very old, then get born again and do more at it.

PR 47

*That they may be one, even as we are one.* John 17:22

The conception which Jesus Christ had of society was that men might be one with Him as He was one with the Father. The full-orbed meaning of the term 'personality' in its fundamental aspect is a being created by God who has lived on this earth and formed his character. The majority of us are not personalities as yet, we are beginning to be, and our value to God in His Kingdom depends on the development and growth of our personality. There is a difference between being saved and sanctified by the sheer sovereign grace of God and choosing to be the choice ones, not for heaven, but down here. The average view of Christianity, that we only need to have faith and we are saved, is a stumbling block. How many of us care anything about being witnesses to Jesus Christ? How many of us are willing to spend every ounce of energy we have, every bit of mental, moral and spiritual life for Jesus Christ? That is the meaning of a worker in God's sense. God has left us on earth, what for? To be saved and sanctified? No, to be at it for Him...

My life as a worker is the way I say 'Thank you' to God for His unspeakable salvation.

AUG 18

115

*If a man therefore purge himself... he shall be a vessel unto honour, sanctified, and meet for the master's use.* 2 Timothy 2:21

The vessels in a household have their honour from the use made of them by the head of the house. As a worker I have to separate myself for one purpose—for Jesus Christ to use me for what He likes. Imitation, doing what other people do, is an unmitigated curse. Am I allowing anyone to mould my ideas of Christian service? Am I taking my ideals from some servant of God or from God Himself? We are here for one thing only—to be vessels 'meet for the master's use'. We are not here to work for God because we have chosen to do so, but because God has apprehended us. Natural ability has nothing to do with service; consequently there is never any thought of, 'Oh well, I am not fitted for this.'

Is He going to help Himself to your life, or are you taken up with your conception of what you are going to do? God is responsible for our lives, and the one great keynote is reckless reliance upon Him.

AUG 34

*And it came to pass... that these made war... Twelve years they served Chedorlaomer, and in the thirteenth year they rebelled.* Genesis 14:1–4

Life without conflict is impossible, either in nature or in grace. This is an open fact of life. The basis of physical, mental, moral and spiritual life is antagonism. Physical life is maintained according to the power of fight in the corpuscles of the blood. If I have sufficient vital force within to overcome the forces without, I produce the balance of health. The same is true of mental life. If I want to maintain a clear, vigorous, mental life, I have to fight, and in this way I produce the balance of thought. Morally it is the same. Virtue is the result of fight; I am only virtuous according to the moral stability I have within. If I have sufficient moral fighting capacity, I produce the moral balance of virtue. We make virtue out of necessity, but no one is virtuous who is good because he cannot help it. Virtue is the outcome of conflict. And spiritually it is the same. 'In the world ye shall have tribulation'; i.e., everything that is not spiritual makes for my undoing; 'but be of good cheer; I have overcome the world.' When once this is understood it is a perfect delight to meet opposi-

116

tion, and as we learn to score off the things that come against us, we produce the balance of holiness. Faith must be tried, and it is the trial of faith that is precious. If you are faint-hearted, it is a sign you won't play the game, you are fit for neither God nor man because you will face nothing.

NKW 36

## June 15

*Why dost thou not pardon my transgression, and take away mine iquity?* Job 7:21

Job gives utterance to a mood which is not foreign to us when he says, 'Am I a sea, or a whale, that thou settest a watch over me?' In certain moods of anguish the human heart says to God, 'I wish You would let me alone, why should I be used for things which have no appeal to me?' In the Christian life we are not being used for our own designs at all, but for the fulfilment of the prayer of Jesus Christ. He has prayed that we might be 'one with him as he is one with the Father', consequently God is concerned only about that one thing, and He never says 'By your leave'. Whether we like it or not, God will burn us in His fire until we are as pure as He is, and it is during the process that we cry, as Job did, 'I wish You would leave me alone.'

We have the idea that prosperity, or happiness, or morality, is the end of a man's existence; according to the Bible it is something other, viz., 'to glorify God and enjoy him for ever'. When a man is right with God, God puts His honour in that man's keeping. Job was one of those in whom God staked His honour, and it was during the process of His inexplicable ways that Job makes his appeal for mercy, and yet all through there comes out his implicit confidence in God. 'And blessed is he, whosoever shall not be offended in me,' said our Lord.

BFB 28

## June 16

*Better is the sight of the eyes than the wandering of the desire: this is also vanity and vexation of spirit.* Ecclesiastes 6:9

Lust means literally—'I must have it at once, and I don't care what the consequences are.' It may be a low, animal lust, or it may be a

117

mental lust, or a moral or spiritual lust; but it is a characteristic that does not belong to the life hid with Christ in God. Love is the opposite; love can wait endlessly. 'Better is the sight of the eyes, than the wandering of the desire.' One of the first things Jesus Christ does is to open a man's eyes and he sees things as they are. Until then he is not satisfied with the seeing of his eyes, he wants more, anything that is hidden he must drag to the light, and the wandering of desire is the burning waste of a man's life until he finds God. His heart lusts, his mind lusts, his eyes lust, everything in him lusts until he is related to God. It is the demand for an infinite satisfaction and it ends in the perdition of a man's life.

Jesus Christ says, 'Come unto me, and I will give you rest', i.e., I will put you in the place where your eyes are open. And notice what Jesus Christ says we will look at—lilies, and sparrows, and grass. What man in his senses bothers about these things! We consider aeroplanes and tanks and shells, because these demand our attention, the other things do not. The great emancipation in the salvation of God is that it gives a man the sight of his eyes, and he sees for the first time the handiwork of God in a daisy.

'But their eyes were holden that they should not know him.'... 'And their eyes were opened, and they knew him' (Luke 24:16, 31). The salvation of Jesus Christ enables a man to see for the first time in his life, and it is a wonderful thing.

SSH 72


### June 17

*Many will say to me in that day, Lord, Lord, have we not prophesied in thy name? and in thy name have cast out devils? and in thy name done many wonderful works?* Matthew 7:22

If we are able to cast out devils and to do wonderful works, surely we are the servants of God? Not at all, says Jesus, our lives must bear evidence in every detail. Our Lord warns here against those who utilize His words and His ways to remedy the evils of men whilst they are disloyal to Himself. 'Have we not prophesied in thy name ... cast out devils ... done many wonderful works'—not one word of confessing Jesus Christ; one thing only, they have preached Him as a remedy. In Luke 10:20 our Lord told the disciples not to rejoice because the devils were subject to them, but to rejoice because they were rightly related to Himself. We are brought back to the one point
118

all the time—an unsullied relationship to Jesus Christ in every detail, private and public.

SSM 106

### June 18

*A time to keep silence, and a time to speak.* Ecclesiastes 3:7
Sometimes it is cowardly to speak, and sometimes it is cowardly to keep silence. In the Bible the great test of a man's character is his tongue (see James 1:26). The tongue only came to its right place within the lips of the Lord Jesus Christ, because He never spoke from His right to Himself. He who was the Wisdom of God Incarnate, said 'the words that I speak unto you, I speak not of myself', i.e., from the disposition of my right to Myself, but from My relationship to My Father. We are either too hasty or too slow; either we won't speak at all, or we speak too much, or we speak in the wrong mood. The thing that makes us speak is the lust to vindicate ourselves. '... leaving you an example... who did no sin neither was guile found in his mouth.' Guile has the ingredient of self-vindication in it—My word, I'll make him smart for saying that about me! That spirit never was in Jesus Christ. The great deliverance for a man in time is to learn the programmes of speech and of silence.

SHH 27

### June 19

*That they may be one, even as we are one.* John 17:22
Christianity is personal, therefore it is un-individual. An individual remains definitely segregated from every other individual; when you come to the teaching of our Lord there is no individuality in that sense at all, but only personality, 'that they may be *one*'. Two *individuals* can never merge; two *persons* can become one without losing their identity. Personality is the characteristic of the spiritual man as individuality is the characteristic of the natural man. When the Holy Spirit comes in He emancipates our personal spirit into union with God, and individuality ultimately becomes so interdependent that it loses all its self-assertiveness. Jesus Christ prayed for our identification with Himself in His oneness with the Father— 'that they may be one, *even as we are one*'. That is infinitely beyond experience. Identification is a revelation—the exposition of the ex-

119

perience. The standard Revelation with regard to identification is our Lord Himself, and you can never define Him in terms of individuality, but only in terms of personality. When Jesus Christ emancipates the personality individuality is not destroyed, it is trans-figured, and the transfiguring, incalculable element is love, personal passionate devotion to Himself, and to others for His sake.

BE 31

**June 20**

*I will be as the dew unto Israel: he shall blossom as the lily.* Hosea 14:5 (RV)

The New Testament notices things which from our standpoint do not seem to count. For instance, Our Lord called only twelve disciples, but what about all those other disciples of His who were not specially called? The twelve disciples were called for a special purpose; but there were hundreds who followed Jesus and were sincere believers in Him who were unnoticed. We are apt to have a disproportionate view of a Christian because we look only at the exceptions. The exceptions stand out *as* exceptions. The extra-ordinary conversions and phenomenal experiences are magnificent specimen studies of what happens in the life of everyone, but not one in a million has an experience such as the Apostle Paul had. The majority of us are unnoticed and unnoticeable people. If we take the extraordinary experiences as a model for the Christian life, we erect a wrong standard without knowing it, and in the passing of the years we produce that worst abortion, the spiritual prig—an intoler-able un-likeness to Jesus Christ. The man or woman who becomes a spiritual prig does so by imperceptible degrees, but the starting-point is a departure from the evangel of the New Testament and a building up on the evangel of Protestantism.

MU 35

**June 21**

*O wretched man that I am! Who shall deliver me from the body of this death?* Romans 7:24

Be careful not to be caught up in the clap-trap of today which says, 'I believe in the teachings of Jesus, but I don't see any need for the Atonement.' Men talk pleasant, patronizing things about Jesus

120

Christ's teaching while they ignore His Cross. By all means let us study Christ's teaching, we do not think nearly enough along New Testament lines, we are swamped by pagan standards, and as Christians we ought to allow Jesus Christ's principles to work out in our brains as well as in our lives; but the teaching of Jesus apart from His Atonement simply adds an ideal that leads to despair. What is the good of telling me that only the pure in heart can see God when I am impure? of telling me to love my enemies when I hate them? I may keep it down but the spirit is there. Does Jesus Christ make it easier? He makes it a hundredfold more difficult! The purity God demands is impossible unless we can be re-made from within, and that is what Jesus Christ undertakes to do through the Atonement. Jesus Christ did not come to tell men they ought to be holy—there is an 'ought' in every man that tells him that, and whenever he sees a holy character he may bluster and excuse himself as he likes, but he knows that is what he ought to be: He came to put us in the place where we can be holy, that is, He came to *make* us what He teaches we should be, that is the difference.

BE 10–11

June 22

*If thine eye offend thee, pluck it out.* Mark 9:47

Sanctification means not only that we are delivered from sin, but that we start on a life of stern discipline. It is not a question of praying but of performing, of deliberately disciplining ourselves. There is no royal road there; we each have it entirely in our own hands. It is not wrong things that have to be sacrificed, but right things. 'The good is the enemy of the best', not the bad, but the good that is not good enough. The danger is to argue on the line of giving up only what is wrong; Jesus Christ selected things essential to a full-orbed life—the right hand and the eye, these are not bad things, they are creations of God. Jesus Christ talked rugged, unmitigated truth, He was never ambiguous, and He says it is better to be maimed than damned. There was never a saint yet who did not have to start with a maimed life. Anyone will give up wrong things if he knows how to, but will I give up the best I have for Jesus Christ? If I am only willing to give up wrong things, never let me talk about being in love with Him! We say, 'Why shouldn't I do it, there is no harm in it?' For pity's sake, go and do it, but

121

remember that the construction of a spiritual character is doomed once you take that line.

BE 48

**June 23**

*These things saith he that is holy, he that is true.* Revelation 3:7
The disciple's Lord is the supreme Authority in every relationship of life the disciple is in or can be in. That is a very obvious point, but think what it means—it means recognizing it as impertinent to say, 'Oh, well, Jesus Christ does not know my circumstances; the principles involved in His teachings are altogether impracticable for me where I am.' That thought never came from the Spirit of God, and it has to be gripped in a vice on the threshold of the mind and allowed no way. If as we obey God such a circumstance is possible where Jesus Christ's precepts and principles are impracticable, then He has misled us. The idea insinuates itself—'Oh, well, I can be justified from my present conduct because of—so and so.' We are never justified as disciples in taking any line of action other than that indicated by the teaching of our Lord and made possible for us by His Spirit. The providence of God fits us into various settings of life to see if we will be disciples in those relationships.

IWP 123

**June 24**

*Philip saith unto him, Lord, shew us the Father, and it sufficeth us.* John 14:9
*And he findeth Philip, and Jesus saith unto him, Follow me.* John 1:43
You may have had no reluctance in obeying the Lord's command, and yet it is probable you are hurting Him because you look for God to manifest Himself where He never can—'Lord, shew us the Father.' We look to God to manifest Himself to His children: God manifests Himself *in* His children, consequently the manifestation is seen by others, not by us. It is a snare to want to be conscious of God; you cannot be conscious of your consciousness and remain sane. You have obeyed Christ's command, then are you hurting Him by asking some profoundly perverse question? I believe our Lord is repeatedly astounded at the stupidity we display. It is notions of

122

our own that make us stupid; when we are simple we are never stupid, we discern all the time. 'Lord, shew us the Father'; 'Shew me Thy face'; 'Expound this thing to me'; and His answer comes straight back to our heart: 'Have I been so long time with you, and yet hast thou not known *me*?'

GW 25

**June 25**

*And he must needs go through Samaria.* John 4:4

One great thing to notice is that God's order comes to us in the haphazard. We try to plan our ways and work things out for ourselves, but they go wrong because there are more facts than we know; whereas if we just go on with the days as they come, we find that God's order comes to us in that apparently haphazard way. The man who does not know God depends entirely on his own wits and forecasting. If instead of arranging our own programmes we will trust to the wisdom of God and concentrate all our efforts on the duty that lies nearest, we shall find that we meet God in that way and in no other. When we become 'amateur providences' and arrange times and meetings, we may cause certain things to happen, but we very rarely meet God in that way; we meet Him most effectively as we go on in the ordinary ways. Where you look for God, He does not appear; where you do not look for Him, there He is—a trick of the weather, a letter, and suddenly you are face to face with the best thing you ever met. This comes out all through the life of Jesus Christ; it was the most natural thing for Him to go through Samaria.

HGM 31

**June 26**

*There is an evil which I have seen under the sun, and it is common among men: a man to whom God has given riches, wealth, and honour, so that he wanteth nothing for his soul of all that he desireth, yet God giveth him not power to eat thereof, but a stranger eateth it: this is vanity, and it is an evil disease.* Ecclesiastes 6:1, 2

The inevitable barriers are there in every one of our lives. They may not be of an intense order, such as a terrible maiming, or blindness, or deafness, or something that knocks a man out of fulfilling his ambitions, they may be hereditary incapabilities; but the

123

peril is lest we lie down and whine and are of no more good. The thing to do is to recognize that the barriers are inscrutable, that they are there not by chance but entirely by God's permission, and they should be faced and not ignored. Was there ever a more severely handicapped life on this earth than Helen Keller's? The peril of the inevitable barriers is that if I have not faced the facts sufficiently, I am apt to blame God for them. There is one fact more that I do not know, and that fact lies entirely with God, not with me. It is no use to spend my time saying, I wish I was not like this. I am just like it. The practical point in Christianity is—Can Jesus Christ and His religion be of any use to me as I am, not as I am not? Can He deal with me where I am, in the condition I am in?

SHH 70

## June 27

*And when he is come, he will reprove the world of sin, of righteousness and of judgment.* John 16:8

The subject of human free will is nearly always either overstated or understated. There is a pre-determination in man's spirit which makes him will along certain lines; but no man has the power to make an act of pure free will. When the Spirit of God comes into a man, He brings His own generating will power and causes him to will with God, and we have the amazing revelation that the saint's free choices are the pre-determinations of God. That is a most wonderful thing in Christian psychology, viz., that a saint chooses exactly what God pre-determined he should choose. If you have never received the Spirit of God this will be one of the things which is 'foolishness' to you; but if you have received the Spirit and are obeying Him, you find He brings your spirit into complete harmony with God and the sound of your goings and the sound of God's goings are one and the same.

BP 215

## June 28

*If I had not come and spoken unto them, they had not had sin: but now they have no cloke for their sin.* John 15:22

We have, as Christian disciples, to continually recognize that much

124

of what is called Christianity today is not the Christianity of the New Testament; it is distinctly different in generation and manifestation. Jesus is not the fountain-head of modern Christianity; He is scarcely thought about. Christian preachers, Sunday School teachers, religious books, all without any apology patronize Jesus Christ and put Him on one side. We have to learn that to stand true to Jesus Christ's point of view means ostracism, the ostracism that was brought on Him; most of us know nothing whatever about it. The modern view looks upon human nature as pathetic: men and women are poor ignorant babes in the wood who have lost themselves. Jesus Christ's view is totally different, He does not look on men and women as babes in the wood, but as sinners who need saving, and the modern mind detests His view. Our Lord's teaching is based on something we violently hate, viz., His doctrine of sin; we do not believe it unless we have had a radical dealing with God on the line of His teaching.

Remember that a disciple is committed to much more than belief in Jesus; he is committed to his Lord's view of the world, of men, of God and of sin. Take stock of your views and compare them with the New Testament, and never get tricked into thinking that the Bible does not mean what it says when it disagrees with you. Disagree with what our Lord says by all means if you like, but never say that the Bible does not mean what it says.

HG 63


June 29

*Whosoever hateth his brother is a murderer.* 1 John 3:15.

Few of us are actually murderers, but we are all criminals in potentiality; and one of the greatest humiliations in work for God is that we are never free from the reminder by the Holy Spirit of what we might be in actuality but for the grace of God.

CHI 24


The Bible never deals with proportionate sin; according to the Bible an impure thought is as bad as adultery; a covetous thought is as bad as a theft. It takes a long education in the things of God before we believe that is true. Never trust innocence when it is contradicted by the word of God. The tiniest bit of sin is an indication of the vast corruption that is in the human heart. ('For from within, out of the heart of man, proceed ...' Mark 7:21–3.) That is why we must keep in the light all the time. Never allow horror at crime to blind you to the fact that it is human nature like your own that committed it. A saint is never horror-stricken because although he knows that what our Lord says about the human heart is true, he knows also of a Saviour who can save to the uttermost.

CHI 71

**June 30**

*For from within, out of the heart of men, proceed evil thoughts, adulteries, fornications, murders ...* Mark 7:21–2

This passage is detestable to an unspiritual person, it is in absolutely bad taste, nine out of every ten people do not believe it because they are grossly ignorant about the heart. In these verses Jesus Christ says, to put it in modern language, 'No crime has ever been committed that every human being is not capable of committing.' Do I believe that? Do you? If we do not, remember we pass a verdict straight off on the Lord Jesus Christ, we tell Him He does not know what He is talking about. We read that Jesus 'knew what was in man', meaning that He knew men's hearts; and the Apostle Paul emphasizes the same thing—'Don't glory in man; trust only the grace of God in yourself and in other people.' No wonder Jesus Christ pleads with us to give over the keeping of our hearts to Him so that He can fill them with a new life! Every characteristic seen in the life of Jesus Christ becomes possible in our lives when once we hand over our hearts to Him to be filled with the Holy Spirit.

BP 104

**July 1**

*Whatsoever things are pure ...* Philippians 4:8

Purity is not innocence, it is much more. Purity means stainlessness, an unblemishedness that has stood the test. Purity is learned in private, never in public. Jesus Christ demands purity of mind and imagination, chastity of bodily and mental habits. The only men and women it is safe to trust are those who have been tried and have stood the test; purity is the outcome of conflict, not of necessity. You cannot trust innocence or natural goodness; you cannot trust possibilities. This explains Jesus Christ's attitude. Our Lord trusted no man (see John 2:24–5), yet He was never suspicious, never bitter; His confidence in what God's grace could do for any man was so perfect that He never despaired of anyone. If our trust is placed in human beings, we will end in despairing of every one. But when we limit our thinking to the things of purity we shall think only of what God's grace has done in others, and put our confidence in that and in nothing else.

MFL 88

### July 2

*Whatsoever things are lovely* ... Philippians 4:8
The things of loveliness, i.e. the things that are morally agreeable and pleasant. The word 'lovely' has the meaning of juicy and delicious. That is the definition given by Calvin, and he is supposed to be a moloch of severity! We have the idea that our duty must always be disagreeable, and we make any number of duties out of diseased sensibilities. If our duty is disagreeable, it is a sign that we are in a disjointed relationship to God. If God gave some people a fully sweet cup, they would go carefully into a churchyard and turn the cup upside down and empty it, and say, 'No, that could never be meant for me.' The idea has become incorporated into their make-up that their lot must always be miserable. Once we become rightly related to God, duty will never be a disagreeable thing of which we have to say with a sigh, 'Oh, well, I must do my duty.' Duty is the daughter of God. Never take your estimate of duty after a sleepless night, or after a dose of indigestion; take your sense of duty from the Spirit of God and the word of Jesus. There are people whose lives are diseased and twisted by a sense of duty which God never inspired; but once let them begin to think about the things of loveliness, and the healing forces that will come into their lives will be amazing. The very essence of godliness is in the things of loveliness; think about these things, says Paul.

MFL 89

### July 3

*Whatsoever things are of good report* ... Philippians 4:8
When we do think about the things of good report we shall be

127

astonished to realize where they are to be found; they are found where we only expected to find the opposite. When our eyes are fixed on Jesus Christ we begin to see qualities blossoming in the lives of others that we never saw there before. We see people whom we have tabooed and put on the other side exhibiting qualities we have never exhibited, although we call ourselves saved and sanctified. Never look for other people to be holy; it is a cruel thing to do, it distorts your view of yourself and of others. Could anyone have had a sterner view of sin than Jesus had, and yet had anyone a more loving, tender patience with the worst of men than He had? The difference in the attitude is that Jesus Christ never expected men to be holy; He knew they could not be: *He came to make men holy*. All He asks of men is that they acknowledge they are not right, then He will do all the rest—'Blessed are the poor in spirit'.

MFL 90

### July 4

*I keep under my body, and bring it into subjection.* 1 Corinthians 9:27

The way to examine whether we are doing what Jesus Christ wants us to do is to look at the habits of our life in three domains—physical, emotional, and intellectual. The best scrutiny we can give ourselves is along this line: Are my bodily habits chaste? is my emotional nature inordinate? is my intellectual life insubordinate? When we begin to work out what God has worked in, we are faced with the problem that this physical body, this mechanism, has been used by habit to obeying another rule called sin; when Jesus Christ delivers us from that rule, He does not give us a new body, He gives us power to break and then re-mould every habit formed while we were under the dominion of sin. Much of the misery in our Christian life comes not because the devil tackles us, but because we have never understood the simple laws of our make-up. We have to treat the body as the servant of Jesus Christ: when the body says 'Sit', and He says 'Go', go! When the body says 'Eat', and He says 'Fast', fast! When the body says 'Yawn', and He says 'Pray', pray!

BE 57

*Now unto him who is able ... to present you faultless before the presence of his glory ...* Jude 24

There is no such thing as God overlooking sin. That is where people make a great mistake with regard to God's love; they say 'God is love and of course He will forgive sin': God is *holy* love and of course He *cannot* forgive sin. Therefore if God does forgive, there must be a reason that justifies Him in doing it. Unless there is a possibility of forgiveness establishing an order of holiness and rectitude in a man, it would be a mean and abominable thing to be forgiven. If I am forgiven without being altered by the forgiveness, forgiveness is a damage to me and a sign of unmitigated weakness on the part of God. A man has to clear God's character in forgiving him. The revelation of forgiveness in the Bible is not that God puts snow over a rubbish heap, but that He turns a man into the standard of Himself, the Forgiver. If I receive forgiveness and yet go on being bad, I prove that God is not justified in forgiving me. When God forgives a man He gives him the heredity of His own Son, and there is no man on earth but can be presented 'perfect in Christ Jesus'. Then on the ground of the Redemption, it is up to me to live as a son of God. The reason my sins are forgiven so easily is because the Redemption cost God so much.

HGM 102

*The kingdom of God is within you.* Luke 17:21

The blessedness of the gospel of the kingdom of God in this dispensation is that a man is born from above while he is below, and he actually sees with the eyes of his spirit the rule of God in the devil's territory. You will see how far we have got away from Jesus Christ's teaching. We bring in all kinds of things, we talk about salvation and sanctification and forgiveness of sins; Jesus did not mention these things to Nicodemus (He mentioned them later to the disciples), He said, 'Be born from above and you will see the rule of God.' It is an attitude of essential simplicity all through. Preaching what we call the Gospel, i.e. salvation from hell does not appeal to men; but once get Jesus Christ to preach His own Gospel and the Spirit of God to expound it, then men are hauled up at once.

HG 51

*For the word of God is quick and powerful and sharper than any two-edged sword, piercing even to the dividing asunder of soul and spirit, and of the joints and marrow, and is a discerner of the thoughts and intents of the heart.* Hebrews 4:12

'Why should I believe a thing because it is in the Bible?' That is a perfectly legitimate question. There is no reason why you should believe it, it is only when the Spirit of God applies the Scriptures to the inward consciousness that a man begins to understand their living efficacy. If we try from the outside to fit the Bible to an external standard, or to a theory of verbal inspiration or any other theory, we are wrong. 'Ye search the scriptures, because ye think that in them ye have eternal life; and these are they which bear witness of me; and ye will not come to me, that ye may have life' (John 5:39–40).

There is another dangerous tendency, that of closing all questions by saying, 'Let us get back to the external authority of the Bible.' That attitude lacks courage and the power of the Spirit of God; it is a literalism that does not produce 'written epistles', but persons who are more or less incarnate dictionaries; it produces not saints but fossils, people without life, with none of the living reality of the Lord Jesus. There must be the Incarnate Word and the interpreting word, i.e. people whose lives back up what they preach, 'written epistles, known and read of all men'. Only when we receive the Holy Spirit and are lifted into a total readjustment to God do the words of God become 'quick and powerful' to us. The only way the words of God can be understood is by contact with the Word of God. The connection between our Lord Himself, who is the Word, and His spoken words is so close that to divorce them is fatal. 'The words that I speak unto you, they are spirit, and they are life.'

BE122

*And Jesus went into the temple, and began to cast out them that sold and them that bought in the temple, and overthrew the tables of the money-changers ...* Mark 11:15 (cf. John 2:13–17)

We bring to the New Testament a sentimental conception of our Lord; we think of Him as the 'meek and mild and gentle Jesus' and make it mean that He was of no practical account whatever.

Our Lord *was* 'meek and lowly in heart', yet watch Him in the Temple, meekness and gentleness were not the striking features there. We see instead a terrible Being with a whip of small cords in His hands, overturning the money-changers' tables and driving out men and cattle. Is He the 'meek and gentle Jesus' there? He is absolutely terrifying; no one dare interfere with Him. Why could He not have driven them out in a gentler way? Because passionate zeal had eaten Him up, with a detestation of everything that dared to call His Father's honour into disrepute. 'Make not my Father's house an house of merchandise'—the deification of commercial enterprise. Everything of the nature of wrong must go when Jesus Christ begins to cleanse His Father's house.

SHL 70

July 9

*And they are they which testify of me.* John 5:39
*For had ye believed Moses, ye would have believed me, for he wrote of me.* John 5:46

To believe in Jesus means much more than the experience of salvation in any form, it entails a mental and moral commitment to our Lord Jesus Christ's view of God and man, of sin and the devil, and of the Scriptures.

How much intellectual impertinence there is today among many Christians relative to the Scriptures, because they forget that to 'believe also' in Jesus means that they are committed beforehand to His attitude to the Bible. He said that He was the context of the Scriptures, '... they are they which testify of me.' We hear much about 'key words' to the Scriptures, but there is only one 'key word' to the Scriptures for a believer, and that is our Lord Jesus Christ Himself. All the intellectual arrogance about the Bible is a clear proof of disbelief in Jesus. How many Sunday School teachers today believe as Jesus believed in the Old Testament? How many have succumbed to the insolence of intellectual partisanship about the Person of our Lord and His limitations, and say airily, 'Of course, there is no such thing as demon possession or hell, and no such being as the devil.' To 'believe also' in Jesus means that we submit our intelligence to Him as He submitted His intelligence to His Father. This does not mean that we do not exercise our reason, but it does mean that we exercise it in submission to Reason

131

Incarnate. Beware of interpreters of the Scriptures who take any other context than our Lord Jesus Christ.

AUG 104

**July 10**

*When Jesus came to the place, he looked up, and saw him, and said unto him, Zacchaeus, make haste, and come down; for today I must abide at thy house.* Luke 19:5

The thing we have to learn by contact with Jesus Christ is this, that if the whole human race—everybody, good, bad and indifferent—is lost, we must have the boundless confidence of Jesus Christ Himself about us, that is, we must know that He can save anybody and everybody. There is a great deal of importance to be attached to this point. Just reflect in your mind and think of some lives you know that are frozen; there is no conviction of sin; they are dishonourable, and they know it; they are abnormal, off the main track altogether, but they are not a bit troubled about it; talk to them about their wrong doing and they are totally indifferent to you. You have to learn how to introduce the atmosphere of the Lord Jesus Christ around those souls. As soon as you do, something happens. Look what happened to Zacchaeus—'And Zacchaeus stood, and said unto the Lord, Behold, Lord, the half of my goods I give to the poor; and if I have wrongfully exacted aught of any man, I restore him fourfold.' Who had been talking to him about his doings? Not a soul. Jesus had never said a word about his evil doings. What awakened him? What suddenly made him know where he was? The presence of Jesus!

WG 23

**July 11**

*But the Comforter, which is the Holy Ghost, whom the Father will send in my name, he shall teach you all things, and bring to your remembrance whatsoever I have said unto you.* John 14:26

Every mind has two compartments—conscious and subconscious. We say that the things we hear and read slip away from memory; they do not really, they pass into the subconscious mind. It is the work of the Holy Spirit to bring back into the conscious mind the things that are stored in the subconscious. In studying the Bible

132

never think that because you do not understand it, therefore it is of no use. A truth may be of no use to you just now, but when the circumstances arise in which that truth is needed, the Holy Spirit will bring it back to your remembrance. This accounts for the curious emergence of the statements of Jesus; we say, 'I wonder where that word came from?' Jesus said that the Holy Spirit would 'bring all things to your remembrance, whatsoever I have said unto you'. The point is, will I obey Him when He does bring it to my remembrance? If I discuss the matter with someone else the probability is that I will not obey. 'Immediately I conferred not with flesh and blood ...' Always trust the originality of the Holy Spirit when He brings a word to your remembrance.

SSM 13

### July 12

*But we have this treasure in earthen vessels, that the excellency of the power may be of God, and not of us.* 2 Corinthians 4:7

In the Incarnation we see the amalgam of the Divine and the human. Pure gold cannot be used as coin, it is too soft; in order to make gold serviceable for use it must be mixed with an alloy. The pure gold of the Divine is of no use in human affairs; there must be an alloy, and the alloy does not stand for sin, but for that which makes the Divine serviceable for use. God Almighty is nothing but a mental abstraction to me unless He can become actual, and the revelation of the New Testament is that God did become actual: 'the Word was made flesh'. Jesus Christ was not pure Divine, He was unique: Divine and human ...

Holiness Movements are apt to ignore the human and bank all on the Divine; they tell us that human nature is sinful, forgetting that Jesus Christ took on Him our human nature, and 'in Him is no sin'. It was God who made human nature, not the devil; sin came into human nature and cut it off from the Divine, and Jesus Christ brings the pure Divine and the pure human together. Sin is a wrong thing altogether and is not to be allowed for a moment. Human nature is earthly, it is sordid, but it is not bad, the thing that makes it bad is sin.

No man is constituted to live a pure Divine life on earth; he is constituted to live a human life on earth presenced with Divinity. When the pure Divine comes into us we have the difficulty of making our human nature the obedient servant of the new disposition, it is difficult, and thank God it is! God gives us the fighting chance. A saint is not an ethereal creature too refined for life on this earth; a saint is a mixture of the Divine and the human that can stand anything.

BE 51–2

**July 13**

*A city that is set on an hill cannot be hid.* Matthew 5:14

The illustrations our Lord uses are all conspicuous, viz., salt, light, and a city set on a hill. There is no possibility of mistaking them. Salt to preserve from corruption has to be placed in the midst of it, and before it can do its work it causes excessive irritation which spells persecution. Light attracts bats and night-moths, and points out the way for burglars as well as honest people: Jesus would have us remember that men will certainly defraud us. A city is a gathering place for all the human drift-wood that will not work for its own living, and a Christian will have any number of parasites and ungrateful hangers-on. All these considerations form a powerful temptation to make us pretend we are not salt, to make us put our light under a bushel, and cover our city with a fog, but Jesus will have nothing in the nature of covert discipleship.

SSM 19–20

**July 14**

*Simon Peter answered him, Lord, to whom shall we go? Thou hast the words of eternal life.* John 6:68

John 6 contains a description of the sifting out of the disciples from the crowd round about, until there were just the twelve left, and to them Jesus says—'Would ye also go away?' Some who had been following Jesus had not gone too far to turn back, and 'they went back, and walked no more with him'. But Peter has gone too far to turn back and he says, 'Lord, to whom shall we go?' There is a stage like that in our spiritual experience, we do not see the Guide ahead of us, we do not feel the joy of the Lord, there is no exhilaration, yet we have gone too far to go back, we are up against it now. It might be illustrated in the spiritual life by Tennyson's phrase, 'a white funeral'. When we go through the moral death to self-will

134

we find we have committed ourselves, there are many things that must go to the 'white funeral'. At the first we have the idea that everything apart from Christ is bad; but there is much in our former life that is fascinating, any amount of paganism that is clear and vigorous, virtues that are good morally. But we have to discover they are not stamped with the right image and superscription, and if we are going to live the life of a saint we must go to the moral death of those things, make a termination of them, turn these good natural things into the spiritual.

PH 159

July 15

*And ye shall hear of wars and rumours of wars, see that ye be not troubled.* Matthew 24:6

That is either the statement of a madman or of a Being who has power to put something into a man and keep him free from panic, even in the midst of the awful terror of war. The basis of panic is always cowardice. Our Lord teaches us to look things full in the face. He says – 'When you hear of wars, don't be scared.' It is the most natural thing in the world to be scared, and the clearest evidence that God's grace is at work in our hearts is when we do not get into panics. Our Lord insists on the inevitableness of peril. He says, 'You must lay your account with war, with hatred, and with death.' Men may have lived undisturbed over a volcano for a long while, when suddenly an eruption occurs. Jesus Christ did not say—'You will understand why war has come,' but– 'Don't be scared when it does come, do not be in a panic.' It is astonishing how we ignore Jesus Christ's words. He said that nations would end in war and bloodshed and havoc. We ignore His warnings; and when war comes we lose our wits and exhibit panic.

SA 54

July 16

*For we know that the law is spiritual; but I am carnal, sold under sin. For that which I do I allow not: for what I would, that I do not; but what I hate, that do I.* Romans 7:14–15

A lot of tawdry stuff has been written on this chapter simply because Christians so misunderstand what conviction of sin really is. Conviction of sin such as the apostle Paul is describing does not

135

come when a man is born again, nor even when he is sanctified, but long after, and then only to a few. It came to Paul as an apostle and saint, and he could diagnose sin as no other. Knowledge of what sin is is in inverse ratio to its presence; only as sin goes do you realize what it is; when it is present you do not realize what it is because the nature of sin is that it destroys the capacity to know you sin.

BE 75

When once a man really sees himself as the Lord Jesus Christ sees him, it is not the abominable social sins of the flesh that shock him, it is the awful nature of the pride of his own heart against the Lord Jesus Christ—the shame, the horror, the desperate conviction that comes when we realize ourselves in the light of Jesus Christ as the Spirit of God reveals Him to us. That is the true gift of repentance and the real meaning of it.

DP 131

July 17

*He that believeth on me, out of his belly shall flow rivers of living water.* John 7:38

We must distinguish between the revelation of Redemption and the experience of regeneration. We don't *experience* life; we are alive. We don't *experience* Redemption; we experience regeneration, that is, we experience the life of God coming into our human nature, and immediately the life of God comes in it produces a surface of consciousness, but Redemption means a great deal more than a man is conscious of. The Redemption is not only for mankind, it is for the universe, for the material earth; everything that sin and the devil have touched and marred has been completely redeemed by Jesus Christ. There is a day coming when the Redemption will be actually manifested, when there will be 'a new heaven and a new earth', with a new humanity upon it.... What the Redemption deals with is the sin of the whole human race, not primarily with the sins of individuals, but something far more fundamental, viz., the heredity of sin. Pseudo-evangelism singles out the individual, it prostitutes the terrific meaning of the Redemption into an individual possession, the salvation of *my* soul.

CHI 9–10

*Faith cometh by hearing, and hearing by the word of God.* Romans 10:17.

Our idea of faith has a good deal to do with the harmful way faith is often spoken of. Faith is looked upon as an attitude of mind whereby we assent to a testimony on the authority of the one who testifies. We say that because Jesus says these things, we believe in Him. The faith of the New Testament is infinitely more than that; it is the means by which sanctification is manifested, the means of introducing the life of God into us, not the effect of our understanding only. In Romans 3:24-5, Paul speaks about faith in the blood of Jesus, and faith is the instrument the Spirit of God uses. Faith is more than an attitude of the mind; faith is the complete, passionate, earnest trust of our whole nature in the Gospel of God's grace as it is presented in the Life and Death and Resurrection of our Lord Jesus Christ.

OBH 20

*And Peter answered and said to Jesus, Master, it is good for us to be here; and let us make three tabernacles; one for thee, and one for Moses, and one for Elias.* Mark 9:5

The test of spiritual life is the power to descend; if we have power to rise only, there is something wrong. We all have had times on the mount when we have seen things from God's standpoint and we wanted to stay there; but if we are disciples of Jesus Christ, He will never allow us to stay there. Spiritual selfishness makes us want to stay on the mount; we feel so good, as if we could do anything— talk like angels and live like angels, if only we could stay there. But there must be the power to descend; the mountain is not the place for us to live, we were built for the valleys. This is one of the hardest things to learn because spiritual selfishness always wants repeated moments on the mount.

MU 51

Being seated together in heavenly places in Christ Jesus does not mean lolling about on the mount of transfiguration, singing ecstatic hymns, and letting demon-possessed boys go to the devil in the valley; it means being in the accursed places of this earth as far as the walk of the feet is concerned, but in undisturbed communion with God.

IWP 70

**July 20**

*As it is written, For thy sake we are killed all the day long; we are accounted as sheep for the slaughter.* Romans 8:36
Life is a far greater danger than death. I want to say something, crudely, but very definitely: the Bible nowhere says that men are damned; the Bible says that men are damnable. There is always the possibility of damnation in any life, always the possibility of disobedience; but, thank God, there is also always the possibility of being made 'more than conqueror'. The possibilities of life are awful. Think—are you absolutely certain that you are not going to topple headlong over a moral precipice before you are three years older? Look back on your life and ask yourself how it was you escaped when you were set on the wrong course—the tiniest turn and you would have been a moral ruin? Disease cut off with a tremendous fell swoop your companions—why did it not cut you off? The men with you in your youth who were so brilliant—where are they now? Out in the gutter some of them, all but damned while they live. Why are you not there? Why am I not there? Oh, it does us good, although it frightens us, to look at the possibilities of life. May God help us to face the issues.

SHL 26

**July 21**

*Except your righteousness shall exceed the righteousness of the scribes and Pharisees, ye shall in no case enter into the kingdom of heaven.* Matthew 5:20
The Sermon on the Mount is quite unlike the Ten Commandments in the sense of its being absolutely unworkable unless Jesus Christ can remake us.
There are teachers who argue that the Sermon on the Mount supersedes the Ten Commandments, and that, because 'we are not under law, but under grace', it does not matter whether we honour our father and mother, whether we covet, etc. Beware of statements like this: There is no need nowadays to observe giving the tenth

138

either of money or of time; we are in a new dispensation and everything belongs to God. That, in practical application, is sentimental dust-throwing. The giving of the tenth is not a sign that all belongs to God, but a sign that the tenth belongs to God and the rest is ours, and we are held responsible for what we do with it. To be 'not under the law, but under grace' does not mean that we can do as we like.

SSM 21

## July 22

*And this is the condemnation, that light is come into the world, and men loved darkness rather than light.* John 3:19

I am not judged by the light I have, but by the light I have refused to accept. There is no man but can have the knowledge, perfectly clearly obtainable, of the standard of Jesus Christ. Whether I am a Christian or not, or whether I am conscientious or not, is not the question; it is whether I have refused the light of the finest moral character who ever lived, Jesus Christ. *This* is the condemnation, that the Light, Jesus Christ, has come into the world, and I prefer darkness, i.e. my own point of view. The characteristic of a man who begins to walk in the light is that he drags himself into the light all the time. He does not make excuses for things done in the dark, he brings everything to the light, and says, 'This is to be condemned; this does not belong to Jesus Christ', and so keeps in the light ...

'But if we walk in the light, as he is in the light ...' (1 John 1:7); that is, don't have anything folded up, don't juggle things, don't pretend you have not done anything shady. John says, if you have committed sin, confess it; walk in the light, and you will have fellowship with everyone else who is there. Natural affinity does not count here at all. Watch how God has altered your affinities since you were filled with the Spirit; you have fellowship with people you have no natural affinity for at all; you have fellowship with everybody who is in the light. Light is the description of clear, beautiful, moral character from God's standpoint, and if we walk in the light, 'the blood of Jesus Christ cleanses us from all sin'; God Almighty can find nothing to censure.

SA 49, 52

*Lovest thou me ... Feed my sheep.* John 21:16

'If you love Me', says Jesus, 'Feed my sheep.' 'Don't make converts to your way of thinking, but look after My sheep, see that they are nourished in the knowledge of Me.' Our Lord's first obedience was to the will of His Father, and He said, 'As the Father hath sent me, even so send I you.' It sounds the right thing to say that Jesus Christ came here to help mankind: but His great desire was to do the will of His Father, and our Lord was misunderstood because He would not put the needs of men first. He said the first commandment is 'Thou shalt love the Lord thy God with all thy heart, and with all thy soul, and with all thy mind, and with all thy strength.'

Jesus Christ is a source of deep offence to the educated trained mind of today that does not want Him in any other way than as a Comrade. Many do not want to be devoted to Him, but only to the cause He started. If I am only devoted to the cause of humanity, I will soon be exhausted and come to the point where my love will falter, but if I love Jesus Christ I will serve humanity, though men and women treat me like a door-mat.

PH 145

*Peter ... walked upon the waters to come to Jesus.* Matthew 14:29

Passionate, genuine affection for Jesus will lead to all sorts of vows and promises which it is impossible to fulfil. It is an attitude of mind and heart that sees only the heroic. We are called to be unobtrusive disciples, not heroes. When we are right with God, the tiniest thing done out of love to Him is more precious to Him than any eloquent preaching of a sermon.... We all have a lurking desire to be exhibitions for God, to be put, as it were, in His show room. Jesus does not want us to be specimens, He wants us to be so taken up with Him that we never think about ourselves, and the only impression left on others by our life is that Jesus Christ is having unhindered way.

Walking on water is easy to impulsive pluck, but walking on dry land as a disciple of Jesus Christ is different. Peter walked on the water to go to Jesus, but he followed Him afar off on the land.

We do not need the grace of God to stand crises; human nature and our pride will do it. We can buck up and face the music of a crisis magnificently, but it does require the supernatural grace of God to live twenty-four hours of the day as a saint, to go through drudgery as a saint, to go through poverty as a saint, to go through an ordinary, unobtrusive, ignored existence as a saint, unnoted and unnoticeable. The 'show business', which is so incorporated into our view of Christian work today, has caused us to drift far from our Lord's conception of discipleship. It is instilled in us to think that we have to do exceptional things for God; we have not. We have to be exceptional in ordinary things, to be holy in mean streets, among mean people, surrounded by sordid sinners. That is not learned in five minutes.

SSY 68

## July 25

*The blood of Jesus Christ his Son cleanseth us from all sin.* 1 John 1:7

When we speak of the blood of Jesus Christ cleansing us from all sin, we do not mean the physical blood shed on Calvary, but the whole life of the Son of God which was poured out to redeem the world. All the perfections of the essential nature of God were in that blood, and all the holiest attainments of mankind as well. It was the life of the perfection of Deity that was poured out on Calvary, '...the church of God, which he purchased with his own blood' (Acts 20:28). We are apt to look upon the blood of Jesus Christ as a magic-working power instead of its being the very life of the Son of God poured forth for men. The whole meaning of our being identified with the death of Jesus is that His blood may flow through our mortal bodies. Identification with the death of Jesus Christ means identification with Him to the death of everything that never was in Him, and it is the blood of Christ, in the sense of the whole personal life of the Son of God, that comes into us and 'cleanseth us from all sin'.

PH 162

141

*Whosoever shall keep the whole law, and yet offend in one point, he is guilty of all.* James 2:10

Every man has an imperative something within him which makes him say 'I ought,' even in the most degraded specimens of humanity the 'ought' is there, and the Bible tells us where it comes from—it comes from God. The modern tendency is to leave God out and make our standard what is most useful to man. The utilitarian says that these distinct laws of conduct have been evolved by man for the benefit of man—the greatest use to the greatest number. That is not the reason a thing is right; the reason a thing is right is that God is behind it. God's 'ought's' never alter; we never grow out of them. Our difficulty is that we find in ourselves this attitude— 'I ought to do this, but I won't;' 'I ought to do that, but I don't want to.' That puts out of court the idea that if you teach men what is right they will do it—they won't; what is needed is a power which will enable a man to do what he knows is right. We may say 'Oh I won't count this time', but every bit of moral wrong is counted by God. The moral law exerts no coercion, neither does it allow any compromise. 'For whosoever shall keep the whole law, and yet offend in one point, he is guilt of all.' Once we realize this we see why it was necessary for Jesus Christ to come. The Redemption is the Reality which alters inability into ability.

BE 8

*When it was yet dark* ... John 20:1

There is twilight before night, and an infinitely deeper dark before dawn; but there are hours in spiritual experience darker than either of these, when the new day looks like disaster, and light and illumination have not yet come. There is no possible progress in personal life or national life without cataclysms, big crises, breaks. In our ordinary life we have the idea that things should gradually progress, but there comes a time when there is a tumble-up, a mixture of God and man and friends, of crime and abomination, and all our idea of steady progress is done for, although there may be progress in individual lives. In the Bible there is the same idea. For instance, take what our Lord says about new birth—'Verily, verily, I say unto thee, Except a man be born again, he cannot see the kingdom of

142

God' (John 3:3). Some teachers make new birth a simple and natural thing, they say it is necessary, but a necessity along the line of natural development. When Jesus Christ talks about it He implies that the need to be born again is an indication of something radically wrong—'Marvel not that I said unto thee, Ye must be born again.' It is a crisis. We like to talk about the light of God coming like the dawn, but it never does to begin with, it comes in a lightning flash, in terrific upheaval. Things do not go unless they are started, and the start of everything in history and in men's souls proves that the basis of things is not rational but tragic; consequently there must be a crisis.

HGM 54


**July 28**

*Ye must be born again.* John 3:7

The natural man does not want to be born again. If a man's morality is well within his own grasp and he has enough religion to give the right tone to his natural life, to talk about being born again seems utterly needless. The natural man is not in distress, he is not conscious of conviction of sin, or of any disharmony, he is quite contented and at peace. Conviction of sin is the realization that my natural life is based on a disposition that will not have Jesus Christ. The Gospel does not present what the natural man wants but what he needs, and the Gospel awakens an intense resentment as well as an intense craving. We will take God's blessings and loving-kindnesses and prosperities, but when it comes to the need of having our disposition altered, there is opposition at once.

No man can have his state of mind altered without suffering for it in his body, and that is why men do anything to avoid conviction of sin. When a worldly man who is happy, moral and upright, comes in contact with Jesus Christ, his 'beauty', i.e. the perfectly ordered completeness of his nature, is destroyed and that man must be persuaded that Jesus Christ has a better kind of life for him otherwise he feels he had better not have come across Him.... Thank God, we are coming to the end of the shallow presentation of Christianity that makes out that Jesus Christ came only to give us peace. Thousands of people are happy without God in this world, but that kind of happiness and peace is on a wrong level. Jesus Christ came to send a sword through every peace that is not based

143

on a personal relationship to Himself. He came to put us right with God that His own peace might reign.

SHL 40–1

**July 29**

*The sun also ariseth, and the sun goeth down, and hasteneth to his place where he arose. The wind goeth toward the south, and turneth about unto the north; it whirleth about continually, and the wind returneth again according to his circuits.* Ecclesiastes 1:5–6.

Everything that happens in Nature is continually being obliterated and beginning again. What Solomon says is not merely a poetical statement. A sunset or a sunrise may thrill you for half a minute, so may beautiful music or a song, but the sudden aftermath is a terrific, and almost eternal sadness. Lovers always think of what one would do if the other died; it is more than drivel. Immediately you strike the elemental in war or in Nature or in love, you come to the basis of ineffable sadness and tragedy. You feel that things ought to be full of joy and brightness, but they are not. You will never find the abiding order of joy in the haphazard, and yet the meaning of Christianity is that God's order comes to a man in the haphazard.

There is a difference between God's will and God's order. Take the case of two boys born in the slums, one determines to get out of it, and carves out for himself an honourable career, he gets at God's order in the middle of His permissive will. The other sinks down in despair and remains where he is. God's order is—no sin, no sickness, no devil, no war: His permissive will is things as they are.

SHH 6

**July 30**

*Mortify therefore your members which are upon the earth; fornication, uncleanness, passion, evil desire, and covetousness, which is idolatry.* Colossians 3:5

In this passage Paul mentions things that are of the nature of rubbish, and he mentions them in their complete ugliness. They are the abortion of the stuff human nature is made of, and he says, 'Mortify them, destroy them by neglect.' Certain things can only be dealt with by ignoring them; if you face them you increase their

144

power. It is absurd to say, Pray about them; when once a thing is seen to be wrong, don't pray about it, it fixes the mind on it; never for a second brood on it, destroy it by neglect. We have no business to harbour an emotion which we can see will end in any of the things Paul mentions. No man or woman on earth is immune, each one of us knows the things we should not think about, or pray about, but resolutely neglect. It is a great thing for our moral character to have something to ignore. It is because these things are not understood that there is so much inefficiency in spiritual life. What Christianity supplies is 'the expulsive power of a new affection'. We cannot destroy sin by neglect; God deals with sin, and we can get the effective measure of His dealing with it in our actual life.

BE 47

## July 31

*Let not sin therefore reign in your mortal body, that ye should obey it in the lusts thereof.* Romans 6:12.

Paul is strong in urging us to realize what salvation means in our bodily lives; it means that we command our bodies to obey the new disposition. That is where you find the problems on the margins of the sanctified life. Paul argues in Romans 6:19, 'You are perfectly adjusted to God on the inside by a perfect Saviour, but your members have been used as servants of the wrong disposition; now begin to make those same members obey the new disposition.' As we go on, we find every place God brings us into is the means of enabling us to realize with growing joy that the life of Christ within is more than a match, not only for the enemy on the outside, but for the impaired body that comes between. Paul urges with passionate pleading, that we present our bodies a living sacrifice, and then realize, not presumptuously, but with slow, sure, overwhelming certainty that every command of Christ can be obeyed in our bodily life through the Atonement.

IWP 28

## August 1

*What, could ye not watch with me one hour?* Matthew 26:40
*For this cause many among you are weak and sickly, and not a few sleep.* 1 Corinthians 11:30

There are many today who are suffering from spiritual sleeping sickness, and the sorrow of the world which works death is witnessed in all directions. If personal sorrow does not work itself out along the appropriate line, it will lull us to a pessimistic sleep. For instance, when we see our brother 'sinning a sin not unto death' do we get to prayer for him, probed by the searching sorrow of his sin? (see 1 John 5:16). Most of us are so shallow spiritually that when our Lord in answer to some outrageous request we have made, asks us—'Are ye able to drink the cup that I drink? or to be baptized with the baptism that I am baptized with?' we say 'We are able.' Then He begins to show us what the cup and the baptism meant to Him—'But I have a baptism to be baptized with; and how am I straitened till it be accomplished!' (Luke 12:50). And Jesus said unto them, 'Ye shall indeed drink of the cup that I drink of; and with the baptism that I am baptized withal shall ye be baptized'—and there begins to dawn for the disciple the great solemn day of martyrdom which closes for ever the day of exuberant undisciplined service, and opens the patient pilgrimage of pain and joy, with 'more of the first than the last'.

HGM 119

### August 2

*If thou wilt be perfect, go and sell that thou hast ... and come and follow me.* Matthew 19:21

Numbers of people say, 'I have asked God to sanctify me and He has not done it.' Of course He has not! Do we find one word in the Bible which tells us to pray, 'Lord, sanctify me?' What we do read is that God sanctifies what we give. An unconditional 'give up' is the condition of sanctification, not claiming something for ourselves. This is where unscriptural holiness teaching has played so much havoc with spiritual experience. We receive from God on one condition only, viz., that we yield ourselves to Him and are willing to receive nothing. Immediately we state conditions and say, 'I want to be filled with the Holy Spirit,' 'I want to be delivered from sin,' 'I want to be the means of saving souls'—we may pray to further orders, but an answer will never come that way. That is all the energy of the flesh, it has no thought of the claims of Jesus on the life. Are we willing to be baptized into His death? How much struggle is there in a dead man?

IWP 17

*Praying in the Holy Ghost ...* Jude 20

When we pray in the Holy Ghost we begin to have a more intimate conception of God; the Holy Ghost brings all through us the sense of His resources. For instance, we may be called to a definite purpose for our life which the Holy Ghost reveals and we know that it means a decision, a reckless fling over on to God, a burning of our bridges behind us; and there is not a soul to advise us when we take that step saving the Holy Ghost. Our clingings come in this way—we put one foot on God's side and one on the side of human reasoning; then God widens the space until we either drop down in between or jump on to one side or the other. We have to take a leap, a reckless leap, and if we have learned to rely on the Holy Ghost, it will be a reckless leap on to God's side. So many of us limit our praying because we are not reckless in our confidence in God. In the eyes of those who do not know God, it is madness to trust Him, but when we pray in the Holy Ghost we begin to realize the resources of God, that He is our perfect heavenly Father, and we are His children.

Always keep an inner recollectedness that God is our Father through the Lord Jesus Christ.

IYA 62


August 4

*He that hath seen me hath seen the Father.* John 14:9

An ideal has no power over us until it becomes incarnate. The idea of beauty lies unawakened until we see a thing we call beautiful. God may be a mere mental abstraction; He may be spoken of in terms of culture or poetry or philosophy, but He has not the slightest meaning for us until He becomes incarnate. When once we know that God has 'trod this earth with naked feet, and woven with human hands the creed of creeds', then we are arrested. When once we know that the Almighty Being Who reigns and rules over His creation does not do so in calm disdain, but puts His back to the wall of the world, so to speak, and receives all the downcast, the outcast, the sin-defiled, the wrong, the wicked and the sinful into His arms, then we are arrested. An intellectual conception of God may be found in a bad vicious character. The knowledge and vision of God is dependent entirely on a pure heart. Character determines the revelation of God to the individual. 'The pure in heart see God.' Jesus Christ changes the worst into the best and gives the moral readjustment that enables a man to love and delight in the true God. Of a great almighty incomprehensible Being we know nothing, but of our Lord Jesus Christ we do know, and the New Testament reveals that the Almighty God is nothing that Jesus was not.

BE 104

### August 5

*Thou shalt not hate thy brother in thine heart.* Leviticus 19:17.

A good way to use the 'cursing' Psalms is in some such way as this—'Do not I hate them, O Lord, that hate Thee? ... I hate them with perfect hatred.' Ask yourself what is it that hates God? Nothing and no one hates God half as much as the wrong disposition in you does. The carnal mind is *'enmity against God'*; what we should hate is this principle that lusts against the Spirit of God and is determined to have our bodies and minds and rule them away from God. The Spirit of God awakens in us an unmeasured hatred of that power until we are not only sick of it, but sick to death of it, and we will gladly make the moral choice of going to its funeral. The meaning of Romans 6:6 is just this put into Scriptural language —'Knowing this, that our old man is crucified with him.' The 'old man' is the thing the Spirit of God will teach us to hate, and the love of God in our hearts concentrates our soul in horror against the wrong thing. Make no excuse for it. The next time you read those Psalms, which people think are so terrible, bring this interpretation to bear on them.

BP 120

### August 6

*And looking on Jesus as he walked, he saith, Behold the Lamb of God.* John 1:36

The real life of the saint on this earth, and the life that is most glorifying to Jesus, is the life that steadfastly goes on through common days and common ways, with no mountain-top experiences. We read that John the Baptist 'looked upon Jesus *as he walked ...*'

148

—not at Jesus in a prayer meeting or in a revival service, or Jesus performing miracles; he did not watch Him on the Mount of Transfiguration, he did not see Him in any great moment at all, he saw Him on an ordinary day when Jesus was walking in an ordinary common way, and he said, 'Behold, the Lamb of God!' That is the test of reality. Mounting up with wings as eagles, running and not being weary, are indications that something more than usual is at work. Walking and not fainting is the life that glorifies God and satisfies the heart of Jesus to the full—the plain daylight life, unmarked, unknown, only occasionally, if ever, does the marvel of it break on other people.

PS 38

### August 7

*That the life also of Jesus might be made manifest in our mortal flesh.* 2 Corinthians 4:11

We look for God to manifest Himself to His children: God only manifests Himself *in* His children, consequently others see the manifestation, the child of God does not. You say, 'I am not conscious of God's blessing now'—thank God! 'I am not conscious now of the touches of God'—thank God! 'I am not conscious now that God is answering my prayers'—thank God! If you are conscious of these things it means you have put yourself outside God. 'That the life also of Jesus might be made manifest in our mortal flesh'—'I am not conscious that His life is being manifested,' you say, but if you are a saint it surely is. When a little child becomes conscious of being a little child, the child-likeness is gone; and when a saint becomes conscious of being a saint, something has gone wrong. 'Oh but I'm not good enough.' You never will be good enough! that is why the Lord had to come and save you. Go to your own funeral and ever after let God be all in all, and life will become the simple life of a child in which God's order comes moment by moment.

Never live on memories. Do not remember in your testimony what you once were; let the word of God be always living and active in you, and give the best you have every time and all the time.

GH 66

149

*The reproaches of them that reproached thee fell upon me.* Romans 15:3

What reproaches fell on Jesus? Everything that was hurled in slander against God hurt our Lord. The slanders that were hurled against Himself made no impression on Him; His suffering was on account of His Father. On what account do you suffer? Do you suffer because men speak ill of you? Read Hebrews 12:3: 'For consider him that hath endured such gainsaying of sinners against himself, that ye wax not weary, fainting in your souls.' Perfect love takes no account of the evil done unto it. It was the reproaches that hit and scandalized the true centre of His life that Jesus Christ noticed in pain. What was that true centre? Absolute devotion to God the Father and to His will; and as surely as you get Christ-centred you will understand what the Apostle Paul meant when he talks about 'filling up that which is lacking of the afflictions of Christ'. Jesus Christ could not be touched on the line of self-pity. The practical emphasis here is that our service is not to be that of pity, but of personal, passionate love to God, and a longing to see many more brought to the centre where God has brought us.

BP 183

*One thing thou lackest: go ... sell whatsoever thou hast, and give to the poor ... and come, take up the cross, and follow me.* Mark 10:21

These words mean a voluntary abandoning of riches and a deliberate, devoted attachment to Jesus Christ. We are so desperately wise in our own conceit that we continually make out that Jesus did not mean what He said, and we spiritualize His meaning into thin air. Jesus saw that this man depended on his riches. If He came to you or to me He might not say that, but He would say something that dealt with whatever He saw we were depending on. 'Sell that thou hast,' strip yourself of every possession, disengage yourself from all things until you are a naked soul; be a man merely and then give your manhood to God. Reduce yourself until nothing remains but your consciousness of yourself, and then cast that consciousness at the feet of Jesus Christ ...

Am I prepared to strip myself of what I possess in property, in virtues, in the estimation of others—to count all things to be loss in order to win Christ? I can be so rich in poverty, so rich in the consciousness that I am nobody, that I shall never be a disciple; and I can be so rich in the consciousness that I am somebody that I shall never be a disciple. Am I willing to be destitute even of the sense that I am destitute? It is not a question of giving up outside things, but of making myself destitute to myself, reducing myself to a mere consciousness and giving that to Jesus Christ. I must reduce myself until I am a mere conscious man, fundamentally renounce possessions of all kinds—not to save my soul, only one thing saves a man's soul, absolute reliance on the Lord Jesus—and then give that manhood to Jesus.

SSY 58

### August 10

*For thou shalt eat the labour of thine hands: happy shalt thou be, and it shall be well with thee.* Psalm 128:2

This verse reveals the connection between the natural creation and the regenerated creation. We have to be awake strenuously to the fact that our body is the temple of the Holy Ghost, not only in the spiritual sense, but in the physical sense. When we are born from above we are apt to despise the clay of which we are made. The natural creation and the creation of grace work together, and what we are apt to call the sordid things, labouring with our hands, and eating and drinking, have to be turned into spiritual exercises by obedience, then we shall 'eat and drink, and do all to the glory of God'. There must be a uniting in personal experience of the two creations. It cannot be done all at once, there are whole tracts of life which have to be disciplined. 'Your body is the temple of the Holy Ghost', it is the handiwork of God, and it is in these bodies we are to find satisfaction, and that means strenuousness. Every power of mind and heart should go into the strenuousness of turning the natural into the spiritual by obeying the word of God regarding it. If we do not make the natural spiritual, it will become sordid; but when we become spiritual the natural is shot through with the glory of God.

PSB 43

151

*For I say unto you, That except your righteousness shall exceed the righteousness of the scribes and Pharisees, ye shall in no case enter into the kingdom of heaven.* Matthew 5:20

'Except your righteousness shall exceed'—not be different from but *'exceed'*, that is, we have to be all they are and infinitely more! We have to be right in our external behaviour, but we have to be as right, and 'righter', in our internal behaviour. We have to be right in our words and actions, but we have to be as right in our thoughts and feelings. We have to be right according to the conventions of the society of godly people, but we have also to be right in conscience towards God. Nominal Christians are often without the ordinary moral integrity of the man who does not care a bit about Jesus Christ; not because they are hypocrites, but because we have been taught for generations to think on one aspect only of Jesus Christ's salvation, viz., the revelation that salvation is not merited by us, but is the sheer sovereign act of God's grace in Christ Jesus. A grand marvellous revelation fact, but Jesus says we have got to say 'Thank you' for our salvation, and the 'Thank you' is that our righteousness is to exceed the righteousness of the most moral man on earth.

Jesus not only demands that our external life is above censure but that we are above censure where God sees us. We see the meaning now of saying that Jesus is the most tantalizing Teacher: He demands that we be so pure that God who sees to the inmost springs of our motives, the inmost dreams of our dreams, sees nothing to censure. We may go on evolving and evolving, but we shall never produce that kind of purity. Then what is the good of teaching it? Listen: 'If we walk in the light, as he is in the light, we have fellowship with one another, *and the blood of Jesus Christ his Son cleanseth us from all sin.*' That is the Gospel.

HG 59

*When ye pray, say, Our Father which art in heaven ...* Luke 11:2

Words are full of revelation when we do not simply recall or memorize them but receive them. Receive these words from Jesus— 'Father', 'heaven', 'Hallowed be thy name', 'kingdom', 'will', there is all the vocabulary of the Deity and Dominion and Disposition of Almighty God in relation to men in these words. Or take the words—

'bread', 'forgiveness', 'debts', 'temptation', 'deliverance', 'evil', in these words the primary psychological colours which portray the perplexing puzzles and problems of personal life, are all spelled out before our Father.

Or lastly, look at such words as 'power', 'glory', 'for ever', 'Amen' —in them there sounds the transcendent triumphant truth that all is well, that God reigns and rules and rejoices, and His joy is our strength. What a rapturous grammar class our Lord Jesus conducts when we go to His school of prayer and learn of Him!

DPR 26

### August 13

*We are troubled on every side, yet not distressed; we are perplexed, but not in despair.* 2 Corinthians 4:8

By Actual is meant the things we come in contact with by our senses, and by Real that which lies behind, that which we cannot get at by our senses. The fanatic sees the real only and ignores the actual; the materialist looks at the actual only and ignores the real. The only sane Being who ever trod this earth was Jesus Christ, because in Him the actual and the real were one. Jesus Christ does not stand first in the actual world, He stands first in the real world; that is why the natural man does not bother his head about Him— 'the natural man receiveth not the things of the Spirit of God: for they are foolishness unto him'. When we are born from above we begin to see the actual things in the light of the real. We say that prayer alters things, but prayer does not alter actual things nearly so much as it alters the man who sees the actual things. In the Sermon on the Mount our Lord brings the actual and the real together.

SSM 25–6

### August 14

*Praying always with all prayer and supplication in the Spirit.* Ephesians 6:18

Prayer '*in the Spirit*' is not meditation, it is not reverie; it is being filled with the Holy Ghost who brings us as we pray into perfect union before God, and this union manifests itself in '*perseverance and supplication for all saints*'. Every saint of God knows those

153

times when in closest communion with God nothing is articulated, and yet there seems to be an absolute intimacy not so much between God's mind and their mind as between God's Spirit and their spirit.

The conscious and the subconscious life of our Lord is explained perhaps in this way. Our Lord's subconscious life was Deity, and only occasionally when He was on earth did the subconscious burst up into His conscious life. The subconscious life of the saint is the Holy Ghost, and in such moments of prayer as are alluded to in Romans 8:26-8, there is an uprush of communion with God into the consciousness of the saint, the only explanation of which is that the Holy Ghost in the saint is communicating prayers which cannot be uttered.

DPR 53

### August 15

*Behold, God exalteth by his power: who teacheth like him?* Job 36:22

There is always a tendency to produce an absolute authority; we accept the authority of the Church, or of the Bible, or of a creed, and often refuse to do any more thinking on the matter; and in so doing we ignore the essential nature of Christianity which is based on a personal relationship to Jesus Christ, and works on the basis of our responsibility. On the grounds of the Redemption I am saved and God puts His Holy Spirit into me, then He expects me to react on the basis of that relationship. I can evade it by dumping my responsibility on to a Church, or a Book or a creed, forgetting what Jesus said—'Ye search the scriptures, because ye think that in them ye have eternal life; and these are they which bear witness of me; and ye will not come to me, that ye may have life.' The only way to understand the Scriptures is not to accept them blindly, but to read them in the light of a personal relationship to Jesus Christ. If we insist that a man must believe the doctrine of the Trinity and the inspiration of the Scriptures before he can be saved, we are putting the cart before the horse. All that is the effect of being a Christian, not the cause of it; and if we put the effect first we produce difficulties because we are putting thinking before life. Jesus says, 'Come unto me, and if you want to know whether my teaching is of God, do his will.' A scientist can explain the universe in which common-sense men live, but the scientific explanation is not first;

154

life is first. The same with theology; theology is the systematizing of the intellectual expression of life from God; it is a mighty thing, but it is second, not first.

BFB 91

*Even to them that believe on his name.* John 1:12

A great thinker has said, 'The seal and end of true conscious life is joy,' not pleasure, nor happiness. Jesus Christ said to His disciples, 'These things have I spoken unto you, that my joy might remain in you, and that your joy might be full'—identity with Jesus Christ and with His joy.

What was the joy of the Lord Jesus Christ? His joy was in having completely finished the work His Father gave Him to do; and the same type of joy will be granted to every man and woman who is born of God the Holy Ghost and sanctified, when they fulfil the work God has given them to do. What is that work? To be a saint, a walking, talking, living, practical epistle of what God Almighty can do through the Atonement of the Lord Jesus Christ one in identity with the faith of Jesus, one in identity with the love of Jesus, one in identity with the Spirit of Jesus until we are so one in Him that the high-priestly prayer not only begins to be answered, but is clearly manifest in its answering—'that they may be one, even as we are one'.

AUG 112

*All things were made by him; and without him was not anything made. That which hath been made was life in him; and the life was the light of men.* John 1:3–4 (RV marg.)

By creation we are the children of God; we are not the sons and daughters of God by creation; Jesus Christ makes us sons and daughters of God by regeneration (John 1:12). The idea of the Father-hood of Jesus is revealed in the Bible, though rarely mentioned. 'Everlasting Father' refers to the Being we know as the Son of God. Paul in talking to the Athenians said, 'We are the offspring of God.' But the creator-power in Jesus Christ is vested in a more marvellous way even than when God created the world through

155

him for He has that in Himself whereby He can create His own image. God created the world and everything that was made through the Son, and 'that which hath been made was life in Him'; therefore just as God created the world through Him, the Son is able to create His own image in anyone and everyone.

OBH 25

*If ye love me, keep my commandments.* John 14:15

'If you love me, you will keep my commandments,' said Jesus; that is the practical simple test. Our Lord did not say, 'If a man *obeys* me, he will keep my commandments'; but, 'If you *love* me, you will keep my commandments.' In the early stages of Christian experience we are inclined to hunt with an overplus of zeal for commands of our Lord to obey; but as we mature in the life of God conscious obedience becomes so assimilated into our make-up that we begin to obey the commands of God unconsciously, until in the maturest stage of all we are simply children of God through whom God does His will for the most part unconsciously. Many of us are on the borders of consciousness—consciously serving, consciously devoted to God; all that is immature, it is not the life yet. The first stages of spiritual life are passed in conscientious carefulness; the mature life is lived in unconscious consecration. The term 'obey' would be better expressed by the word 'use'. For instance, a scientist, strictly speaking, 'uses' the laws of nature; that is, he more than obeys them, he causes them to fulfil their destiny in his work. That is exactly what happens in the saint's life, he 'uses' the commands of the Lord and they fulfil God's destiny in his life.

MFL 53

*Worthy is the Lamb that was slain to receive power, and riches, and wisdom, and strength, and honour, and glory, and blessing.* Revelation 5:12

The childish idea that because God is great He can do anything, good or bad, right or wrong, and we must say nothing, is erroneous. The meaning of moral worth is that certain things are impossible

156

to it: 'it is impossible for God to lie'; it is impossible for Jesus Christ to contradict His own holiness or to become other than He is. The profound truth for us is that Jesus Christ is the Worthy One not because He was God Incarnate, but because He was God Incarnate on the human plane. 'Being made in the likeness of men' He accepted our limitations and lived on this earth a life of perfect holiness. Napoleon said of Jesus Christ that He had succeeded in making of every human soul an appendage of His own—why? Because He had the genius of holiness. There have been great military geniuses, intellectual giants, geniuses of statesmen, but these only exercise influence over a limited number of men; Jesus Christ exercises unlimited sway over all men because He is the altogether worthy one.

CHI 119

August 20

*If any man come to me, and hate not his own father, and mother, and wife, and children, and brethren, and sisters, yea, and his own life also, he cannot be my disciple.* Luke 14:26

You cannot consecrate yourself *and* your friends. If at the altar your heart imagines that loving arms are still around you, and that together, lovers as lovers, and friends as friends, can enter through this mighty gate of supreme Sanctification, it is a fond dream, doomed to disillusionment. Alone! Relinquish all! You cannot consecrate your children, your wife, your lover, your friend, your father, your mother or your own life as yours. You must abandon all and fling yourself on God as a mere conscious being, and unperplexed, seeking you'll find Him. The teaching that presents consecration as giving to God our gifts, our possessions, our comrades, is a profound error. These are all abandoned, and we give up for ever *our right to ourselves.* A sanctified soul may be an artist, or a musician; but he is not a sanctified artist or musician: he is one who expresses the message of God through a particular medium. As long as the artist or musician imagines he can consecrate his artistic gifts to God, he is deluded. Abandonment of ourselves is the kernel of consecration, not presenting our gifts, but presenting ourselves without reserve.

DL 88

157

*If any man would come after me, let him deny himself, and take up his cross, and follow me.* Matthew 16:24

Is there any use in beating about the bush? We call ourselves Christians, what does our Christianity amount to practically? Has it made any difference to my natural individual life? It cannot unless I deliberately give up my right to myself to Jesus, and as His disciple begin to work out the personal salvation He has worked in. Independence must be blasted right out of a saint. God's providence seems to pay no attention whatever to our individual ideas because He is after only one thing—'that they may be one, even as we are one'. It may look like a thorough breaking up of the life, but it will end in a manifestation of the Christian self in oneness with God. Sanctification is the work of Christ in me, the sign that I am no longer independent, but completely dependent upon Him. Sin in its essential working is independence of God: personal dependence upon God is the attitude of the Holy Ghost in my soul.

SHL 87

*Let him deny himself.* Matthew 16:24

The critical moment in a man or woman's life is when they realize they are individually separate from other people. When I realize I am separate from everyone else, the danger is that I think I am different from everyone else. Immediately I think that, I become a law to myself; that means I excuse everything I do, but nothing anyone else does. 'My temptations are peculiar,' I say; 'my setting is very strange; no one knows but myself the peculiar forces that are in me.' When first that big sense awakens that I am different from everyone else, it is the seed of all lawlessness and all immoralities...

It would serve us well if we thought a great deal more from the ethical side of our Christian work than we do. We think of it always from the spiritual side because that is the natural way for us, but when we think of it from the ethical side we get at it from a different angle. More damage is done because souls have been left alone on the moral side than Christian workers ever dream, simply because their eyes are blinded by seeing only along the spiritual line. When once the powers of a nature, young or old, begin to awaken it realizes that it is an individual; that it has a power of knowing without reasoning, and it begins to be afraid because it is alone and looks for a companion, and the devil is there always to supply the need. Remember the old proverb—'If you knock long enough at a door the devil may open it.' The Bible indicates that there is a wrong as well as a right perseverance.

PS 33

### August 23

*Ye are the light of the world.* Matthew 5:14

Individuality is a smaller term than personality. Possibly the best illustration we can use is that of a lamp. A lamp unlighted will illustrate individuality; a lighted lamp will illustrate personality. The lighted lamp takes up no more room, but the light permeates far and wide; so the influence of personality goes far beyond that of individuality. 'Ye are the light of the world,' said our Lord. Individually we do not take up much room, but our influence is far beyond our calculation. When we use the term 'personality', we use the biggest mental conception we have, that is why we call God a Person, because the word 'person' has the biggest import we know. We do not call God an individual; we call God a Person. He may be a great deal more, but at least He must be that. It is necessary to remember this when the personality of God is denied and He is taken to be a tendency. If God is only a tendency, He is much less than we are. Our personality is always too big for us.

BP 150

### August 24

*And he gave some to be apostles; and some prophets; and some, evangelists; and some, pastors and teachers;...till we all attain unto the unity of the faith.* Ephesians 4:11–13

These verses do not refer to individual Christian lives but to the collective life of the saints. The individual saint cannot be perfected apart from others. 'He gave some to be apostles...' for what purpose? To show how clever they were, what gifts they had? No, 'for the perfecting of the saints'. In looking back over the history of the Church we find that every one of these 'gifts' has been tackled. Paul says that apostles, prophets, evangelists, pastors and teachers, are all meant for one thing by God, viz., 'for the perfecting of the saints ...

159

unto the building up of the body of Christ'. No saint can ever be perfected in isolation or in any other way than God has laid down. There are very few who are willing to apprehend that for which they were apprehended, they thank God for salvation and sanctification and then stagnate, consequently the perfecting of the saints is hindered.

PS 44

**August 25**

*And for their sakes I sanctify myself.* John 17:19

How does that statement of our Lord fit in with our idea of sanctification? Sanctification must never be made synonymous with purification; Jesus Christ had no need of purification, and yet He used the word 'sanctify'. In the words, 'I sanctify myself', Jesus gives the key to the saint's life. Self is not sinful; if it were, how could Jesus say 'I sanctify myself'? Jesus Christ had no sin to deny, no wrong self to deny; He had only a holy Self. It was that Self He denied all the time, and it was that Self that Satan tried to make Him obey. What could be holier than the will of the holy Son of God? and yet all through He said, 'not as I will, but as thou wilt'. It was the denying of His holy Self that made the marvellous beauty of our Lord's life.

If we have entered into the experience of sanctification, what are we doing with our holy selves? Do we every morning we waken thank God that we have a self to give to Him, a self that He has purified and adjusted and baptized with the Holy Ghost so that we might sacrifice it to Him? Sacrifice in its essence is the exuberant, passionate love-gift of the best I have to the one I love best. The best gift the Son of God had was His Holy Manhood, and He gave that as a love-gift to God that He might use it as an Atonement for the world. He poured out His soul unto death, and that is to be the characteristic of our lives. God is at perfect liberty to waste us if He chooses. We are sanctified for one purpose only, that we might sanctify our sanctification and give it to God.

MFL 107

**August 26**

*It is enough for the disciple that he be as his master.* Matthew 10:25
At first sight this looks like an enormous honour: to be 'as his

160

master' is marvellous glory—is it? Look at Jesus as He was when He was here, it was anything but glory. He was easily ignorable, saving to those who knew Him intimately; to the majority of men He was 'as a root out of a dry ground'. For thirty years He was obscure, then for three years He went through popularity, scandal, and hatred; He succeeded in gathering a handful of fishermen as disciples, one of whom betrayed Him, one denied Him, and all forsook Him; and He says, 'It is enough for you to be like that.' The idea of evangelical success, Church prosperity, civilized manifestation, does not come into it at all. When we fulfil the conditions of spiritual life we become unobtrusively real.

SHL 105

Many who knew our Lord while He was on earth saw nothing in Him; only after their disposition had been altered did they realize Who He was. Our Lord lived so ordinary a life that no one noticed Him... Could anything more startling be imagined than for someone to point out a Nazarene carpenter and say, 'That man is God Incarnate'? It would sound blasphemous to a Pharisee.

MU 43

**August 27**

*Casting down imaginations, and every high thing that exalteth itself against the knowledge of God, and bringing into captivity every thought to the obedience of Christ.* 2 Corinthians 10:5

Obedience to the Holy Spirit will mean that we have power to direct our ideas. It is astonishing how we sit down under the dominance of an idea, whether a right or a wrong idea, and saints have sat down under this idea more than any other, that they cannot help thoughts of evil. Thank God that's a lie, we can. If you have never realized this before, put it to the test and ask yourself why the Spirit of God through the apostle Paul should say, '... bringing every thought into captivity to the obedience of Christ' if we cannot do it? Never sit down under ideas that have no part or lot in God's Book; trace the idea to its foundation and see where it comes from. The Bible makes it plain that we can help thoughts of evil; it is Satan's interest to make us think we cannot. God grant the devil may be kept off the brains of the saints!

BE 71

*Then the waters had overwhelmed us, the stream had gone over our soul.* Psalm 124:4

One element in the alternative danger that attends the saints of God is the agony it produces. It is strange that God should make it that 'through the shadow of an agony cometh Redemption'; strange that God's Son should be made perfect through suffering; strange that suffering should be one of the golden pathways for God's children. There are times in personal life when we are brought into an understanding of what Abraham experienced. 'Get thee out of thy country...' It is not so much that we are misunderstood, but that suffering is brought on others through our being loyal to God, and it produces agony for which there is no relief on the human side, only on God's side. When we pray 'Thy Kingdom come' we have to share in the pain of the world being born again; it is a desperate pain. God's servants are, as it were, the birth-throes of the new age. 'My little children, of whom I travail in birth again until Christ be formed in you' (Galatians 4:19). Many of us receive the Holy Ghost, but immediately the throes begin we misunderstand God's purpose. We have to enter into the travail with Him until the world is born again. The world must be born again just as individuals are.

PSB 24

*They that sow in tears shall reap in joy. He that goeth forth and weepeth, bearing precious seed, shall doubtless come again with rejoicing, bringing his sheaves with him.* Psalm 126:5-6

We make the blunder of wanting to sow and plough and reap all at the same time. We forget what our Lord said, that 'one soweth, and another reapeth'. 'They that sow in tears...'—it looks as if the seed were drowned. You can see the seed when it is in the basket, but when it falls into the ground, it disappears (see John 12:24). The same thing is true with regard to Sunday school work or meetings, it looks as if everything were flung away, you cannot see anything happening; but the seed is there. 'They that sow in tears *shall reap in joy.*' 'Cast thy bread upon the waters: for thou shalt find it after many days.' The seed is the word of God, and no word of God is ever fruitless. If I know that the sowing is going to bring forth fruit, I am blessed in the drudgery. Drudgery is never blessed, but drudgery can be enlightened. The Psalmist says, 'Thou hast enlarged me in distress'; the enlargement comes through knowing that God is looking after everything. Before, when I came to a difficult bit of the way, I was staggered, but now through the affliction and suffering I can put my foot down more firmly (see Romans 8:35–9).

PSB 36

*Though our outward man perish, yet the inward man is renewed day by day.* 2 Corinthians 4:16

The apostle Paul continually had external depression, he had agonies and distresses, terrible persecution and tumults in his life, but he never had the 'blues', simply because he had learned the secret that the measure of the inner glory is the wasting of the outward man. The outer man was being wasted, Paul knew it and felt it, but the inner man was being renewed, every wasting meant a corresponding winging on the inside. Some of us are so amazingly lazy, so comfortably placed in life, that we get no inner winging. The natural life, apart altogether from sin, must be sacrificed to the will and the word of God, otherwise there is no spiritual glory for the individual. With some of us the body is not wearing away, our souls are stagnant, and the vision spiritually is not getting brighter; but once we get into the heavenlies, live there, and work from that standpoint, we find we have the glorious opportunity of spending all our bodily energies in God's service, and a corresponding weight of moral and spiritual glory remains all the time.

MIC 81

*Even to them that are called according to his purpose.* Romans 8:28

To talk about our intercession for another soul being the means of doing what the Bible says, 'the effectual fervent prayer of a righteous man availeth much', sounds utterly ridiculous until we get the basal thinking revealed through the Atonement and the indwelling Holy Ghost, then it is an amazing revelation of the marvellous love and condescension of God—that in Christ Jesus and by the reception of the Holy Spirit, He can take us, sin-broken, sin-diseased, wrong creatures, and re-make us entirely until we are really the ones in whom the Holy Spirit intercedes as we do our part. Are we making

163

it easy for the Holy Spirit to work out God's will in us, or are we continually putting Him on one side by the empty requests of our natural hearts, Christians though we be? Are we learning to bring ourselves into such obedience that our every thought and imagination is brought into captivity to the Lord Jesus Christ, and is the Holy Spirit having an easy way through us more and more? Remember, your intercessions can never be mine, and my intercessions can never be yours, but the Holy Ghost makes intercession in our particular editions, without which intercession someone will be impoverished. Let us remember the depth and height and solemnity of our calling as saints.

IYA 108

### September 1

*And they heard the voice ('sound', RV marg.) of the Lord God walking in the garden in the cool of the day.* Genesis 3:8

Until Adam fell, he was not *interested in* God, he was *one with* God in communion—a man is never interested in that which he is; when Adam fell, he became so appallingly interested in God that he was afraid of Him—'and the man and his wife hid themselves from the presence of the Lord God amongst the trees of the garden'. Sin finds us severed from God and interested only in anything we can be told about Him, consequently there is an element of fear; when we become children of God, there is no fear. As long as a child has not done wrong he enjoys perfect freedom and confidence towards his parents, but let him disobey, and the one he disobeys becomes someone in whom he is interested, with an element of fear. Conscious piety springs from being interested in God—'I want to know whether I am right with God'; if you are right with God, you are so one with Him that you are unconscious of it, the relationship is deeper than consciousness because you are being disposed by the very nature of God.

OPG 6

### September 2

*As ye have therefore received Christ Jesus the Lord, so walk ye in him.* Colossians 2:6

Our right standing is proved by the fact that we can walk; if we are not rightly related to God in our thinking we cannot walk

164

properly. Walk means character. If we have only our own energy and devotion and earnestness to go on we cannot walk at all; but if we are based on the revelation that if we receive Christ Jesus the Lord we are complete in Him, then we can begin to walk according to the perfection we have in Him. When God brings us up against difficult circumstances that reveal the inability of our human nature it is not that we may sink back and say, 'Oh dear, I thought I should have been all right by now'; it is that we may learn to draw on our union with Jesus Christ and claim that we have sufficient grace to do this particular thing according to God's will. If we are vitally connected with God in our thinking we shall find we can walk; but if we have not been thinking rightly we will succumb—'I can't do this'. If we are thinking along the line of God's grace, that He is able to make all grace abound unto us, we will not only stand, but walk as a son or daughter of God and prove that His grace is sufficient. To be weak in God's strength is a crime.

GW 13

September 3

...*so walk ye in him.* Colossians 2:6
   God has to deal with us on the death side as well as on the life side. It is all very well to know in theory that there are things we must not trust in, but another thing to know it in fact. When God deals with us on the death side He puts the sentence of death on everything we should not trust in, and we have a miserable time until we learn never any more to trust in it, never any more to look anywhere else than to God. It sometimes happens that hardly a day passes without God saying, 'Don't trust there, that is dead.'
   Then He deals with us on the life side and reveals to us all that is ours in Christ Jesus, and there comes in the overflowing strength of God, the unsearchable riches in Christ Jesus. Whether God is dealing with us on the death side or the life side, it is all in order to teach us how to walk, how to try our standing in Christ Jesus. God is teaching us to try our steps in faith, and it is a very tottering business to begin with, we clutch hold of everything; God gives us any amount of encouragement, 'ribbons' of blessings, of feelings and touches that make us know His presence; then He withdraws them and slowly we get strengthened on our feet and learn how to walk in Him.

GW 13

165

*Ye were running well; who did hinder you....?* Galatians 5:7

An undertow is an undercurrent flowing in a different direction from the water at the surface. It is the undercurrent that drowns; a swimmer will never plunge into an undercurrent, a fool will. The spiritual undertow that switched away the Galatians was Judaism, formalism. It was not dominant, but hidden; it ran in exactly the opposite direction to the current of liberty into which they were being brought by Christ. Instead of going out to sea, out into the glorious liberty of the children of God, they were being switched away. 'Ye were running well...' they had been heading straight for the ocean, but the undercurrent of ritualism bewitched them, hindered them from obeying the truth. After a big transaction with God the current of your life heads you straight out to sea, right over the harbour bar, every sail set; now be alert for the spiritual undertow that would suck you back. The undercurrent is always most dangerous just where the river merges with the sea. The undercurrent is of the same nature as the river and will take you back into its swirling current; not out into the main stream, but back to the shipwrecks on the bank. The most pitiable of all wrecks are those inside the harbour...

Be alert for the spiritual undertow, the current that sets in another direction. It is after the floodtide of a spiritual transaction that the undertow begins to tell, and to tell terribly. The undercurrent for each one of us is different. It is only felt at certain stages of the tide; when the tide is full there is no undercurrent.

PH 48

*And it came to pass in those days, when Moses was grown, that he went out unto his brethren, and looked on their burdens.* Exodus 2:11

That is an indication of the vision of God's purpose for Moses, viz., the deliverance of his brethren. It is a great moment in a man's life when he realizes that he has to go a solitary way alone. Moses was 'learned in all the wisdom of the Egyptians', a man in a royal setting by the providence of God, and he saw the burden of God's people, and his whole heart and mind was ablaze with the vision that he was the man to deliver them. He *was* the man to deliver his people, but not yet, there was something in the road, and God sent him into the wilderness to feed sheep for forty years. Imagine what those years

166

must have meant to Moses, realizing on the threshold of his manhood the vision of what he was to do; seeing, as no one else could see, the burdens of his people, and feeling in himself the certainty that he was the one to deliver them; how he would ponder over God's ways during those forty years...

Think of the enormous leisure of God! He never is in a hurry. We are in such a frantic hurry. We get down before God and pray, then we get up and say, 'It is all done now', and in the light of the glory of the vision we go forth to do the thing. But it is not real, and God has to take us into the valley and put us through fires and floods to batter us into shape, until we get into the condition in which He can trust us with the reality of His recognition of us.

SSY 29, 31

## September 6

*Take heed, and beware of covetousness; for a man's life consisteth not in the abundance of the things which he possesseth.* Luke 12:15

The thing about our Lord and His teaching which puts Him immeasurably away from us nowadays is that He is opposed to all possessions, not only of money and property, but any kind of possession. That is the thing that makes Him such a deep-rooted enemy to the modern attitude to things. The two things around which our Lord centred His most scathing teaching were money and marriage, because they are the two things that make men and women devils or saints. Covetousness is the root of all evil, whether it shows itself in money matters or in any way.

Jesus Christ nowhere stands with the anti-property league. It is an easy business for me to mentally satirize the man who owns land and money when I don't. It is easy for me to talk about what I could do with a thousand pounds if I had it; the test is what I do with the two-and-a-half pence I have got. It may be hard for a rich man to enter into the kingdom of heaven, but it is just as hard for a poor man to seek first the kingdom of God. It is not eternal perdition, it is the perdition of losing the soul for this life. Jesus thought as much of the possibility of losing the highest good through poverty as through riches. His own followers were poor, yet He said to them, 'Seek ye first'—bread and cheese? money? a new situation? clothing? food? No, 'the kingdom of God and his righteousness, and all these things shall be added unto you'. Did He know what He was talking

167

about, this poor Carpenter who had not a pillow of His own and never enough money to pay a night's lodging and yet spoke like that, and who also said that 'the cares of this world, and the deceitfulness of riches, and the lusts of other things entering in, choke the word, and it becometh unfruitful'?

HG 67

### September 7

*...be ye transformed by the renewing of your mind.* Romans 12:2

To renew means to transform to new life. This passage makes it clear that we can be renewed in our mind when we choose. We have no choice about being born into this world, but to be born again, if we will but come to Jesus and receive His Spirit, is within our own power. This is true all along in the Christian life, you can be renewed in the spirit of your mind when you choose, you can revive your mind on any line you like by sheer force of will. Always remember that Jesus Christ's statements force an issue of will and conscience first, and only as we obey is there the understanding with the mind (see John 7:17). The challenge to the will comes in the matter of study, as long as you remain in the 'stodge' state there is no mental progress —'I am overwhelmed by the tremendous amount there is to know and it's no use my going on.' If you will forge through that stage you will suddenly turn a corner where everything that was difficult and perplexing becomes as clear as a lightning flash, but it all depends on whether you will forge ahead. When people say, 'Preach us the simple Gospel', what they mean is, 'Preach us the thing we have always heard, the thing that keeps us sound asleep, we don't want to see things differently'; then the sooner the Spirit of God sends a thrust through their stagnant minds the better. Continual renewal of mind is the only healthy state for a Christian. Beware of the ban of finality about your present views.

BE 39

### September 8

*I am crucified with Christ.* Galatians 2:20

The evidence that I have accepted the Cross of Christ as the revelation of Redemption is that the regenerating life of God is manifested in my mortal flesh. Immediately I accept the Cross of Christ

168

as the revelation of Redemption I am not, I must not be, the same man, I must be another man, and I must take up my cross from my Lord. The cross is the gift of Jesus to His disciples and it can only bear one aspect: 'I am not my own.' The whole attitude of the life is that I have given up my right to myself. I live like a crucified man. Unless that crisis is reached it is perilously possible for my religious life to end as a sentimental fiasco. 'I don't mind being saved from hell and receiving the Holy Spirit, but it is too much to expect me to give up my right to myself to Jesus Christ, to give up my manhood, my womanhood, all my ambitions.' Jesus said, If any man will be my disciple, those are the conditions. It is that kind of thing that offended the historic disciples, and it will offend you and me. It is a slander to the Cross of Christ to say we believe in Jesus and please ourselves all the time, choosing our own way.

TGR 99

### September 9

*Ye are a chosen generation, a royal priesthood, an holy nation, a peculiar people.* 1 Peter 2:9

To say that the doctrine of sanctification is unnatural is not true, it is based on the way God has made us. When we are born again we become natural for the first time; as long as we are in sin we are abnormal, because sin is not normal. When we are restored by the grace of God it becomes the most natural thing to be holy, we are not forcing ourselves to be unnatural. When we are rightly related to God all our natural instincts help us to obey Him and become the greatest ally of the Holy Spirit. We disobey whenever we become independent. Independence is not strength but unrealized weakness, and is the very essence of sin. There was no independence in our Lord, the great characteristic of His life was submission to His Father.

MFL 72

Jesus Christ belonged to the order of things God originally intended for mankind; He was easily Master of the life of the sea and air and earth. If we want to know what the human race will be like on the basis of Redemption, we shall find it mirrored in Jesus Christ, a perfect oneness between God and man.

LG 25

169

*Awake, thou that sleepest, and arise from the dead.* Ephesians 5:14

The Bible reveals that apart from the Spirit of God men have no moving emotion towards God, they are described as 'dead'; the preaching of the Gospel, the reading of the Word of God, has no answering emotion. Religious enterprise that has not learned to rely on the Holy Spirit makes everything depend on the human intellect —'God has said so-and-so, now believe it and it will be all right', but it won't. The basis of Jesus Christ's religion is the acceptance of a new Spirit, not a new creed, and the first thing the Holy Spirit does is to awaken us out of sleep. We have to learn to rely on the Holy Spirit because He alone gives the Word of God life. All our effort to pump up faith in the word of God is without quickening, without illumination. You reason to yourself and say, 'Now God says this and I am going to believe it', and you believe it, and re-believe it, and re-re-believe it, and nothing happens, simply because the vital power that makes the words living is not there. The Spirit of God always comes in surprising ways—'The wind bloweth where it listeth ...so is everyone that is born of the Spirit.' No creed or school of thought or experience can monopolize the Spirit of God.

BE 72

*As the Father hath sent me, even so send I you.* John 20:21

If we are not in full conscious allegiance to our Lord, it has nothing to do with our personal salvation, but with the 'broken bread and poured out wine' aspect of life. God can never make me wine if I object to the fingers He uses to crush me with. If God would only crush me with His own fingers and say, 'Now, my son, I am going to make you broken bread and poured out wine in a particular way and everyone will know what I am doing...' But when He uses someone who is not a Christian, or someone I particularly dislike, or some set of circumstances which I said I would never submit to, and begins to make *these* the crushers, I object. I must never choose the scene of my own martyrdom, nor must I choose the things God will use in order to make me broken bread and poured out wine. His own Son did not choose. God chose for His Son that He should have a devil in His company for three years. We say— I want angels, I want people better than myself, I want everything to be significantly from

170

God, otherwise I cannot live the life, or do the thing properly; I want to be always gilt-edged. Let God do as He likes. If you are ever going to be wine to drink, you must be crushed. Grapes cannot be drunk, grapes are only wine when they have been crushed. I wonder what kind of coarse finger and thumb God has been using to squeeze you, and you have been like a marble and escaped? You are not ripe yet, and if God *had* squeezed you, the wine that came out would have been remarkably bitter. Let God go on with His crushing, because it will work His purpose in the end.

SSY 19

### September 12

*...and he builded a city.* Genesis 4:17

The first civilization was founded by a murderer, and the whole basis of civilized life is a vast, complicated, more or less gilded-over system of murder. We find it more conducive to human welfare not to murder men outright, we do it by a system of competition. It is ingrained in our thinking that competition and rivalry are essential to the carrying on of civilized life; that is why Jesus Christ's statements seem wild and ridiculous. They are the statements either of a madman or of God Incarnate. To carry out the Sermon on the Mount is frankly impossible to anyone but a fool, and who is the fool? The man who has been born again and who dares to carry out in his individual life the teaching of Jesus. And what will happen? The inevitable result, not the success he would otherwise have. A hard saying, but true.

OPG 15

### September 13

*What is man that thou art mindful of him?* Psalm 8:4

The way we see the world outside us depends entirely upon our nervous system, and the marvel of God's construction of us is that we see things outside us as we do. For instance, the existence to us of beauty and colour and sound is due entirely to our nervous system: there is no colour to me when my eyes are shut, no sound when I am deaf, no sensation when I am asleep. If you want to know the most marvellous thing in the whole of creation, it is not the heavens, the moon and the stars, but—'What is man that thou art mindful of

171

him?...Thou madest him to have dominion over the works of thy hands.' The whole of creation was designed for man, and God intended man to be master of the life upon the earth, in the air and in the sea; the reason he is not master is because of sin, but he will yet be. (See Romans 8:19–22.) Paul indicates that the problems of the grave seclusion we are in are accounted for by sin, yet it remains true that our nervous system is not a disease, but is designed by God to be the temple of the Holy Ghost.

HGM 82

### September 14

*I am debtor both to Greeks, and to Barbarians.* Romans 1:14

Do I feel this sense of indebtedness to Christ that Paul felt with regard to every unsaved soul I meet, every unsaved nation? Is it a point of spiritual honour with me that I do not hoard blessings for myself? The point of spiritual honour in my life as a saint is the realization that I am a debtor to every man on the face of the earth because of the Redemption of the Lord Jesus Christ...

The great characteristic of Paul's life was that he realized he was not his own: he had been bought with a price, and he never forgot it...

'I am made all things to all men, that I might by all means save some.' Paul attracted to Jesus all the time, never to himself. He became a sacramental personality, that is, wherever he went Jesus Christ helped Himself to his life (cf. 2 Corinthians 2:14). Many of us are subtly serving our own ends, and Jesus Christ cannot help Himself to our lives; if I am abandoned to Jesus, I have no ends of my own to serve...

The great motive and inspiration of service is not that God has saved and sanctified me, or healed me; all that is a fact, but the great motive of service is the realization that every bit of my life that is of value I owe to the Redemption; therefore I am a bondslave of Jesus. I realize with joy that I cannot live my own life; I am a debtor to Christ, and as such I can only realize the fulfilment of His purposes in my life. To realize this sense of spiritual honour means I am spoilt for this age, for this life, spoilt from every standpoint but this one, that I can disciple men and women to the Lord Jesus.

SSY 21–3

*And as ye would that men should do to you, do ye also to them likewise.* Luke 6:31

Over and over again we blame God for His neglect of people by our sympathy with them, we may not put it into words but by our attitude we imply that we are filling up what God has forgotten to do. Never allow that idea, never allow it to come into your mind. In all probability the Spirit of God will begin to show us that people are where they are because we have neglected to do what we ought. Today the great craze is socialism, and men are saying that Jesus Christ came as a social reformer. Nonsense! We are the social reformers; Jesus Christ came to alter us, and we try to shirk our responsibility by putting our work on Him. Jesus alters us and puts us right; then these principles of His instantly make us social reformers. They begin to work straightway where we live, in our relationship to our fathers and mothers, to our brothers and sisters, our friends, our employers, or employees. 'Consider how God has dealt with you,' says Jesus, 'and then consider that you do likewise to others.'

SSM 87

*We know not what we should pray for as we ought: but the Spirit itself maketh intercession for us.* Romans 8:26

An abiding way of maintaining our relation to Reality is intercession. Intercession means that I strive earnestly to have my human soul moved by the attitude of my Lord to the particular person I am praying for. That is where our work lies, and we shirk it by becoming active workers, we do the things that can be tabulated and scheduled, and we won't do the one thing that has no snares. Intercession keeps the relationship to God completely open. You cannot intercede if you do not believe in the Reality of Redemption, you will turn intercession into futile sympathy with human beings which only increases their submissive content to being out of touch with God. Intercession means getting the mind of Christ about the one for whom we pray, that is what is meant by 'filling up that which is behind of the afflictions of Christ'; and that is why there are so few intercessors. Be careful not to enmesh yourself in more difficulties than God has engineered for you to know; if you know too much, more than God has engineered, you cannot pray, the condition of the people is so crushing that you can't get through to Reality. The true intercessor is the one who realizes Paul's meaning when he says, 'for we know not what we should pray for as we ought: but the Spirit itself maketh intercession for us with groanings which cannot be uttered'.

CHI 32

## September 17

*My soul is exceeding sorrowful, even unto death.* Matthew 26:38
Have we for one second watched Jesus pray? Have we ever understood why the Holy Ghost and our Lord Himself were so exceptionally careful about the recording of the agony in Gethsemane? This is not the agony of a man or a martyr; this is the agony of God as Man. It is God, as Man, going through the last lap of the supreme, supernatural Redemption of the human race. We ought to give much more time than we do—a great deal more time than we do—to brooding on the fundamental truths on which the Spirit of God works the simplicity of our Christian experience...

Remember, what makes prayer easy is not our wits or our understanding, but the tremendous agony of God in Redemption. A thing is worth just what it costs. Prayer is not what it costs us, but what it cost God to enable us to pray. It cost God so much that a little child can pray. It cost God Almighty so much that anyone can pray. But it is time those of us who name His Name knew the secret of the cost, and the secret is here, 'My soul is exceeding sorrowful, even unto death.' These words open the door to the autobiography of our Lord's agony.

IYA 21

## September 18

*Strive to enter in at the strait gate.* 13:24
If you make a moral struggle and gain a moral victory, you will be a benefit to all you come across, whereas if you do not struggle, you act as a moral miasma. Gain a moral victory in chastity or in your emotional life, it may be known to no one but yourself, and you are an untold benefit to everyone else; but if you refuse to struggle everyone else is enervated. This is a recognized psychological law, although little known. Struggle to gain the mastery over
174

selfishness, and you will be a tremendous assistance; but if you don't overcome the tendency to spiritual sluggishness and self-indulgence, you are a hindrance to all around you. These things are intangible, but they are there, and Jesus says to us, 'Strive to enter in at the strait gate.' You never get through alone. If you struggle to get through, others are the stronger and better for knowing you. The men and women who lift and inspire us are those who struggle for self, not for self-assertiveness, that is a sign of weakness, but for the development of personality. There are some people in whose company you cannot have a mean thought without being instantly rebuked.

PH 79

## September 19

*It is vain for you that ye rise up early and so late take rest, and eat the bread of toil: for so he giveth unto his beloved sleep.* Psalm 127:2

I wonder if we have ever considered the Bible implications about sleep? It is not true to say that sleep is simply meant for physical recuperation; surely much less time than God has ordered would have served that purpose. The Revised Version suggests a deeper, profounder ministry for sleep than mere physical recuperation. 'For so he giveth unto his beloved *in* sleep' (marg.). The deepest concerns of our souls, whether they be good or bad, are furthered during sleep. It is not merely a physical fact that you go to bed perplexed and wake clear-minded; God has been ministering to you during sleep. Sometimes God cannot get at us until we are asleep. In the Bible there are times when in the deep slumber of the body God has taken the souls of His servants into deeper communion with Himself (e.g. Genesis 2:21, 15:12). Often when a problem or perplexity harasses the mind and there seems no solution, after a night's rest you find the solution easy, and the problem has no further perplexity. Think of the security of the saint in sleeping or in waking, 'Thou shalt not be afraid for the terror by night, nor for the arrow that flieth by day.' Sleep is God's celestial nurse who croons away our consciousness, and God deals with the unconscious life of the soul in places where only He and His angels have charge. As you retire to rest, give your soul and God a time together, and commit your life to God with a conscious peace for the hours of sleep, and deep

175

and profound developments will go on in spirit, soul and body by the kind creating hand of our God.

PSB 38

### September 20

*Therefore take no thought...for your heavenly Father knoweth.* Matthew 6:31–2

To have faith tests a man for all he is worth, he has to stand in the common-sense universe in the midst of things which conflict with his faith, and place his confidence in the God whose character is revealed in Jesus Christ. Jesus Christ's statements reveal that God is a Being of love and justice and truth; the actual happenings in our immediate circumstances seem to prove He is not; are we going to remain true to the revelation that God is good? Are we going to be true to His honour, whatever may happen in the actual domain? If we are, we shall find that God in His providence makes the two universes, the universe of revelation and the universe of common sense, work together in perfect harmony. Most of us are pagans in a crisis; we think and act like pagans, only one out of a hundred is daring enough to bank his faith in the character of God.

The golden rule for understanding in spiritual matters is not intellect, but obedience. Discernment in the spiritual world is never gained by intellect; in the common-sense world it is. If a man wants scientific knowledge, intellectual curiosity is his guide; but if he wants insight into what Jesus Christ teaches, he can only get it by obedience. If things are dark to us spiritually, it is because there is something we will not do. Intellectual darkness comes because of ignorance; spiritual darkness comes because of something I do not intend to obey.

SSM 66

### September 21

*Jesus, knowing that the Father had given all things into his hands, and that he came forth from God and goeth unto God...*John 13:3

We might have expected the record to go on: 'He was transfigured before them'; but we read that the next thing our Lord did was of the most menial commonplace order—'he took a towel, and girdeth himself... and began to wash the disciples' feet'. Can we use a towel as our Lord did? Towels and basins and feet and sandals, all the

176

ordinary sordid things of our lives, reveal more quickly than anything what we are made of. It is not the big occasions that reveal us, but the little occasions. It takes God Incarnate to do the most menial commonplace things properly.

'If I then, the Lord and the Master, have washed your feet, ye also ought to wash one another's feet.' Our Lord did not say: 'I have been the means of the salvation of thousands, I have been most successful in my service, now you go and do the same thing'—He said: '*I have washed your feet; you go and wash one another's feet.*' We try to get out of it by washing the feet of those who do not belong to our own set—we will wash the heathen's feet, or feet in the slums, but fancy washing my brother's feet, my wife's, my husband's, the feet of the minister of my church! Our Lord said—'*one another's feet*'.

Watch the humour of our Heavenly Father. It is seen in the way He brings across our path the type of person who exhibits to us what we have been like to Him. 'Now,' He says, 'show that one the same love that I have shown you.' If Jesus Christ has lifted us in love and grace, we must show that love to someone else.

SSY 83

September 22

*Know ye not that your body is the temple of the Holy Ghost?*
1 Corinthians 6:19

My body is designed to be 'a temple of the Holy Ghost', and it is up to me to stand for the honour of Jesus Christ in my bodily practices. When the Spirit of God comes in, He cleanses the temple and does not let one darling sin lurk. The one thing Jesus Christ insists on in my bodily life is chastity. As individuals we must not desecrate the temple of God by tampering with anything we ought not to tamper with; if we do, the scourge of God will come. Immediately the Spirit of God comes in we begin to realize what it means—everything that is not of God has to be turned clean out. People are surprised and say, 'I was told God would give the Holy Spirit to them that ask Him; well, I asked for the Holy Spirit and expected that He would bring me joy and peace, but I have had a terrible time ever since.' That is the sign He has come, He is turning out the 'money-changers and the cattle', i.e. the things that were making the temple into a trafficking place for self-realization. We

177

soon find why the Gospel can never be welcome. As long as we speak winsomely about the 'meek and gentle Jesus', and the beautiful ideas the Holy Spirit produces when He comes in, people are captivated, but that is not the Gospel. The Gospel does away with any other ground to stand on than that of the Atonement. Speak about the peace of heaven and the joy of the Lord, and men will listen to you; but tell them that the Holy Spirit has to come in and turn out their claim to their right to themselves, and instantly there is resentment— 'I can do what I like with my body; I can go where I choose.' The majority of people are not blackguards and criminals, living in external sin, they are clean-living and respectable, and it is to such that the scourge of God is the most terrible thing because it reveals .that the natural virtues may be in idolatrous opposition to God.

SHL 71–2

**September 23**

*Submitting yourselves one to another in the fear of God.* Ephesians 5:21

When the Holy Spirit first comes into us He seems to put us into a prison house; then He opens our eyes and causes us to expand in the realization that 'all things are yours', from the tiniest flower that blooms to God on His throne. When we have learnt the secret that God Himself is the Source of our life, then He can trust us with the expansion of our nature. Every expansion of our nature transforms selfhood into unselfishness. It is not peculiar to Christians, it is true of human nature apart altogether from the grace of God. Inspiration, either true or false, unites the personality, makes a man feel at one with himself and with everyone else, and he is unselfish as long as the inspiration lasts. Paul says, 'Don't be drunk with wine,' which is the counterfeit of the true transformation, 'but be filled with the Spirit', and all self-interested considerations are transformed at once, you will think only, without trying to, of the good of others and of the glory of God. Be careful what you allow to unite you and make you feel unselfish; the only power we must allow as Christians is the Holy Spirit who will so transform us that it will be easy to submit one to another in the fear of God.

BE 74

*Think not that I came to send peace on the earth: I came not to send peace, but a sword.* Matthew 10:34

The natural pagan, a man whose word is as good as his bond, a moral and upright man, is more delightful to meet than the Christian who has enough of the Spirit of God to spoil his sin but not enough to deliver him from it.

PH 168

You will never find in the Bible that things are destroyed for the sake of destruction. Human beings destroy for the sake of destruction, and so does the devil; God never does, He destroys the wrong and the evil for one purpose only, the deliverance of the good.

The purpose of the sword is to destroy everything that hinders a man being delivered. The first thing in salvation is the element of destruction, and it is this that men object to. With this thought in mind, recall what our Lord said about His own mission: 'Think not that I am come to send peace on earth: I came not to send peace, but a sword.' Our Lord reveals Himself as the destroyer of all peace and happiness, and of ignorance, wherever these are the cloak for sin (cf. Matthew 3:10). It sounds a startling and amazing thing to say that Jesus did not come to send peace, but He said He did not. The one thing Jesus Christ is after is the destruction of everything that would hinder the emancipation of men. The fact that people are happy and peaceful and prosperous is no sign that they are free from the sword of God. If their happiness and peace and well-being and complacency rests on an undelivered life, they will meet the sword before long, and all their peace and rest and joy will be destroyed.

PS 24

*For I say unto you, that except your righteousness shall exceed the righteousness of the scribes and Pharisees, ye shall in no wise enter into the kingdom of heaven.* Matthew 5:20

Take Saul of Tarsus as an example of Pharisaism; he says of himself in writing to the Philippians, 'as touching the law, a Pharisee; ... touching the righteousness which is in the law, blameless ...' (Philippians 3:5–6): Jesus Christ says as disciples we have to exceed that. No wonder we find His statements absolutely shattering. Our righteousness has to be in excess of the righteousness of the man whose external conduct is blameless according to the law—what does that produce? despair straightaway. When we hear Jesus say 'Blessed are the pure in heart', our answer, if we are awake is, 'My God, how am I going to be pure in heart? If ever I am to be blameless down to the deepest recesses of my intentions, You must do something mighty in me.' That is exactly what Jesus Christ came to do. He did not come to *tell us* to be holy, but to *make* us holy, undeserving of censure in the sight of God. If any man or woman gets there it is by the sheer supernatural grace of God. You can't indulge in pious pretence when you come to the atmosphere of the Bible. If there is one thing the Spirit of God does it is to purge us from all sanctimonious humbug, there is no room for it.

BE 22


## September 26

*And the Lord God formed man of the dust of the ground, and breathed into his nostrils the breath of life: and man became a living soul.* Genesis 2:7

God made man a mixture of dust and Deity. The dust of a man's body is his glory, not his shame. Jesus Christ manifested Himself in that dust, and He claims that He can presence any man with His own divinity. The New Testament teaches us how to keep the body under and make it a servant.

Drudgery is the outcome of sin, but it has no right to be the rule of life. It becomes the rule of life because we ignore the fact that the dust of the earth belongs to God, and that man's chief end is to glorify God. Unless we can maintain the presence of Divinity in our dust, life becomes a miserable drudgery. If a man lives in order to hoard up the means of living, he does not live at all, he has no time to, he is taken up with one form of drudgery or another to keep things going.

SHH 57


## September 27

*As he came forth of his mother's womb, naked shall he return to go as he came, and shall take nothing of his labour.* Ecclesiastes 5:15

When a man dies he can take nothing he has done or made in his lifetime with him. The only thing he can take with him is what he *is*. There is no warrant in the Bible for the modern speculation of a second chance after death. There may be a second chance. There may be numbers of interesting things—but it is not taught in the Bible. The stage between birth and death is the probation stage.

SHH 65

The Sermon on the Mount produces despair in the heart of the natural man, and that is the very thing Jesus means it to do, because immediately we reach the point of despair we are willing to come to Jesus Christ as paupers and receive from Him. 'Blessed are the poor in spirit'—that is the first principle of the Kingdom. As long as we have a conceited, self-righteous idea that we can do the thing if God will help us, God has to allow us to go on until we break the neck of our ignorance over some obstacle, then we will be willing to come and receive from Him. The bed-rock of Jesus Christ's Kingdom is poverty, not possession; not decisions for Jesus Christ, but a sense of futility, 'I cannot begin to do it.' Then, says Jesus, 'Blessed are you.' That is the entrance, and it takes us a long while to believe we are poor. The knowledge of our own poverty brings us to the moral frontier where Jesus Christ works.

SSM 12

**September 28**

*Wilt thou also disannul my judgment? wilt thou condemn me that thou mayest be righteous?* Job 40:8

Whatever the universe is, it is not tame. A certain type of modern science would have us believe it is, that we can harness the sea and air and earth. Quite true, you can, if you only read scientific manuals and deal with successful experiments; but before long you discover elements which knock all your calculations on the head and prove that the universe is wild and unmanageable. And yet in the beginning God intended man to control it; the reason he cannot is because he twisted God's order; instead of recognizing God's dominion over himself, man became his own god, and by so doing lost control of everything else. (See Genesis 3.)

When Jesus Christ came He was easily Master of the life in the air and earth and sky, and in Him we see the order God originally

181

intended for man. If you want to know what the human race is to be like on the basis of the Redemption, you will find it mirrored in Jesus Christ—a perfect oneness between God and man, no gap; in the meantime there is a gap, and the universe is wild, not tame. Every type of superstition pretends it can rule the universe, the scientific quack proclaims he can control the weather, that he has occult powers and can take the untameable universe and tame it. God says it cannot be done.

BFB 97

*For we wrestle not against flesh and blood, but ... against spiritual wickedness in high places.* Ephesians 6:12

Today spiritualism is having tremendous vogue; men and women are getting into communication with departed spirits and putting themselves in league with the unseen powers. If you have got as far as reading fortunes in tea-cups, *stop.* If you have gone as far as telling fortunes by cards, *stop.* I will tell you why—the devil uses these apparently harmless things to create a fearful curiosity in the minds of men and women, especially young men and women, and it may bring them into league with the angelic forces that hate God, into league with the principalities and the rulers of this world's darkness. Never say, 'What is the harm in it?' Push it to its logical conclusion and ask—'Where will this end?' You are absolutely safe as long as you remain under the shelter of the Atonement; but if you do not—I don't care what your experiences are—you are absolutely unsafe. At any minute dangers may beset you, terrors and darkness may take hold of you and rack your life with terrific perils.

God grant we may keep as far away from these things as we can. But if in the strange providence of God you find you are near a spiritualist meeting, pray, and keep on your praying, and you will paralyse every power of the medium if he is genuine. No spiritualistic séance can continue if there is a Christian anywhere near who knows how to lay hold of God in prayer; no spirits will communicate. I could tell you wonderful stories of how God's power has worked. Blessed be God; Jesus Christ's salvation makes us more than conqueror over the angelic forces.

SHL 29

*And he did not many mighty works there because of their unbelief.*
Matthew 13:58

Redemption is the great outside fact of the Christian faith; it has to do not only with a man's experience of salvation, but with the basis of his thinking. The revelation of Redemption means that Jesus Christ came here in order that by means of His Death on the Cross He might put the whole human race on a redemptive basis, so making it possible for every man to get back into perfect communion with God. 'I have finished the work which thou gavest me to do.' What was finished? The redemption of the world. Men are not *going* to be redeemed; they *are* redeemed. 'It is finished.' It was not the salvation of individual men and women like you and me that was finished: the whole human race was put on the basis of Redemption. Do I believe it? Let me think of the worst man I know, the man for whom I have no affinity, the man who is a continual thorn in my flesh, who is as mean as can be; can I imagine that man being presented 'perfect in Christ Jesus'? If I can, I have got the beginning of Christian thinking. It ought to be an easy thing for the Christian who thinks to conceive of any and every kind of man being presented 'perfect in Christ Jesus', but how seldom we do think! If I am an earnest evangelical preacher I may say to a man, 'Oh yes, I believe God can save you', while in my heart of hearts I don't believe there is much hope for him. Our unbelief stands as the supreme barrier to Jesus Christ's work in men's souls. 'And he did not many mighty works there because of their unbelief.'

CHI 8

*Not as though I had already attained, either were already perfect: but I follow after, if that I may apprehend that for which also I am apprehended of Christ Jesus.* Philippians 3:12

We have to build up useful associations in our minds, to learn to associate things for ourselves, and it can only be done by determination. There are ideas associated in each of our minds that are not associated in the mind of anyone else, and this accounts for the difference in individuals. For instance, learn to associate the chair you sit in with nothing else but study; associate a selected secret place with nothing but prayer. We do not sufficiently realize the power we have to infect the places in which we live and work by our prevailing habits in those places.

The law of associated ideas applied spiritually means that we must drill our minds in godly connections. How many of us have learned to associate our summer holidays with God's Divine purposes? to associate the early dawn with the early dawn on the Sea of Galilee after the Resurrection? If we learn to associate ideas that are worthy of God with all that happens in Nature, our imagination will never be at the mercy of our impulses. Spiritually, it is not a different law that works, but the same law. When once we have become accustomed to connecting these things, every ordinary occurrence will serve to fructify our minds in godly thinking because we have developed our minds along the lines laid down by the Spirit of God. It is not done once for always; it is only done *always*. Never imagine that the difficulty of doing these things belongs peculiarly to you, it belongs to everyone. The character of a person is nothing more than the habitual form of his associations.

MFL 99

**October 2**

*Jesus, the author and perfecter of our faith.* Hebrews 12:2 RV

The business of faith is to convert Truth into reality. What do you really believe? Take time and catalogue it up; are you converting your belief into reality? You say, 'I believe God has sanctified me' —does your actual life prove He has? 'I believe God has baptized me with the Holy Ghost'—why? Because you had cold shivers and visions and marvellous times of prayer? The proof that we are baptized with the Holy Ghost is that we bear a strong family like-ness to Jesus, and men take knowledge of us, as they did of the disciples after Pentecost, that we have been with Jesus, they can recognize the family likeness at once ...

There is a great snare especially in evangelical circles of knowing the will of God as expressed in the Bible without the slightest practical working of it out in the life. The Christian religion is the most practical thing on earth. If the Holy Spirit has given you a vision in your private Bible study or during a meeting which made your heart glow, and your mind expand, and your will stir itself to grasp, you will have to pay to the last farthing in concentration along that line until all you saw in vision is made actual.

CHI 58

### October 3

*Furnish your ... brotherliness with Christian love.* 2 Peter 1:7 (Moffatt)

Love, to most of us, is an indefinite thing; we do not know what we mean when we speak of love. The love Paul mentions in 1 Corinthians 13 means the sovereign preference of my person for another person, and everything depends on who the other person is. Jesus demands that the sovereign preference be for Him. We cannot love to order, and yet His word stands—'If any come to me, and *hate not* his father, and mother, and wife, and children, and brethren, and sisters, yea, and his own life also' (i.e. a hatred of every loyalty that would divide the heart from loyalty to Jesus), 'he cannot be my disciple.' Devotion to a Person is the only thing that tells; and no man on earth has the love which Jesus demands, unless it has been imparted to him. We may admire Jesus Christ, we may respect Him and reverence Him; but apart from the Holy Ghost we do not love Him.

GH 57

### October 4

*Who shall ascend into the hill of the Lord? and who shall stand in his holy place? He that hath clean hands, and a pure heart ...* Psalm 24:3–4

Today we are in danger of being caught up in the lure of wrong roads to the Kingdom—'Things must be worked out at once, we cannot wait, there must be results immediately.' If to benefit mankind is the whole purpose of God, quicker results could be produced apart from the Redemption, because the Redemption works appallingly slowly, according to our human standards. If all that is necessary is this hand-to-mouth business there is no need for all the teaching of Jesus, no need for patience until God's purposes are fully worked out. To look on the precepts of the Sermon on the Mount as referring to a future dispensation is to rob the Cross of its meaning. If Jesus Christ cannot alter me now, so that the altera-

185

tion shows externally in my home life, in my business life, when is He going to alter me? What is going to transform me so that I can love my enemies, can pray for those that persecute me, if I cannot do it now? No suffering or discipline on my part will make me any different; the only thing that will make me different is being born again into the Kingdom of God. To look for death to make me holy is to make out that death, which is 'the last enemy', is going to do what the Atonement cannot do. The Cross of Christ alone makes me holy, and it does so the second I am willing to let it.

The Kingdom of God is latent in the Cross, but don't spiritualize the Kingdom into vagueness, and don't materialize it into non-spirituality ... To say that the Kingdom is going to be brought in by the earth being swept clean through wars and cataclysms is not true; you cannot introduce the Kingdom in that way, it is impossible. Nothing can bring in the Kingdom saving the Redemption, which works in personal lives through the Cross and in no other way.

GW 53

### October 5

*Again I say unto you, That if two of you shall agree on earth ...*
Matthew 18:19

Agreement in purpose on earth must not be taken to mean a predetermination to agree together to storm God's fort doggedly till He yields. It is far from right to agree beforehand over what we want, and then go to God and wait, not until He gives us His mind about the matter, but until we extort from Him permission to do what we had made up our minds to do before we prayed; we should rather agree to ask God to convey His mind and meaning to us in regard to the matter. Agreement in purpose on earth is not a public presentation of persistent begging which knows no limit, but a prayer which is conscious that it is limited through the moral nature of the Holy Ghost. It is really 'symphonizing' on earth with our Father who is in heaven.

DPR 41

Be yourself exactly before God, and present your problems, the things you know you have come to your wits' end about. Ask what you *will*, and Jesus Christ says your prayers will be answered. We

186

can always tell whether our will is in what we ask by the way we live when we are not praying.

IYA 13

## October 6

*I am the way, and the truth, and the life.* John 14:6

However far we may drift, we must always come back to these words of our Lord: 'I am the way'—not a road that we leave behind us, but the way itself. Jesus Christ is the way *of* God, not a way that leads to God; that is why He says—'Come unto *me*'; 'abide in *me*'. 'I am the truth', not the truth about God, not a set of principles, but the truth itself. Jesus Christ is the Truth *of* God. 'No man cometh unto the Father, but by me.' We can get to God as Creator in other ways, but no man can come to God as Father in any other way than by Jesus Christ (cf. Matthew 11:27). 'I am the life.' Jesus Christ is the Life *of* God as He is the Way and the Truth of God. Eternal life is not a gift *from* God, it is the gift of *God Himself.* The life imparted to me by Jesus is the life of God. 'He that hath the Son hath the life'; 'I am come that they might have life'; 'And this is life eternal, that they should know thee the only true God'. We have to abide in the *way*; to be incorporated into the *truth*; to be infused by the *life.*

SSY 92

## October 7

*I am the way* ... John 14:6

Our Lord said, '*I am the way*,' not the way to any one or anything; He is not a road we leave behind us, He is the Way to the Father in which we abide (John 15:4). He *is* the Way, not He was the Way, and there is not any way of living in the Fatherhood of God except by living in Christ. 'Whoso findeth himself in Christ findeth life.' The Way to the Father is not by the law, nor by obedience, or creed, but Jesus Christ Himself, He is the Way of the Father whereby any and every soul may be in peace, in joy, and in divine courage.

DP 137

*I am* ... *the truth.* John 14:6

Truth is not a system, not a constitution, nor even a creed; the Truth is the Lord Jesus Christ Himself, and He is the Truth about the

187

Father just as He is the Way of the Father. Our tendency is to make truth a logical statement, to make it a principle instead of a Person. Profoundly speaking there are no Christian principles, but the saint by abiding in Christ in the Way of the Fatherhood of God discerns the Truth of God in the passing moments.

DP 138

*I am ... the life.* John 14:6
The superb declaration of our Lord, 'I am the life,' comes with eternal succour. He is the Life of the Father just as He is the Father's Way and the Father's Truth....

Let us remember that Jesus Christ is Life, and our life, 'all our fresh springs are in Him', so that whether we eat or drink, or whatsoever we do, let us do all to the glory of God.

DP 139

October 8

*I am the door ...* John 10:9
This is a picture of the life we are to live as God's children—entering in by our Lord, who is the Door, not once for all, but every day, for everything. Is there trouble in the physical domain? enter in by the Door and be saved. Trouble in mental matters? enter in and be saved. A thousand and one things make up life as it is and in them all we have to learn to enter in by the Door. Entering in, in the Name of Jesus, is the condition of daily salvation, not salvation from sin only, but a salvation that keeps us manifestly the Lord's sheep.

Are you experiencing daily salvation, or are you shut out from Jesus Christ just now in your bodily life, in your mind, in your circumstances? is there any fog, any darkness, any weariness, any trouble? Every day there are things that seem to shut the way up, but you can always enter in by the Door and experience salvation. In the East it is the body of the shepherd himself that is the door of the fold.

We are apt to have the idea that salvation is a kind of watertight compartment and if we enter in all our liberty will be destroyed. That is not our Lord's conception; He says 'he shall go in and go out'. Are we entering in by the Door for our daily work or only at a devotional meeting? The going in and out is our Lord's picture of the freedom of a son. A servant cannot go in and out as he likes, but Jesus says, 'Henceforth I call you not servants ... but I have called you friends.' Nothing is closed to you once you enter in by the Door.

GW 110

**October 9**

*And he from within shall answer and say, Trouble me not: the door is now shut ...* Luke 11:7

There is a time in spiritual life when God does not seem to be a friend. Everything was clear and easily marked and understood for a while, but now we find ourselves in a condition of darkness and desolation. The parable of the importunate friend is the illustration Jesus gives of how the Heavenly Father will appear in times of spiritual confusion—as a man who does not care for his friends. We are in need, or our friends or our homes are in need, and though we go to God who has been our Friend all through, He does nothing at all. It is as if Jesus said to His disciples—'There are times when the Heavenly Father will look like that, but don't give up, remember I have told you—*everyone that asks receives.*' In the meantime the friendship of God is completely shrouded. There are things that have no explanation, but maintain your relationship to God, 'hang in' in confidence in Him, and the time will come when everything will be explained. It is only by going through the confusion that we shall get at what God wants us to get at.

Never say God has done what He has not done because it sounds better to say it; never pretend to have an answer when you have not. Jesus said 'Everyone that asketh receiveth'; we say—'I have asked but I have not received.' It is because we ask in spiritual confusion. Jesus said to James and John: 'Ye know not what ye ask'; they were brought into fellowship with Jesus Christ's cup and baptism, but not in the way they expected.

PH 95

**October 10**

*Whither shall I go from thy spirit? or whither shall I flee from thy presence?* Psalm 139:7

The Psalmist states that the presence of God is the secure accompaniment of His knowledge; not only does God know everything

189

about him, but He is with him in the knowledge. Where is the place that God is not?—hell? No, hell is God; if there were no God, there would be no hell. 'If I make my bed in hell, behold, thou art there.' The first thing 'the fool' does is to get rid of God ('The fool hath said in his heart, There is no God,' Psalm 14:1); then he gets rid of heaven and hell; then he gets rid of all moral consequences—no such thing as right and wrong. The Psalmist is stating that wherever he may go in accordance with the indecipherable Providence of God, there the surprising presence of God will meet him. Immediately you begin to forecast and plan for yourself God will break up your programme, He delights to do it, until we learn to live like children based on the knowledge that God is ruling and reigning and rejoicing, and His joy is our strength. When we say—'even there shall thy hand lead me, and thy right hand shall hold me', there is no foreboding anxiety, because 'His love in times past' enables us to rest confidently in Him. The only rest there is is in this abandon to the love of God. There is security from yesterday—'Thou hast beset me behind'; security for tomorrow—'and before'; and security for today, 'and laid thine hand upon me'. It was this knowledge that gave our Lord the imperturbable peace He always had. We must be like a plague of mosquitoes to the Almighty, with our fussy little worries and anxieties, and the perplexities we imagine, all because we won't get into the elemental life with God which Jesus came to give.

BE 86–7

## October 11

*Therefore we will sing my songs to the stringed instruments all the days of our life in the house of the Lord.* Isaiah 38:20

Jesus Christ taught hypocrisy to His disciples! 'But thou, when thou fastest, anoint thy head, and wash thy face, that thou be not seen of men to fast.' Don't say you are fasting, or that you spent the night in prayer, wash your face; and never let your dearest friend know what you put yourself through. Natural stoicism was created by God, and when it is transfigured by the indwelling Holy Ghost, people will never think of you. 'He must increase, but I must decrease.' John is not saying that with a quivering mouth, or out of modesty; he is expressing the spiritual delight of his life. I am to decrease because He has come! He says it with a manly thrill. Is Jesus Christ

190

increasing in my life, or am I taking everything for myself? When I get disillusioned I see Him and Him alone, there are no illusions left. It is a matter of indifference how I am hurt, the one thing I am concerned about is that every man may be presented 'perfect in Christ Jesus'.

PH 57

October 12

*But when thou doest alms, let not thy left hand know what thy right hand doeth.* Matthew 6:3

Do good until it is an unconscious habit of the life and you do not know you are doing it, you will be covered with confusion when Jesus Christ detects it. 'Lord, when saw we thee an hungred, and fed thee? ... Inasmuch as ye have done it unto one of the least of these my brethren, ye have done it unto me.' That is our Lord's magnanimous interpretation of kind acts that people have never allowed themselves to think of. Get into the habit of having such a relationship to God that you do good without knowing you do it, then you will no longer trust your own impulse, or your own judgment, you will trust only the inspiration of the Spirit of God. The mainspring of your motives will be the Father's heart, not your own; the Father's understanding, not your own. When once you are rightly related to God, He will use you as a channel through which His disposition will flow.

SSM 57

Much of our modern philanthropy is based on the motive of giving to the poor man because he deserves it, or because we are distressed at seeing him poor. Jesus never taught charity from those motives: He said, 'Give to him that asketh thee, not because he deserves it, but because I tell you to.' The great motive in all giving is Jesus Christ's command. We can always find a hundred and one reasons for not obeying our Lord's commands, because we will trust our reasoning rather than His reason, and our reason does not take God into calculation. How does civilization argue? 'Does this man deserve what I am giving him?' Immediately you talk like that, the Spirit of God says, 'Who are you? Do *you* deserve more than other men the blessings you have?'

SSM 46

191

*The Son of man is come eating and drinking: and ye say, Behold a gluttonous man, and a winebibber.* Luke 7:34

We are all so abominably serious, so interested in our own characters, that we refuse to behave like Christians in the shallow concerns of life. Our safeguard is the God-given shallowness. It is the attitude of a spiritual prig to go about with a countenance that is a rebuke to others because you have the idea that they are shallower than you. Live the surface common-sense life in a common-sense way, and remember that the shallow concerns of life are as much of God as the profound concerns. It is not our devotion to God or our holiness that makes us refuse to be shallow, but our wish to impress others that we are not shallow, which is a sure sign that we are prigs. We are to be of the stamp of our Lord and Master, and the prigs of His day called Him a glutton and a winebibber, they said He was not dealing with the profound things. Beware of the production of contempt for others by thinking that they are shallow. To be shallow is not a sign of being wicked: the ocean has a shore. The shallow amenities of life are appointed of God and are the things in which our Lord lived, and He lived in them as the Son of God. It is easier for personal pride not to live in them. Beware of posing as a profound person; God became a Baby.

NKW 68

*Verily I say unto you, That the publicans and the harlots go into the kingdom of God before you.* Matthew 21:31

Read the New Testament, and you will find that Jesus Christ did not get into a moral panic over the things that rouse us. We are staggered at immorality, but Jesus faced those things in the most amazingly calm way. When He was roused to a state of passionate indignation it was by people who were never guilty of such things. What our Lord continually faced was the disposition behind either the morality or the immorality. 'If I had not come and spoken unto them, they had not had sin ...' (John 15:22). Any man would have known without His coming that it was wrong to take life, the law is written in him; any man would have known that immorality was wrong; but no man apart from Jesus Christ would believe that 'my right to myself' is the very essence of sin. When we realize what Jesus means when He says, 'If you would be my disciple, give up your right to yourself to me', we begin to understand that 'the carnal mind is enmity against God'. 'I will not give up my right to myself; I will serve God as I choose.' Jesus Christ came to remove this disposition of self-realization.

BSG 12

### October 15

*But of him are ye in Christ Jesus, who was made unto us ... sanctification.* 1 Corinthians 1:30

The stars do their work without fuss; God does His work without fuss, and saints do their work without fuss. The people who are always desperately active are a nuisance; it is through the saints who are one with Him that God is doing things all the time. The broken and the jaded and the twisted are being ministered to by God through the saints who are not overcome by their own panic, who because of their oneness with Him are absolutely at rest, consequently He can work through them. A sanctified saint remains perfectly confident in God, because sanctification is not something the Lord gives me, sanctification is *Himself in me*. There is only one holiness, the holiness of God, and only one sanctification, the sanctification that has its origin in Jesus Christ. A sanctified saint is at leisure from himself and his own affairs, confident that God is bringing all things out well.

PH 41

### October 16

*Search me, O God, and know my heart: try me and know my thoughts ...* Psalm 139:23

We must live scrutinized by God, and if you want to know what the scrutiny of God is like, listen to Jesus Christ: 'for from within, out of the heart of men evil thoughts proceed ...', and then follows a rugged catalogue of things few of us know anything about in conscious life, consequently we are apt to be indignant and resent Jesus Christ's diagnosis—'I have never felt like a murderer, or an adulterer, therefore those things cannot be in me.' To talk in that way is proof that we are grossly ignorant of ourselves. If we prefer

193

to trust our ignorant innocence we pass a verdict on the only Master of the human heart there is, we tell Him He does not know what He is talking about. The one right thing to do is to listen to Jesus Christ and then hand our hearts over to God to be searched and guarded, and filled with the Holy Spirit, then the wonderful thing is that we never need know and never shall know in actual experience the truth of Jesus Christ's revelation about the human heart. But if we stand on our own rights and wisdom at any second an eruption may occur in our personal life and we shall discover to our unutterable horror that what Jesus said is appallingly true.

SHL 47–8

### October 17

*Then goeth he, and taketh to him seven other spirits more wicked than himself: and they enter in, and dwell there: and the last state of that man is worse than the first.* Luke 11:26

Men say—'I can't help committing sin'; 'I can't help doing this thing'. Are they right? Perfectly right. You may talk to further orders about a weak will; there is nothing more absurd. It is not the man's weak will; he has got into league with a power stronger than he is, and when once a man gets in league with the prince of this world, I defy all his strength of will to stand before the terrific power of this world's darkness for one second. According to the New Testament, there is such a thing as obsession by unclean, malicious, wicked spirits who will damn and ruin body and soul in hell. A moral empty heart is the resort of these spirits when a man is off his guard. But if a man has been born again of the Spirit of God and is keeping in the light, he cannot help going right because he is backed by the tremendous power of Almighty God. What does the Apostle John say?—'the evil one toucheth him not'. What a marvellous certainty! God grant we may be so filled with the Holy Spirit that we listen to His checks along every line. No power can deceive a child of God who keeps in the light with God.

SHL 31

194

*How much more shall the blood of Christ, who through the eternal Spirit offered himself without spot to God, purge your conscience from dead works to serve the living God?* Hebrews 9:14

Forgiveness means not merely that I am saved from sin and made right for heaven (no man would accept forgiveness on such a level); forgiveness means that I am forgiven into a recreated relationship, into identification with God in Christ.

The background of God's forgiveness is holiness. If God were not holy there would be nothing in His forgiveness. There is no such thing as God overlooking sin; therefore if God does forgive there must be a reason that justifies His doing so. If I am forgiven without being altered by the forgiveness, forgiveness is a damage to me and a sign of the unmitigated weakness of God. When a man is convicted of sin he knows God dare not forgive him; if He did it would mean that man has a bigger sense of justice than God. God, in forgiving a man, gives him the heredity of His own Son, i.e. He turns him into the standard of the Forgiver. Forgiveness is a revelation—hope for the hopeless; that is the message of the Gospel.

A man may say, 'I don't deny that God will forgive me, but what about the folks I have put wrong? Can God give me a clearing-house for my conscience?' It is because these things are neglected in the presentation of Redemption that men are kept away from Jesus Christ. Men are kept away by honesty more than by dishonesty.

SA 18

*But he that lacketh these things is blind.* 2 Peter 1:9

When Christ is formed in us we have to see that our human nature acts in perfect obedience to all that the Son of God reveals. God does not supply us with character, He gives us the life of His Son and we can either ignore Him and refuse to obey Him, or we can so obey Him, so bring every thought and imagination into captivity, that the life of Jesus is manifested in our mortal flesh. It is not a question of being saved from hell, but of being saved in order to manifest the Son of God in our mortal flesh. Our responsibility is to keep ourselves fit to manifest Him ...

The only way to keep yourself fit is by the discipline of the disagreeable. It is the disagreeable things which make us exhibit whether we are manifesting the life of the Son of God, or living a life which is antagonistic to Him. When disagreeable things happen, do we manifest the essential sweetness of the Son of God or the essential irritation of ourselves apart from Him? Whenever self comes into the ascendant, the life of the Son of God in us is perverted and twisted; there is irritation, and His life suffers. Growth in grace stops the moment we get huffed.

GH 74–5

### October 20

*Ye are a chosen generation ... that ye should shew forth the praises of him who hath called you out of darkness into his marvellous light.*
1 Peter 2:9

Imitation is one of the first reactions of a child, it is not sinful. We come to a right knowledge of ourselves by imitating others. The instinct that makes us afraid of being odd is not a cowardly instinct, it is the only power of self-preservation we have. If you live much by yourself you become an oddity, you never see the quirks in yourself. Some people won't live with others spiritually, they live in holes and corners by themselves. The New Testament warns of those who 'separate themselves' (Jude 19). By the grace of God we are taken out of the fashion we were in and we become more or less speckled birds. Immediately you introduce a standard of imitation which the set to which you belong does not recognize, you will experience what Peter says, 'they think it strange that ye run not with them to the same excess of riot' (1 Peter 4:4).

The Spirit of God lifts the natural reaction of imitation into another domain and by God's grace we begin to imitate our Lord and shew forth His praises. It is the natural instinct of a child to imitate his mother, and when we are born again the Holy Spirit lifts this instinct into the spiritual domain and it becomes the most supernaturally natural thing for us to imitate our Lord. We grow in grace naturally, not artificially. Mimicking is the counterfeit of imitation and produces the 'pi' person, one who tries his level best to be what he is not. When you are good you never try to be. It is natural to be like the one we live with most; then if we spend most of our time with Jesus Christ, we shall begin to be like Him, by the way we are built naturally and by the Spirit God puts in.

MFL 70

*... bringing into captivity every thought to the obedience of Christ.*
2 Corinthians 10:5

Most of us object to giving up the energy of our minds to form the mind of Christ.... We construct the mind of Christ in the same way as we construct the natural mind, viz. by the way our disposition reacts when we come in contact with external things. The mind is closely affiliated with its physical machine, the brain, and we are responsible for getting that machine into right habits. 'Glean your thinking,' says Paul (see Philippians 4:8). Never submit to the tyrannous idea that you cannot look after your mind; you can.... We have to rouse ourselves up to think, to bring 'every thought into captivity to the obedience of Christ'. Never pray about evil thoughts, it will fix them in the mind. 'Quit'—that is the only thing to do with anything that is wrong; to ruthlessly grip it on the threshold of your mind and allow it no more way. If you have received the Holy Spirit, you will find that you have the power to bring 'every thought into captivity to the obedience of Christ'.

MFL 49

Isaiah says that a man takes a tree and cuts it in two, uses part to cook his food, and the other part he carves into an idol to worship. 'None of us do that!' we say; but we *do*. There are other things which are wooden besides trees, viz., our heads! We use one half of our heads to earn our living, and the other half to worship God.

SA 25

*Lay up for yourselves treasures in heaven.* Matthew 6:20

If you are going to succeed in anything in this world, you must concentrate on it, practise it, and the same is true spiritually. There are many things you will find you cannot do if you are going to be concentrated on God, things that may be perfectly legitimate and right for others, but not for you if you are going to concentrate on God. Never let the narrowness of your conscience condemn the other man. Maintain the personal relationship, see that you yourself are concentrated on God, not on your convictions or your point of view, but on God. Whenever you are in doubt about a thing, push it to its logical conclusion—'Is this the kind of thing that Jesus Christ is after or the kind of thing Satan is after?' Immediately your decision is made, act on it.

SSM 63

### October 23

*Having their conscience seared.* 1 Timothy 4:2

The human eye may be damaged by gazing too much on intense whiteness, as in the case of snow blindness when men remain blind for months. And conscience may be damaged by tampering with the occult side of things, giving too much time to speculation; then when we turn to human life we are as blind as bats. It may be all right for angels to spend their time in visions and meditation, but if I am a Christian I find God in the ordinary occurrences of my life. The special times of prayer are of a different order. If I sequester myself and press my mind on one line of things and forget my relation to human life, when I do turn to human affairs I am morally blind. Am I trying to embrace a sensation of God spiritually for myself? When God has saved and sanctified us there is a danger that we are unwilling to let the vision fade; we refuse to take up our ordinary work, and soon we will be completely at a loss because we have hugged an experience to our souls instead of maintaining a right relationship to God who gave us the experience.

GH 70

### October 24

*Meditate upon these things.* 1 Timothy 4:15

Meditation is not being like a pebble in a brook, allowing the waters of thought to flow over us; that is reverie. Meditation is the most intense spiritual act, it brings every part of body and mind into harness. To be spiritual by effort is a sure sign of a false relationship to God; to be obedient by effort in the initial stages is a sure sign that we are determined to obey God at all costs. Take time. Remember we have all the time there is. The majority of us waste time and want to encroach on eternity. 'Oh well, I will think about these things when I have time.' The only time you will have is the day after you are dead, and that will be eternity. An hour, or half an hour, of daily attention to, and meditation on, our own spiritual life is the secret of progress.

MFL 65

*Pray without ceasing.* 1 Thessalonians 5:17

There is a quietism of devotional self-indulgence which takes the place spiritually that loafing does socially. It is easy to call it meditative prayer, but meditation is only attained in actual life by the strenuous discipline of brooding in the centre of a subject.... A saint is never consciously a praying one. A saint endeavours consciously and strenuously to master the technical means of expressing God's life in himself. The place of prayer in the New Testament is just this one of severe technical training in which spiritual sympathies are sustained in unsecular strength, and manifested in the vulgar details of actual life.

DPR 13

### October 25

*And Abraham drew near, and said ...* Genesis 18:23

The meaning of intercession is that we see what God is doing, consequently there is an intimacy between the child and the Father which is never impertinent. We must pour into the bosom of God the cares which give us pain and anxiety in order that He may solve for us, and before us, the difficulties which we cannot solve. We injure our spiritual life when we dump the whole thing down before God and say—You do it. That spirit is blind to the real union with God. We must dump ourselves down in the midst of our problems and watch God solve them for us. 'But I have no faith' bring your problems to God and stay with Him while He solves them, then God Himself and the solution of your problems will be for ever your own. Watch the tendency to pathetic humbug in your approach to God. If we could see the floor of God's immediate presence, we would find it strewn with the 'toys' of God's children who have said—This is broken, I can't play with it any more, please give me another present. Only one in a thousand sits down in the midst of it all and says—I will watch my Father mend this.

NKW 76

I think sometimes we will be covered with shame when we meet the Lord Jesus and think how blind and ignorant we were when He brought people around us to pray for, or gave us opportunities of warning, and instead of praying we tried to find out what was wrong. We have no business to try and find out what is wrong, our business is to pray, so that when the awakening comes Jesus Christ will be the first they meet.

PS 34

### October 26

*And when thou prayest, thou shalt not be as the hypocrites are: for they love to pray standing in the synagogues and in the corners of the streets, that they may be seen of men.* Matthew 6:5

You perhaps have not noticed before that you always take care to tell those to whom it matters how early you rise in the morning to pray, how many all nights of prayer you spend; you have great zealousness in proclaiming your protracted meetings. This is all pious play-acting. Jesus says, 'Don't do it.' Our Lord did not say it was wrong to pray in the corners of the street, but He did say it was wrong to have the motive to be 'seen of men'. It is not wrong to pray in the early morning, but it is wrong to have the motive that it should be known...

Let the words come home to us personally in their New Testament setting, 'But *when* ye pray, use not vain repetitions.' Our Lord prayed the same prayer, using the same words, three times in the Garden of Gethsemane, and He gave the disciples a form of prayer which He knew would be repeated throughout the Christian centuries; so it cannot be mere repetition or the form of words that He is referring to. The latter half of the verse comes home better for personal purposes—'for they think that they shall be heard for their much speaking'—that is, Do not rely on your earnestness as the ground for being heard...

The phrase 'pray through' often means working ourselves up into a frenzy of earnestness in which perspiration is taken for inspiration. It is a mistake to think we are heard on the ground of our earnestness; we are heard on the ground of the evangelical basis, 'Having therefore, brethren, boldness to enter into the holiest by the blood of Jesus' (Hebrews 10:19).

DPR 18–20

*If ye abide in me, and my words abide in you, ye shall ask what ye will, and it shall be done unto you.* John 15.7

We hear it said that a man will suffer in his life if he does not pray; I question it. Prayer is an interruption to personal ambition, and no man who is busy has time to pray. What will suffer is the life of God in him, which is nourished not by food but by prayer. If we look on prayer as a means of developing ourselves, there is nothing in it at all, nor do we find that idea of prayer in the Bible. Prayer is other than meditation; it is that which develops the life of God in us. When a man is born from above, the life of the Son of God begins in him, and he can either starve that life or nourish it. Prayer is the way the life of God is nourished. Our Lord nourished the life of God in Him by prayer; He was continually in contact with His Father. We generally look upon prayer as a means of getting things for ourselves, whereas the Bible idea of prayer is that God's holiness and God's purpose and God's wise order may be brought about, irrespective of who comes or who goes. Our ordinary views of prayer are not found in the New Testament.

IYA 9

*As thou, Father, art in me, and I in thee, that they also may be one in us.* John 17:21

Prayer is not getting things from God, that is a most initial stage; prayer is getting into perfect communion with God; I tell Him what I know He knows in order that I may get to know it as He does. Jesus says, 'Pray because you have a Father, not because it quietens you, and give Him time to answer.'

SSM 59

God does not exist to answer our prayers, but by our prayers we come to discern the mind of God, and that is declared in John 17, 'That they may be one, even as we are one.' Am I as close to Jesus as that? God will not leave me alone until I am. God has one prayer He must answer, and that is the prayer of Jesus Christ. It does not matter how imperfect or immature a disciple may be, if he will hang in, that prayer will be answered.

IYA 55

The great thought which we do not realize sufficiently is the inter-changing action of the Divine Spirit and the human spirit. This inter-changing action of the Divine and human at every stage of our religious life is vividly expressed in Romans 8:26. The best example of the Divine Spirit working in a human spirit is seen in our Lord Jesus Christ in the days of His flesh. According to some expositors, we are so infirm that the Spirit of God brushes aside all our infirmities and prays irrespectively of us, but we find that our Lord recognized the difference between His own Spirit and the Spirit of God, and that His mind was always in subordination to the mind of God. 'I can of mine own self do nothing.'

IYA 99

## October 29

*Men ought always to pray, and not to faint.* Luke 18:1

Jesus also taught the disciples the prayer of patience. If you are right with God and God delays the manifested answer to your prayer, don't misjudge Him, don't think of Him as an unkind friend, or an unnatural father, or an unjust judge, but keep at it, your prayer will certainly be answered, for 'everyone that asketh receiveth'. 'Men ought always to pray, and not to faint,' i.e. not to cave in. 'Your heavenly Father will explain it all one day,' Jesus says, 'He cannot just now because He is developing your character.'

SSM 59

A man will get from life everything he asks for, because he does not ask for that which his will is not in. If a man asks wealth from life, he will get wealth, or he was playing the fool when he asked. 'If ye abide in me,' says Jesus, 'and my words abide in you, ye shall ask *what ye will,* and it shall be done unto you.' We pray pious blether, our will is not in it, and then we say God does not answer; we never *asked* Him for anything. Asking means that our wills are in what we ask.

You say, 'But I asked God to turn my life into a garden of the Lord, and there came the ploughshare of sorrow, and instead of a garden I have been given a wilderness.' God never gives a wrong answer. The garden of your natural life had to be turned into ploughed soil before God could turn it into a garden of the Lord.

He will put the seed in now. Let God's seasons come over your soul, and before long your life will be a garden of the Lord.

SSM 85

**October 30**

*The holy scriptures, which are able to make thee wise unto salvation.* 2 Timothy 3:15
Am I learning how to use my Bible? The way to become complete for the Master's service is to be well soaked in the Bible; some of us only exploit certain passages. Our Lord wants to give us continuous instruction out of His word; continuous instruction turns hearers into disciples. Beware of 'spooned meat' spirituality, of using the Bible for the sake of getting messages; use it to nourish your own soul. Be a continuous learner, don't stop short, and the truth will open to you on the right hand and on the left until you find there is no problem in human life with which the Bible does not deal. But remember that there are certain points of truth our Lord cannot reveal to us until our character is in a fit state to bear it. The discernment of God's truth and the development of character go together.
The life God places in the Christian worker is the life of Jesus Christ, which is continually changing spiritual innocence into glorious practical character.

AUG 34

**October 31**

*My God, my God, why hast thou forsaken me?* Matthew 27:46
The cry on the Cross is unfathomable to us. The only ones—and I want to say this very deliberately—the only ones who come near the threshold of understanding the cry of Jesus are not the martyrs, they knew that God had not forsaken them, His presence was so wonderful; not the lonely missionaries who are killed or forsaken, they experience exultant joy, for God is with them when men forsake them: the only ones who come near the threshold of understanding the experience of God-forsakenness are men like Cain—'My punishment is greater than I can bear', men like Esau, '...an exceeding bitter cry', men like Judas. Jesus Christ knew and tasted to a fuller
203

depth than any man could ever taste what it is to be separated from God by sin. If Jesus Christ was a martyr, our salvation is a myth. We have followed cunningly devised fables if Jesus Christ is not all that this cry represents Him to be—the Incarnate God becoming identified with sin in order to save men from hell and damnation. The depth of this cry of Jesus is deeper than any man can go because it is a cry from the heart of God. The height and depth of our salvation are only measured by God Almighty on His throne and Jesus Christ in the heart of hell.

PS 18

*A Lamb as it had been slain.* Revelation 5:6

In the days of His flesh Jesus Christ exhibited this Divine paradox of the Lion and the Lamb. He was the Lion in majesty, rebuking the winds and demons: He was the Lamb in meekness, 'who when He was reviled, reviled not again'. He was the Lion in power, raising the dead: He was the Lamb in patience—who was 'brought as a lamb to the slaughter, and as a sheep before her shearers is dumb, so He openeth not His mouth'. He was the Lion in authority, 'Ye have heard that it hath been said...*but I say unto you...*': He was the Lamb in gentleness, 'Suffer the little children to come unto me...and he took them up in his arms, put his hand upon them and blessed them.'

In our personal lives Jesus Christ proves Himself to be all this—He is the Lamb to expiate our sins, to lift us out of condemnation and plant within us His own heredity of holiness: He is the Lion to rule over us, so that we gladly say, 'the government of this life shall be upon His shoulders'. And what is true in individual life is to be true also in the universe at large. The time is coming when the Lion of the Tribe of Judah shall reign, and when 'the kingdoms of this world shall become the kingdoms of our Lord, and of his Christ'.

One remaining paradox—In Revelation 6:16 'the wrath of the Lamb' is mentioned. We know what the wrath of a lion is like—but *the wrath of the Lamb!*—it is beyond our conception. All one can say about it is that the wrath of God is the terrible obverse side of the love of God.

CHI 121

204

*To every thing there is a season, and a time to every purpose under heaven.* Ecclesiastes 3:1

The dispensations of God are discernible only to the Spirit of God. If we mistake the dispensations of God to mean something we can see, we are off the track. Solomon is strong on the fact that God has made certain unalterable durations, but he does not say, as St Augustine and Calvin did, that therefore God is tied up by His own laws...

There are certain dispensational things for which God is responsible, e.g. birth and death...Within the limits of birth and death I can do as I like; but I cannot make myself un-born, neither can I escape death, those two limits are there. I have nothing to do with placing the limits, but within them I can produce what my disposition chooses. Whether I have a distressful time or a joyful time depends on what I do in between the limits of the durations.

SHH 22-3

No man's destiny is made for him, each man makes his own. Fatalism is the deification of moral cowardice which arises from a refusal to accept the responsibility for choosing either of the two destined ends for the human race—salvation or damnation. The power of individual choice is the secret of human responsibility. I can choose which line I will go on, but I have no power to alter the destination of that line once I have taken it yet I always have the power to get off one line on to the other.

OPG 50

*And God commanded the man, saying...of the tree of the knowledge of good and evil, thou shalt not eat of it: for in the day that thou eatest thereof thou shalt surely die.* Genesis 2:16–17.

If I am going to find out a thing scientifically, I must find it out by curiosity; but if I want to find out anything on the moral line, I can only do it by obedience. God put man in a garden with the tree of knowledge of good and evil, and said, 'Ye shall not eat of it.' God did not say they were not to know good and evil, but that they were not to know good and evil by eating of the tree. They were intended to know evil in the way Jesus Christ knew it, viz., by contrast with good. They did eat of the tree, consequently the human race knows good by contrast with evil. Adam knew evil positively and good negatively, and none of us knows the order God intended. No man who has eaten of the fruit of the tree knows evil by contrast with good. The curiosity of the human heart finds out the bad things first. The fruit of the tree of the knowledge of good and evil gives the bias of insatiable curiosity on the bad line, and it is only by the readjustment through Jesus Christ that the bias on the other line enters in—a tremendous thirst after God. Jesus Christ knew evil negatively by positively knowing good; He never ate of the tree, and when a man is reborn of the Spirit of God that is the order.

SA 71

### November 4

*Moreover, the profit of the earth is for all: the king himself is served by the field.* Ecclesiastes 5:9

'In the sweat of thy brow shalt thou eat thy bread, cursed is the ground for thy sake, thorns also and thistles shall it bring forth to thee.' The earth is cursed because of man's apostasy, and when that apostasy ceases in actual history, the ground will no longer bring forth the curse. The final redemption includes 'new heavens and a new earth'. 'Instead of the thorn shall come up the fir tree'; and 'the wolf shall dwell with the lamb'. Instead of the savage ferocity of the beasts, there will be the strength without the savageness—an inconceivable order of things just now.

In anything like a revolution or a war, we find what Solomon refers to here is true, that to make profit you must go back to the dust you came from. The curious thing about civilization is that it tends to take men away from the soil, and makes them develop an artificial existence away from the elemental. Civilization has become an elaborate way of doing without God, and when civilized life is hit a smashing blow by any order of tyranny, most of us have not a leg to stand on. Solomon reminds us that king and peasant alike can only gain their profit by proper tillage of the soil. The laws given in the Bible include a scheme for the treatment of the earth and they insist on proper rest being given to the land, and make it clear that that alone will bring profit in actual existence.

SHH 61

*A man's life consisteth not in the abundance of the things which he possesseth.* Luke 12:15

The first thing God does with us after sanctification is to 'force through the channels of a single heart' the interests of the whole world by introducing into us the nature of the Holy Ghost.... When we are born from above the realization dawns that we are built for God, not for ourselves. We are brought, by means of new birth, into the individual realization of God's great purpose for the human race, and all our small, miserable, parochial notions disappear.

If we have been living much in the presence of God, the first thing that strikes us is the smallness of the lives of men and women who do not recognize God. It did not occur to us before, their lives seemed to be broad and generous; but now there seems such a fuss of interests that have nothing whatever to do with God's purpose, and are altogether unrelated to the election of God. It is because people live in the things they possess instead of in their relationship to God, that God at times seems to be cruel. There are a thousand and one interests that God's providential hand has to brush aside as hopelessly irrelevant to His purpose, and if we have been living in those interests, we go with them.

SSY 103

*For ye know the grace of our Lord Jesus Christ, that, though he was rich, yet for your sakes he became poor, that ye through his poverty might be rich.* 2 Corinthians 8:9

Our Lord Jesus Christ became poor for our sakes not as an example, but to give us the unerring secret of His religion. Professional Christianity is a religion of possessions that are devoted to God; the religion of Jesus Christ is a religion of personal relationship to God, and has nothing whatever to do with possessions. The disciple is rich not in possessions, but in personal identity. Voluntary poverty was the marked condition of Jesus (Luke 9:58), and the poverty of God's children in all ages is a significant thing. Today we are ashamed and afraid to be poor. The reason we hear so little about the inner spiritual side of external poverty is that few of us are in the place of Jesus, or of Paul. The scare of poverty will knock the spiritual backbone out of us unless we have the relationship that holds. The attitude of our Lord's life was that He was disconnected with everything to do with things that chain people down to this world, consequently He could go wherever His Father wanted Him to.

AUG 24

### November 7

*There is nothing better for a man than that he should eat and drink, and that he should make his soul enjoy good in his labour. This also I saw, that it was from the hand of God.* Ecclesiastes 2:24

One great essential lesson in Christianity is that God's order comes to us in the haphazard. We are men and women, we have appetites, we have to live on this earth, and things do happen by chance; what is the use of saying they do not? 'One of the most immutable things on earth is mutability.' Your life and mine is a bundle of chance. It is absurd to say it is fore-ordained for you to have so many buttons on your tunic, and if that is not fore-ordained, then nothing is. If things were fore-ordained, there would be no sense of responsibility at all. A false spirituality makes us look to God to perform a miracle instead of doing our duty. We have to see that we do our duty in faith in God. Jesus Christ undertakes to do everything a man cannot do, but not what a man can do. Things do happen by chance, and if we know God, we recognize that His order comes to us in that way. We live in this haphazard order of things, and we have to maintain the abiding order of God in it. The doctrine of the Sacrament teaches the conveying of God's presence to us through the common elements of bread and wine. We are not to seek success or prosperity. If we can get hold of our relationship to God in eating and drinking, we are on the right basis of things.

SHH 17

### November 8

*Naked came I out of my mother's womb, and naked shall I return thither: the Lord gave, and the Lord hath taken away: blessed be the name of the Lord.* Job 1:21

Facing facts as they are produces despair, not frenzy, but real downright despair, and God never blames a man for despair. The man who thinks must be pessimistic; thinking can never produce

208

optimism. The wisest man that ever lived said that 'he that increaseth knowledge increaseth sorrow'. The basis of things is not reasonable, but wild and tragic, and to face things as they are brings a man to the ordeal of despair. Ibsen presents this ordeal, there is no defiance in his presentation, he knows that there is no such thing as forgiveness in Nature, and that every sin has a Nemesis following it. His summing up of life is that of quiet despair because he knows nothing of the revelation given of God by Jesus Christ.

'Blessed are they that mourn.' Our Lord always speaks from that basis, never from the basis of the 'gospel of temperament'. When a man gets to despair he knows that all his thinking will never get him out, he will only get out by the sheer creative effort of God, consequently he is in the right attitude to receive from God that which he cannot gain for himself.

BFB 11

*And Job spoke, and said, Let the day perish wherein I was born, and the night in which it was said, There is a man child conceived.* Job 3:2-3

Optimism is either a matter of accepted revelation or of temperament; to think unimpeded and remain optimistic is not possible. Let a man face facts as they really are, and pessimism is the only possible conclusion. If there is no tragedy at the back of human life, no gap between God and man, then the Redemption of Jesus Christ is 'much ado about nothing'. Job is seeing things exactly as they are. A healthy minded man bases his life on actual conditions, but let him be hit by bereavement, and when he has got beyond the noisy bit and the blasphemous bit, he will find, as Job found, that despair is the basis of human life unless a man accepts a revelation from God and enters into the Kingdom of Jesus Christ.... It is a good thing to be careful in our judgment of other men. A man may utter apparently blasphemous things against God and we say, 'How appalling'; but if we look further we find that the man is in pain, he is maddened and hurt by something. The mood he is talking in is a passing one and out of his suffering will come a totally different relationship to things. Remember, that in the end God said that the friends had not spoken the truth about Him, whilst Job had.

BFB 16, 21

November 10

*God commendeth his love towards us, in that, while we were yet sinners, Christ died for us.* Romans 5:8

If you have had no tension in your life, never been screwed up by problems, your morality well within your own grasp, and someone tells you that God so loved you that He gave His Son to die for you, nothing but good manners will keep you from being amused. The majority of people who have never been touched by affliction see Jesus Christ's death as a thing beside the mark. When a man gets to his wits' end and things go hard with him, his thick hide is pierced and he is stabbed wide awake, then for the first time he begins to see something else—'At last I see; I thought that He was stricken, smitten *of God* and afflicted; but now I see He was wounded for *my* transgressions.'

The great fundamental revelation regarding the human race is that God has redeemed us; and Redemption enters into our lives when we are upset enough to see we need it. It is an insult today to tell some men and women to cheer up. One of the most shallow, petty things that can be said is that 'every cloud has a silver lining'. There are some clouds that are black all through. At the wall of the world stands God with His arms outstretched; and when a man or woman is driven there, the consolations of Jesus Christ are given. Through the agonies in human life we do not make Redemption, but we see why it was necessary for God to make it. It is not necessary for every man to go through these agonies, but it takes a time of agony to get the shallow scepticism knocked out of us. It is a good thing to be reverent with what we do not understand. A moral agony gives a man 'a second wind', and he runs better after it, and is a good deal more likely to win.

SA 16

November 11

*And Jesus was in the hinder part of the ship, asleep on a pillow.* Mark 4:38

The incident recorded in Mark 4:35–41 is not an incident in the life of a man, but in the life of God as Man. This Man asleep in the boat is God Incarnate. Jesus had said to the disciples, 'Let us go over unto the other side,' but when the storm arose, instead of relying upon Him, they failed Him. The actual circumstances were so

210

crushing that their common sense was up in alarm, their panic carried them off their feet, and in terror they awoke Him. When we are in fear, we can do nothing less than pray to God, but our Lord has the right to expect of those who name His Name and have His nature in them, an understanding confidence in Him. Instead of that, when we are at our wits' end we go back to the elementary prayers of those who do not know Him, and prove that we have not the slightest atom of confidence in Him and in His government of the world: He is asleep—the tiller is not in His hand, and we sit down in nervous dread. God expects His children to be so confident in Him that in a crisis they are the ones upon whom He can rely. A great point is reached spiritually when we stop worrying God over personal matters or over any matter. God expects of us the one thing that glorifies Him—and that is to remain absolutely confident in Him, remembering what He has said beforehand, and sure that His purposes will be fulfilled.

PH 39

### November 12

*Peace I leave with you, my peace I give unto you.* John 14:27

We talk about the peace of Jesus, but have we ever realized what that peace was like? Read the story of His life, the thirty years of quiet submission at Nazareth, the three years of service, the slander and spite, backbiting and hatred He endured, all unfathomably worse than anything we shall ever have to go through; and His peace was undisturbed, it could not be violated. It is that peace that God will exhibit in us in the heavenly places; not a peace like it, but that peace. In all the rush of life, in working for our living, in all conditions of bodily life, wherever God engineers our circumstances—'My peace'; the imperturbable, inviolable peace of Jesus imparted to us in every detail of our lives. 'Your life is hid with Christ in God.' Have we allowed the wonder of it to enwrap us round and soak us through until we begin to realize the ample room there is to grow there? 'The secret place of the Most High', absolutely secure and safe.

OBH 34

211

*It is enough for the disciple that he be as his master, and the servant as his lord.* Matthew 10:25

In the East the women sing as they grind the corn between the millstones; and 'the sound of the millstones' is music in the ears of God. The worldling does not think it music, but the saint who is being made into bread knows that his Father knows best, and that He would never allow the suffering if He had not some purpose. Ill-tempered people, hard circumstances, poverty, wilful misunderstandings and estrangements, are all millstones. Had Jesus any of these things in His own life? He had a devil in His company for three years; He lived at home with brothers and sisters who did not believe in Him; He was continually thwarted and misunderstood by the Pharisees, and He says, 'the disciple is not above his master'. If we have the tiniest element of self-pity in us God dare not put us anywhere near the millstones. When these experiences come, remember God has His eyes on every detail.

SHL 117–18

Now we can see why our Lord lived the life He did for thirty-three years. Before He made the entrance into that life possible for any human being, He had to show us what the life of God's normal man was like. The life of Jesus is the life we have to live here, not hereafter. There is no chance to live this kind of life hereafter, we have to live it here.

PR 80

*Whosoever therefore shall humble himself as this little child, the same is greatest in the kingdom of heaven.* Matthew 18:4

When the disciples were discussing who should be the greatest, Jesus took a little child in His arms and said, 'Unless you become like that, you will never see the kingdom of heaven.' He did not put up a little child as an ideal; if He had, He would have destroyed the whole principle of His teaching. If humility were put up as an ideal it would serve only to increase pride. Humility is not an ideal, it is the unconscious result of the life being rightly related to God and centred in Him. Our Lord is dealing with ambition, and had He put up a little child as a standard, it would simply have altered the manifestation of ambition. What is a little child? We all know what a child is until we are asked, and then we find we do not know. We can mention his extra goodness or his extra badness, but none of this is the child himself. We know implicitly what a child is, and we know implicitly what Jesus Christ means, but as soon as we try to put it into words it escapes. A child works from an unconscious principle within, and if we are born again and are obeying the Holy Spirit, we shall unconsciously manifest humility all along the line. We shall easily be the servant of all men, not because it is our ideal, but because we cannot help it. Our eye is not consciously on our service, but on our Saviour.

There is nothing more awful than conscious humility, it is the most Satanic type of pride.

BP 186

### November 15

*Except a grain of wheat fall into the earth and die, it abideth by itself alone; but if it die, it beareth much fruit.* John 12:24

Death is God's delightful way of giving us life. The monks in the early ages shut themselves away from everything to prove they were dead to it all, and when they got away they found themselves more alive than ever. Jesus never shut Himself away from things, the first place He took His disciples to was a marriage feast. He did not cut Himself off from society, He was not aloof, so much was He not aloof that they called Him 'a gluttonous man, and a wine-bibber'! But there was one characteristic of Jesus—He was fundamentally dead to the whole thing, it had no appeal to Him. The 'hundredfold' which Jesus promised means that God can trust a man anywhere and with anything when he is fundamentally dead to things....

We use the phrase 'drawing on the resurrection life of Jesus', but try it, you cannot draw on it when you like. You will never get one breath of that life until you are dead, that is, dead to any desire that you want a blessing for body or soul or spirit. Immediately you die to that, the life of God is in you, and you don't know where you are with the exuberance of it.

IWP 80

*And when he is come he will convict ... of sin.* John 16:8

We are apt to put conviction of sin in the wrong place in a man's life. The man of all men who experienced conviction of sin was the saintly apostle Paul. 'For I was alive without the law once: but when the commandment came, sin revived, and I died' (Romans 7:9). There is no mention of conviction of sin in Paul's account of his conversion, only conviction of darkness and distress and of being out of order. But after Paul had been three years in Arabia with the Holy Ghost blazing through him, he began to write the diagnoses of sin which we have in his Epistles....

If you want to know what sin is, don't ask the convicted sinner, ask the saint, the one who has been awakened to the holiness of God through the Atonement; he is the one who can begin to tell you what sin is. The man writhing at the penitent form is affected because his sins have upset him, but he has very little knowledge of sin. It is only as we walk in the light as God is in the light that we begin to understand the unfathomable depths of cleansing to which the blood of Jesus Christ goes (1 John 1:7).

PS 64–5

*He wakeneth mine ear to hear as the learned.* Isaiah 50:4

Have we learned the habit of listening to what God says? Have we added this resolute hearing in our practical life? We may be able to give a testimony as to what God has done for us, but does the life we live evidence that we are not listening now, but living only in the memory of what we once heard? We have to keep our ears trained to detect God's voice, to be continually renewed in the spirit of our mind. If when a crisis comes we instinctively turn to God, we know that the habit of hearkening has been formed. At the beginning there is the noisy clamour of our own misgivings; we are so taken up with what we have heard that we cannot hear any more. We have to hearken to that which we have not listened to before, and to do it we must be insulated on the inside.

'He wakeneth mine ear to hear as the learned.' Once a week at least read the Sermon on the Mount and see how much you have hearkened to it — 'Love your enemies, bless them that curse you'; we do not listen to it because we do not want to. We have to learn to

214

hearken to Jesus in everything, to get into the habit of finding out what He says. We cannot apply the teachings of Jesus unless we are regenerated, and we cannot apply all His teachings at once. The Holy Spirit will bring back to our remembrance a certain word of our Lord's and apply it to the particular circumstances we are in, the point is—are we going to obey it? 'Whosoever ... heareth my sayings, and *doeth* them ...' When Jesus Christ brings a word home, never shirk it.

GH 54

### November 18

*If any man will do his will, he shall know of the doctrine, whether it be of God, or whether I speak of myself.* John 7:17

*If ye know these things, happy are ye if you do them.* John 13:17

If you believe in Jesus, you will not spend all your time in the smooth waters just inside the harbour, full of exhilaration and delight, but always moored; you will have to go out through the harbour bar into the great deeps of God and begin to know for yourself, begin to get spiritual discernment. If you do not cut the moorings, God will have to break them with a storm and send you out. Why not unloosen and launch all on God and go out on the great swelling tide of His purpose?

'If any man will do his will, he shall know ...' When you know you should do a thing and you do it, immediately you will know more. If you revise where you are stodgy spiritually, you will find it goes back to the point where there was one thing you knew you should do, but you did not do it because there seemed no immediate call to, and now you have no perception, no discernment. Instead of being spiritually self-possessed at the time of crisis, you are spiritually distracted. It is a dangerous thing to refuse to go on knowing.

AHW 118

### November 19

*And the Lord turned the captivity of Job when he prayed for his friends.* Job 42:10

Have you come to 'when' yet? If you are in the position of Job and have shipped some trouble on board that makes you taken up with yourself, remember that when Job prayed for his friends, God

215

emancipated him. Pray for your friends, and God will turn your captivity also. The emancipation comes as you intercede for them; it is not a mere reaction, it is the way God works. It is not a question of getting time for Bible study, but of spontaneous intercession as we go about our daily calling, and we shall see emancipation come all along, not because we understand the problems, but because we recognize that God has chosen the way of intercession to perform His moral miracles in lives. Then get to work and pray, and God will get His chance with other lives; you do not even need to speak to them. God has based the Christian life on Redemption, and as we pray on this basis God's honour is at stake to answer prayer.

BFB 109

### November 20

*Enter into thy closet, and when thou hast shut thy door, pray to thy Father which is in secret.* Matthew 6:6

Prayer that is not an effort of the will is unrecognized by God. 'If ye abide in me, and my words abide in you, ye shall ask what ye will and it shall be done unto you,' said Jesus. That does not mean ask anything you like, but ask what you *will*. What are you actively willing? ask for that. We shall find that we *ask* very few things.

MFL 59

Think how long our Lord has waited for you; you have seen Him in your visions, now pray to Him; get a place, not a mood, but a definite material place and resort to it constantly, and pray to God as His Spirit in you will help you....

Do it now, *'enter into thy closet'*; and remember, it is a place selected to pray in, not to make little addresses in, or for any other purpose than to pray in, never forget that.

DPR 31, 33

### November 21

*Praying...for me, that utterance may be given unto me...* Ephesians 6:19

We naturally suppose it is no use praying for 'Paul', for prominent people, God will look after them all right. The prominent people

216

for God are marked for the wiles of the devil, and we must pray for them all the time; God gives us every now and again an alarming exhibition of what happens if we don't.

IYA 36

The prayers of the saints either enable or disable God in the performance of His wonders. The majority of us in praying for the will of God to be done say, 'In God's good time', meaning 'in my bad time'; consequently there is no silence in heaven produced by our prayers, no results, no performance.

HGM 79

When we pray we give God a chance to work in the unconscious realm of the lives of those for whom we pray. When we come into the secret place it is the Holy Ghost's passion for souls that is at work, not our passion, and He can work through us as He likes.

SSM 59

### November 22

*What is that to thee?* John 21:22

A disciple is one who minds neither his own business nor any one else's business, but looks steadfastly to Jesus and goes on following Him. We read books about the consecration of other men, but it is as so much scaffolding, it all has to go, and the time comes when there is only one thing left—following Jesus. One of the severest lessons we get comes from our stubborn refusal to see that we must not interfere in other people's lives. It takes a long time to realize the danger of being an amateur providence, i.e. interfering with God's order for others. We see a certain person suffering and we say, 'He shall not suffer; I will see that he does not,' and we put our hand straight in front of God's permissive will to prevent it, and He has to say, 'What is that to thee?' We cause delays to God by persistently doing things in our own way.

SSY 70

*Ye that have escaped the sword, go ye, stand not still; remember the Lord from afar and let Jerusalem come into your mind.* Jeremiah 51:50

'And let Jerusalem', the God-lit city, 'come into your mind'. Ask yourself—'What do I let come into my mind?' If a man lets his garden alone, it pretty soon ceases to be a garden; and if a saint lets his mind alone, it will soon become a garbage patch for Satan's scarecrows. Read the terrible things that Paul says will grow in the mind of a saint unless he looks after it (e.g. Colossians 3:5). The command to let Jerusalem come into our mind means we have to watch our intellect and devote it for one purpose; let only those things come in that are worthy of the God-lit city. '*Let*'...it is a command. See to it by the careful watching of your mind that only those thoughts come in that are worthy of God. We do not sufficiently realize the need to pray when we lie down at night, 'Deliver us from the evil one.' It puts us in the attitude of asking the Lord to watch our minds and our dreams, and He will do it.

PS 31

*Yield yourselves unto God, as those that are alive from the dead, and your members as instruments of righteousness unto God.* Romans 6:13

When I am born again my human nature is not different, it is the same as before, I am related to life in the same way, I have the same bodily organs, but the mainspring is different, and I have to see now that all my members are dominated by the new disposition (see Romans 5:13, 19). There is only one kind of human nature, and that is the human nature we have all got; and there is only one kind of holiness, the holiness of Jesus Christ. Give Him 'elbow-room', and He will manifest Himself in you, and other people will recognize Him. Human beings know human beings too well to mistake where goodness comes from; when they see certain characteristics they will know they come only from the indwelling of Jesus. It is not the manifestation of noble human traits, but of a real family likeness of Jesus. It is *His* gentleness, *His* patience, *His* purity, never mine. The whole art of spirituality is that my human nature should retire and let the new disposition have its way.

CHI 21

*Though he slay me, yet will I trust in him.* Job 13:15

We sometimes wrongly illustrate faith in God by the faith of a business man in a cheque. Faith commercially is based on calculation, but religious faith cannot be illustrated by the kind of faith we exhibit in life. Faith in God is a terrific venture in the dark; I have to believe that God is good in spite of all that contradicts it in my experience. It is not easy to say that God is love when everything that happens actually gives the lie to it. Everyone's soul represents some kind of battlefield. The point for each one is whether we will hang in, as Job did, and say 'Though things look black, I will trust in God'...

The basis of a man's faith in God is that God is the Source and Support of all existence, not that He is all existence. Job recognizes this, and maintains that in the end everything will be explained and made clear. Have I this kind of faith—not faith in a principle, but faith in *God*, that He is just and true and right? Many of us have no faith in God at all, but only faith in what He has done for us, and when these things are not apparent we lose our faith and say, 'Why should this happen to me? Why should there be a war? Why should I be wounded and sick? Why should my "cobber" be killed? I am going to chuck up my faith in God.'

BFB 100

*It is good that, thou shouldest take hold of this; yea, also from this withdraw not thine hand: for he that feareth God shall come forth of them all.* Ecclesiastes 7:18

Don't be fanatically religious and don't be irreverently blatant. Remember that the two extremes have to be held in the right balance. If your religion does not make you a better man, it is a rotten religion. The test of true religion is when it touches these four things—food, money, sex and mother earth. These things are the test of a right sane life with God, and the religion that ignores them or abuses them is not right. God made man of the dust of the ground, and that dust can express either Deity or devilishness. Remember we are to be not numbskulls, but holy men, full-blooded and holy to the last degree, not anaemic creatures without enough strength to be bad. The relation to life ordained by Jesus Christ does not unsex men and women but enables them to be holy men and women. 'The love of money is a root of all kinds of evil' (1 Timothy 6:10). Money is a test, another thing which proves a man's religion; and the way a man treats the soil will also prove whether or not he is a son of God. A man needs to hold a right attitude to all these things by means of his personal relationship to God.

SHH 99

### November 27

*I must work the works of him that sent me, while it is day.* John 9:4
The majority of us are blind on certain lines, we see only in the light of our prejudices. A searchlight lights up only what it does and no more, but the daylight reveals a hundred and one facts that the searchlight had not taken into account. An idea acts like a searchlight and becomes tyrannous. Take a man with an idea of evolution; as you listen to him the way seems perfectly clear, life is not difficult at all; but let the daylight of actual experience come across his path, and there are a thousand and one facts which the idea cannot account for, because they do not come into the simple line laid down by the evolutionist. When I am up against problems, I am apt to shut myself up in my own mind and refuse to pay any attention to what anyone says. There are many things which are neither black nor white, but grey. There is nothing simple under heaven saving a man's relationship to God on the ground of the Redemption of Jesus Christ. When Jesus Christ came on the scene, His disciples became impatient and said, 'Why don't you tell us plainly who you are?' Jesus Christ could not, because He could only be discerned through moral obedience. A man who talks like a shell makes the path of a shell, that is, he makes the way straight, but destroys a good deal in doing it. There is another way of reaching the solution of a problem—the long, patient way of solving things. Jesus Christ deliberately took the 'long, long trail'. The temptation of Satan was that He should take the 'short cut'. The temptations of Satan centre round this point: 'You are the Son of God, then do God's work in your own way'; and at the heart of all our Lord's answers was this: 'I came to do My Father's work in His way, not in My own way, although I am the Son of God.'

SA 57

220

*For the word of God ... is a discerner of the thoughts and intents of the heart.* Hebrews 4:12

Thinking takes place in the heart, not in the brain. The real spiritual powers of a man reside in the heart, which is the centre of the physical life, of the soul life, and of the spiritual life. The expression of thinking is referred to the brain and the lips because through these organs thinking becomes articulate.

According to the Bible, thinking exists in the heart, and that is the region with which the Spirit of God deals. We may take it as a general rule that Jesus Christ never answers any questions that spring from a man's head, because the questions which spring from our brains are always borrowed from some book we have read, or from someone we have heard speak; but the questions that spring from our hearts, the real problems that vex us, Jesus Christ answers those. The questions He came to deal with are those that spring from the implicit centre. These problems may be difficult to state in words, but they are the problems Jesus Christ will solve.

BP 122

*Thou shalt love the Lord thy God with all thy heart, and with all thy soul, and with all thy mind, and with all thy strength.* Mark 12:30

The outcome of Mark 12:29-31 is God four times over—God the King of my heart, God the King of my soul, God the King of my mind, God the King of my strength; nothing other than God, and the working out of it is that we show the same love to our fellow-men as God has shown us. That is the external aspect of this internal relationship, the sovereign preference of my person for God. The love of the heart for Jesus, the life laid down for Jesus, the mind thinking only for Jesus, the strength given over to Jesus, the will working only the will of God, and the ear of the personality hearing only what God has to say.

IWP 93

Salvation means not only a pure heart, an enlightened mind, a spirit right with God, but that the whole man is comprehended in the manifestation of the marvellous power and grace of God, body, soul and spirit are brought into fascinating captivity to the Lord

Jesus Christ. An incandescent mantle illustrates the meaning. If the mantle is not rightly adjusted only one bit of it glows, but when the mantle is adjusted exactly and the light shines, the whole thing is comprehended in a blaze of light, and every bit of our being is to be absorbed until we are aglow with the comprehensive goodness of God.

SSM 88

*And the Pharisees and scribes murmured . . . and he spake this parable unto them.* Luke 15:2–3

In interpreting our Lord's teaching, watch carefully who He is talking to; the parable of the prodigal son was a stinging lash to the Pharisees. We need to be reminded of the presentation of Jesus in the New Testament for the Being pictured to us nowadays would not perturb anybody; but He aroused His whole nation to rage. Read the records of His ministry and see how much blazing indignation there is in it. For thirty years Jesus did nothing, then for three years He stormed every time He went down to Jerusalem. Josephus says He tore through the Temple courts like a madman. We hear nothing about that Jesus Christ today. The meek and mild Being pictured today makes us lose altogether the meaning of the Cross. We have to find out why Jesus was beside Himself with rage and indignation at the Pharisees and not with those given over to carnal sins. Which state of society is going to stand a ripping and tearing Being like Jesus Christ who drags to the ground the highest respected pillars of its civilized society, and shows that their respectability and religiosity is built on a much more abominable pride than the harlot's or the publican's? The latter are disgusting and coarse, but these men have the very pride of the devil in their hearts.

Ask yourself, then, what is it that awakens indignation in your heart? Is it the same kind of thing that awakened indignation in Jesus Christ? The thing that awakens indignation in us is the thing that upsets our present state of comfort and society. The thing that made Jesus Christ blaze was pride that defied God and prevented Him from having His right with human hearts. 'Calvary' means 'the place of a skull', and that is where our Lord is always crucified, in the culture and intellect of men who will not have self-knowledge given by the light of Jesus Christ.

HG 78

**December 1**

*A time to kill, and a time to heal; a time to break down, and a time to build up.* Ecclesiastes 3:3

Every art, every healing, and every good, can be used for an opposite purpose. Every possibility I have of producing a fine character in time, I can use to produce the opposite; I have that liberty from the Creator. God will not prevent my disobeying Him; if He did, my obedience would not be worth anything. Some of us complain that God should have made the universe and human life like a foolproof machine, so simple that there would be no possibility of going wrong. If He had, we would have been like jelly-fish. If there is no possibility of being damned, there is no need for salvation.

In the time between birth and death, most of us are in our 'shell'. There is something in us which makes us peck, and when the crack comes, instead of its being the gentle light and dawn of a new day, it is like a lightning flash. The universe we awaken to is not one of order, but a great big howling confusion, and it takes time to get adjusted. The distresses we reap in between God's decrees for us, we, together with other human beings, are personally responsible for. If we make our life a muddle, it is to a large extent because we have not discerned the great underlying relationship to God.

SHH 25

**December 2**

*Then touched he their eyes, saying, According to your faith be it done unto you.* Matthew 9:29

In human sight the thing we soon lose is what Ruskin called 'the innocence of the eye'. An artist records exactly from this 'innocence' of sight, he does not bring in his logical faculties and interfere with what he sees by telling himself what he ought to see. Most of us know what we are looking at, and instead of trusting the 'innocence' of sight, we confuse it by trying to tell ourselves what we see. If ever you have been taught by anyone to *see*, you will know what this means. Drummond says that Ruskin taught him to *see*. An artist does not tell us what he sees, he enables us to see; he communicates the unutterable identity of what he sees. It is a great thing to see *with* anyone. Jesus never tells us what to see, but when His touch is upon our eyes, we know that we see what He is seeing, He restores this pristine

223

innocence of sight. 'Except a man be born again, he cannot *see* the kingdom of God.'

SSY 89

### December 3

*The young man saith unto him, All these things have I kept from my youth up: what lack I yet?* Matthew 19:20

No man thinks so clearly at any time or is ever so thrilled as in his 'teens'. The tragedy begins when he finds his actual life cannot be brought up to the standard of the ideal, and he closes with an agony of his own. Then he goes to preachers who talk about the ideal, or to books, thinking he will find the real thing; but too often he does not. He finds the vision there, but not working out in actual practice; and his agony deepens. The ideal presented by Jesus Christ fascinates some men right away; there is something enthralling about Him; but inevitably, sooner or later, they come to the experience of the early disciples recorded in Mark 14:50: 'They all forsook him and fled.' 'I gave all I had to the ideal presented by Jesus Christ, I honestly tried my best to serve Him, but I cannot go on; the New Testament presents ideals beyond my attainment. I won't lower my ideals, although I realize that I can never hope to make them actual.' No man is so laboured or crushed as the man who, with the religion of ideals, finds he cannot carry them out. There are many more men in that attitude than is supposed. Men are kept away from Jesus Christ by a sense of honesty as much as by dishonesty. 'I don't deny that Jesus Christ saves—but if you only knew me!—the mistakes I have made, the wrong things I have done, the blundering things—I should be a perfect disgrace to Him.' Our Lord says to such a one, 'Come unto me... and I will give you rest.' When a man comes, he will realize that Jesus Christ does not tell him to do his best, but—Surrender to Me, and I will put into you that which will make the ideal and the actual one, and you will be able to work out in actual life what you see by the power of vision. Without Jesus Christ there is an unbridgeable gap between the ideal and the actual.

SA 82

**December 4**

*But ye are not in the flesh, but in the spirit, if so be that the Spirit of God dwell in you.* Romans 8:9

If we have the indwelling identification with Jesus Christ, then we are alive, and more and more alive. In the Christian life the saint is ever young; amazingly and boisterously young, certain that everything is all right. A young Christian is remarkably full of impulse and delight, because he realizes the salvation of God; but this is the real gaiety of knowing that we may cast all our cares on Him and that He careth for us. This is the greatest indication of our identification with Jesus Christ.

AUG 90

The one thing about our Lord that the Pharisees found it hard to understand was His gaiety in connection with the things over which they were appallingly solemn. And what puzzled the religious people of Paul's day was his uncrushable gaiety; he treated buoyantly everything that they treated most seriously. Paul was in earnest over one thing only, and that was his relationship to Jesus Christ. There he was in earnest, and there they were totally indifferent.

AHW 96

**December 5**

*The very God of peace sanctify you wholly.* 1 Thessalonians 5:23

By the Fall man not only died from God, but he fell into disunion with himself.... When a man is born again of the Spirit of God he is introduced to life with God and union with himself. The one thing essential to the new life is obedience to the Spirit of God who has energized our spirits; that obedience must be complete in spirit, soul and body. We must not nourish one part of our being apart from the other parts....

God never develops one part of our being at the expense of the other; spirit, soul and body are kept in harmony. Remember, our spirit does not go further than we bring our body. The Spirit of God always drives us out of the visionary, out of the excitable, out of the ecstasy stages, if we are inclined that way. This blind life of the spirit, a life that delights to live in the dim regions of the spirit, refusing to bring the leadings of the Holy Spirit into the rational life, gives occasion to supernatural forces that are not of God. It is impossible to guard our spirit, the only One who can guard all its entrances is

225

God. Never give way to spiritual ecstasy unless there is a chance of working it out rationally, check it every time. Nights and days of prayer and waiting on God may be a curse to our souls and an occasion for Satan. So always remember that the times we have in communion with God must be worked out in the soul and the body.

IWP 32, 33

### December 6

*For by him were all things created ... and he is before all things, and by him all things consist.* Colossians 1:16–17

Our natural life is a fury of desire for the things we can see. That is the meaning of lust—I must have it at once, a fury of desire without any regard for the consequences. I have to be detached from the things I can see and be brought into a living relationship with the Creator of those things. If I am taken up with the created things and forget Jesus Christ I shall find that things disappoint and I get disillusioned. If my body is 'bossed' by personal self-realization I am defiling the temple of the Holy Ghost; I may be moral and upright but I have become ruler over my own life. 'Give up your right to yourself to me,' says Jesus, 'let me realize myself in you.' He quenches the fury of desire by detaching us from things so that we may know Him. In this way God brings us into the fulness of life. The majority of us are not in the place where God can give us 'the hundredfold more'. We say, 'A bird in the hand is worth two in the bush', while God is wanting to give us the bush with all the birds in it! It is necessary to be detached from things and then come back to them in a right relationship. A sense of property is a hindrance to spiritual growth, that is why so many of us know nothing about communion with Jesus Christ.

HGM 111

### December 7

*If thou wilt be perfect ...* Matthew 19:21

The second 'if' is much more penetrating than the first. Entrance into life is through the recognition of who Jesus is, i.e. all we mean by being born again of the Spirit—'If you would enter into life, that is the way.' The second 'if' is much more searching—'If thou wilt be perfect...'—'If you want to be perfect, perfect as I am, perfect as your Father in Heaven is'—then come the conditions. Do we really want to be perfect? Beware of mental quibbling over the word 'perfect'. Perfection does not mean the full maturity and consummation of a man's powers, but perfect fitness for doing the will of God (cf. Philippians 3:12–15). Supposing Jesus Christ can perfectly adjust me to God, put me so perfectly right that I shall be on the footing where I can do the will of God, do I really want Him to do it? Do I want God at all costs to make me perfect? A great deal depends on what is the real deep desire of our hearts. Can we say with Robert Murray McCheyne—'Lord, make me as holy as Thou canst make a saved sinner'? Is that really the desire of our hearts? Our desires come to light always when we press this 'if' of Jesus—'If thou wilt be perfect...'

IWP 116

### December 8

*A good name is better than precious ointment: and the day of death than the day of one's birth.* Ecclesiastes 7:1

Solomon is speaking of character, not of reputation. Reputation is what other people think of you; 'character is what you are in the dark', where no one sees but yourself. That is where the worth of a man's character lies, and Solomon says that the man who has attained a sagacious character during life is like a most refreshing, soothing, healing ointment. In the New Testament, 'name' frequently has the meaning of 'nature'. 'Where two or three are gathered together in my name', i.e. My nature (Matthew 18:20). Everyone who comes across a good nature is made better by it, unless he is determined to be bad. To say a man has a good nature does not mean he is a pious individual, always quoting texts. The test of a nature is the atmosphere it produces. When we are in contact with a good nature we are uplifted by it. We do not get anything we can state articulately, but the horizon is enlarged, the pressure is removed from the mind and heart and we see things differently.

SHH 77

### December 9

*The life which I now live in the flesh I live by the faith of the Son of God...I do not frustrate the grace of God.* Galatians 2:20–1

We are in danger of forgetting that we cannot do what God does

227

and that God will not do what we can do. We cannot save ourselves or sanctify ourselves; God only can do that; but God does not give us good habits, He does not give us character, He does not make us walk aright; we must do all that. We have to work out what God has worked in (Philippians 2:12–13). Many of us lose out spiritually, not because the devil attacks us, but because we are stupidly ignorant of the way God has made us. Remember, the devil did not make the human body; he may have tampered with it, but the human body was created by God, and its constitution after we are saved remains the same as before. For instance, we are not born with a ready-made habit of dressing ourselves; we have to form that habit. Apply it spiritually—when we are born again, God does not give us a fully fledged series of holy habits, we have to make them; and the forming of habits on the basis of God's supernatural work in our souls is the education of our spiritual life.

Many of us refuse to do it; we are lazy and we frustrate the grace of God.

GH 52

### December 10

*Therefore whosoever heareth these sayings of mine, and doeth them, I will liken him unto a wise man, which built his house upon a rock.* Matthew 7:24

We speak of building castles in the air; that is where a castle should be—whoever heard of a castle underground! The problem is how to get the foundation under your castle in the air so that it can stand upon the earth. The way to put foundations under our castles is by paying attention to the words of Jesus Christ. We may read and listen and not make much of it at the time, but by and by we come into circumstances when the Holy Spirit will bring back to us what Jesus said—are we going to obey? Jesus says that the way to put foundations under spiritual castles is by hearing and doing 'these sayings of mine'. Pay attention to His words, and give time to doing it.

Our spiritual castles must be conspicuous, and the test of a building is not its fair beauty but its foundations. There are beautiful spiritual fabrics raised in the shape of books and of lives, full of the finest diction and activities, but when the test comes, down they go. They have not been built on the sayings of Jesus Christ, but built altogether in the air with no foundations under them.

228

'Build up your character bit by bit by attention to My words,' says Jesus, then when the supreme crisis comes, you will stand like a rock. The crisis does not come always, but when it does come, it is all up in about two seconds, there is no possibility of pretence, you are unearthed immediately. If a man has built himself up in private by listening to the words of Jesus and obeying them, when the crisis comes it is not his strength of will that keeps him, but the tremendous power of God—'kept by the power of God'. Go on building yourself up in the word of God when no one is watching you, and when the crisis comes you will find you will stand like a rock; but if you have not been building yourself up on the word of God, you will go down, however strong your will. All you build will end in disaster unless it is built on the sayings of Jesus Christ; but if you are doing what Jesus told you to do, nourishing your soul on His word, you need not fear the crisis whatever it is.

SSM 108–9

### December 11

*Ye search the scriptures: for in them ye think ye have eternal life: and they are they which testify of me.* John 5:39

The Bible is the universe of revelation facts; the natural world is the universe of common-sense facts, and our means of communication with the two universes is totally different. We come in contact with the natural universe by our senses, our intellect has to be curious. Scientific knowledge, which is systematized common sense, is based on intense intellectual curiosity. Curiosity in the natural world is right, not wrong, and if we are not intellectually curious we shall never know anything, God never encourages laziness.

When we come to the universe of the Bible, the revelation facts about God, intellectual curiosity is not of the slightest use. Our senses are no good here, we cannot find out God by searching. We may have inferences from our common-sense thinking which we call God, but these are mere abstractions. We can only get at the facts· that are revealed in the Bible by faith. Faith is not credulity; faith is my personal spirit obeying God. The Bible does not deal in common-sense facts; the natural universe deals in common-sense facts, and we get at these by our senses. The Bible deals with revelation facts, facts we cannot get at by our common sense, facts we may be pleased to make light of by our common sense. For instance, Jesus Christ is a revelation fact, sin is another, the devil is another, the Holy Spirit is another. Not one of these is a common-sense fact. If a man were merely a common-sense individual, he could do very well without God.

PR 20

### December 12

*Pilate saith unto him, What is truth?* John 18:38

The Personality of Truth is the great revelation of Christianity— 'I am the Truth'. Our Lord did not say He was 'all truth' so that we could go to His statements as to a text-book and verify things; there are domains, such as science and art and history, which are distinctly man's domains and the boundaries of our knowledge must continually alter and be enlarged; God never encourages laziness. The question to be asked is not, 'Does the Bible agree with the findings of modern science?' but, 'Do the findings of modern science help us to a better understanding of the things revealed in the Bible?'...

The Bible is a whole library of literature giving us the final interpretation of the Truth, and to take the Bible apart from that one supreme purpose is to have a book and nothing more; and further, to take our Lord Jesus Christ away from the revelation of Him given in the Bible is to be left with one who is open to all the irreverent slanders of unbelief.

'The Truth' is our Lord Himself; 'the whole truth' is the inspired Scripture interpreting the Truth to us; and 'nothing but the truth' is the Holy Spirit, 'the Spirit of truth', efficaciously regenerating and sanctifying us, and guiding us into 'all the truth'.

GW 33, 35

### December 13

*...and that from a child thou hast known the holy scriptures.* 2 Timothy 3:15

It is not the thing on which we spend most time that moulds us, but the thing that exerts the greatest power. Five minutes with God and His word is worth more than all the rest of the day. Do we come to the Bible to be spoken to by God, to be made 'wise unto salvation', or simply to hunt for texts on which to build addresses? There are people who vagabond through the Bible, taking sufficient only out of it for the making of sermons, they never let the word of God walk out of the Bible and talk to them. Beware of living from hand to mouth in spiritual matters; do not be a spiritual mendicant.

AHW 126

*...and my words abide in you...* John 15:7

Are we in the habit of listening to the words of Jesus? Do we realize that Jesus knows more about our business than we do ourselves? Do we take His word for our clothes, our money, our domestic work; or do we think we can manage these things for ourselves? The Spirit of God has the habit of taking the words of Jesus out of their scriptural setting and putting them into the setting of our personal lives.

AHW 121

**December 14**

*The natural man receiveth not the things of the Spirit of God.*
1 Corinthians 2:14

The Bible is the Word of God only to those who are born from above and who walk in the light. Our Lord Jesus Christ, the *Word* of God, and the Bible, the *words* of God, stand or fall together, they can never be separated without fatal results. A man's attitude to our Lord determines his attitude to the Bible. The 'sayings' of God to a man not born from above are of no moment; to him the Bible is simply a remarkable compilation of literature—'that it is, and nothing more'. All the confusion arises from not recognizing this.

DDG 15

If we present the pearls of God's revelation to unspiritual people, God says they will trample the pearls under their feet; not trample us under their feet, that would not matter so much, but they will trample the truth of God under their feet. These words are not human words, but the words of Jesus Christ, and the Holy Spirit alone can teach us what they mean. There are some truths that God will not make simple. The only thing God makes plain in the Bible is the way of salvation and sanctification, after that our understanding depends entirely on our walking in the light. Over and over again men water down the word of God to suit those who are not spiritual,

231

and consequently the word of God is trampled under the feet of 'swine'.

SSM 82

## December 15

  *...the things of the Spirit of God.* 1 Corinthians 2:14

Everywhere the charge is made against Christian people, not only the generality of Christians, but really spiritual people, that they think in a very slovenly manner. Very few of us in this present dispensation live up to the privilege of thinking spiritually as we ought. This present dispensation is the dispensation of the Holy Ghost. The majority of us do not think according to the tremendous meaning of that; we think ante-Pentecostal thoughts, the Holy Spirit is not a living factor in our thinking; we have only a vague impression that He is here. Many Christian workers would question the statement that we should ask for the Holy Spirit (Luke 11:13). The note struck in the New Testament is not 'Believe in the Holy Spirit', but 'Receive the Holy Spirit'. That does not mean the Holy Spirit is not here; it means He *is* here in all His power, for one purpose, that men who believe in Him might receive Him. So the first thing we have to face is the reception of the Holy Spirit in a practical conscious manner.

Always distinguish between yielding to the Spirit and receiving the Spirit. When the Spirit is at work in a time of mighty revival it is very difficult not to yield to the Spirit, but it is quite another thing to receive Him. If we yield to the power of the Spirit in a time of revival we may feel amazingly blessed, but if we do not receive the Spirit we are left decidedly worse and not better. That is first a psychological fact and then a New Testament fact. So as Christians we have to ask ourselves, does our faith stand 'in demonstration of the Spirit and of power'? Have we linked ourselves up with the power of the Holy Ghost, and are we letting Him have His way in our thinking?

BE 95

## December 16

  *...for the Son of man cometh at an hour when ye think not.* Luke 12:40

The element of surprise is always the note of the life of the Holy Ghost in us. We are born again by the great surprise—'The wind

232

bloweth where it listeth, and thou hearest the voice thereof, but knowest not whence it cometh, and whither it goeth: so is every one that is born of the Spirit' (John 3:8). Men cannot tie up the wind, it blows where it lists; neither can the work of the Holy Spirit be tied up in logical methods. Jesus never comes where we expect Him; if He did He would not have said 'Watch'. 'Be ye also ready: for in an hour when ye think not, the Son of man cometh.' Jesus appears in the most illogical connections, where we least expect Him, and the only way a Christian worker can keep true to God amidst the difficulties of work is to be ready for His surprise visits. We have not to depend on the prayers of other people, not to look for the sympathy of God's children, but to be ready for the Lord. It is this intense reality of expecting Him at every turn that gives life the attitude of child wonder that Jesus wants it to have. When we are rightly related to God, life is full of spontaneous joyful uncertainty and expectancy— we do not know what God is going to do next; and He packs our life with surprises all the time.

SSY 34

### December 17

*But ye shall be baptized with the Holy Ghost...* Acts 1:5

Why do we want to be baptized with the Holy Ghost? All depends on that 'why'. If we want to be baptized with the Holy Ghost that we may be of use, it is all up; or because we want peace and joy and deliverance from sin, it is all up. 'He shall baptize you with the Holy Ghost', not for anything for ourselves at all, but that we may be witnesses unto Him. God will never answer the prayer to be baptized with the Holy Ghost for any other reason than to make us witnesses to Jesus. To be consciously desirous of anything but that one thing is to be off the main track. The Holy Ghost is transparent honesty. When we pray, 'Oh Lord, baptize me with the Holy Ghost whatever it means', God will give us a glimpse of our self-interest and self-seeking until we are willing for everything to go and there is nothing left but Himself. As long as there is self-interest and self-seeking, something has to go. God is amazingly patient. The perplexity is not because of the hardness of the way, but the unwilling pride of sin, the stubborn yielding bit by bit, when it might be done any second. The acceptance of the Divine nature involves in it obedience to the Divine precepts. The commands of God are enablings. God banks entirely on His own Spirit, and when we

233

attempt, His ability is granted immediately. We have a great deal more power than we know, and as we do the overcoming we find He is there all the time until it becomes the habit of our life.

The baptism with the Holy Ghost is the great sovereign work of the personal Holy Ghost; entire sanctification is our personal experience of it.

HGM 30

*What shall a man give in exchange for his soul?* Mark 8:37

The modern Christian laughs at the idea of a final judgment. That shows how far we can stray away if we imbibe the idea that the modern mind is infallible and not our Lord. To His mind at least the finality of moral decision is reached in this life. There is no aspect of our Lord's mind that the modern mind detests so fundamentally as this one....

The parables in the 25th chapter of St Matthew are three aspects of the Divine estimate of life. The parable of the ten virgins reveals that it is fatal from our Lord's standpoint to live this life without preparation for the life to come. That is not the exegesis, it is the obvious underlying principle.

The parable of the talents is our Lord's statement with regard to the danger of leaving undone the work of a lifetime.

And the description of the last judgment is the picture of genuine astonishment on the part of both the losers and the gainers of what they had never once thought about.

To be accustomed to our Lord's teaching is not to ask, 'What must I do to be good?' but, 'What must I do to be saved?' How long does it take us to know what the true meaning of our life is? One half second.

HG 73

*Then will I go unto the altar of God, unto God my exceeding joy.* Psalm 43:4

Joy is the great note all through the Bible. We have the notion of joy that arises from good spirits or good health, but the miracle of the joy of God has nothing to do with a man's life or his circumstances or the condition he is in. Jesus does not come to a man and say 'Cheer up', He plants within a man the miracle of the joy of God's own nature. The stronghold of the Christian faith is *the joy of God*, not *my joy in God*. It is a great thing for a man to have faith in the joy of God, to know that nothing alters the fact of God's joy. God reigns and rules and rejoices, and His joy is our strength. The miracle of the Christian life is that God can give a man joy in the midst of external misery, a joy which gives him power to work until the misery is removed. Joy is different from happiness, because happiness depends on what happens. There are elements in our circumstances we cannot help, joy is independent of them all.

'That my joy might remain in you, and that your joy might be full' (John 15:11).

What was the joy of Jesus? That He did the will of His Father, and He wants that joy to be ours.

HGM 48

## December 20

*Jesus said, 'These things have I spoken unto you ... that your joy may be full.'* John 15:11

The one thing about the apostle Paul that staggered his contemporaries was his unaccountable gaiety of spirit: he would not be serious over anything other than Jesus Christ. They might stone him and imprison him, but whatever they did made no difference to his buoyancy of spirit. The external character of the life of our Lord was that of radiant sociability; so much so, that the popular scandal-mongering about Him was that He was 'a gluttonous man and a winebibber, a friend of publicans and sinners!' The fundamental reason for our Lord's sociability was other than they knew; but His whole life was characterized with a radiant fulness, it was not an exhausted type of life. 'Except ye become as little children ...' If a little child is not full of the spontaneousness of life there is something wrong. The bounding life and restlessness is a sign of health, not of naughtiness. Jesus said, 'I am come that they might have life, and that they might have it more abundantly.' Be being filled with the life Jesus came to give. Men who are radiantly healthy, physically and spiritually, cannot be crushed. They are like the cedars of Lebanon, which have such superabounding vitality in their sap that they intoxicate to death any parasites that try to live on them.

PH 198

235

*For I came not to judge the world, but to save the world.* John 12:47
Jesus Christ did not come to pronounce judgment, He Himself is the judgment; whenever we come across Him we are judged instantly.

One of the most remarkable things about Jesus Christ is that although He was full of love and gentleness, yet in His presence everyone not only felt benefited, but ashamed. It is His presence that judges us; we long to meet Him, yet we dread to...

If you look at a sheep in the summer time you would say it was white, but see it against the background of startling virgin snow and it looks like a blot on the landscape. If we judge ourselves by one another we do not feel condemned (see 2 Corinthians 10:12); but immediately Jesus Christ is in the background—His life, His language, His looks, His labours, we feel judged instantly. 'It is for judgment that I have come into the world.' The judgment that Jesus Christ's presence brings makes us pronounce judgment on ourselves, we feel a sense of shame, or of missing the mark, and we determine never to do that thing again.

HGM 42

*He was in the world, and the world was made by him, and the world knew him not.* John 1:10
In every life there is one place where God must have 'elbow room'. We must not pass judgment on others, nor must we make a principle of judging out of our own experience. It is impossible for a man to know the views of Almighty God. Preaching from prejudice is dangerous, it makes a man dogmatic and certain that he is right. The question for each of us to ask ourselves is this: Would I recognize God if He came in a way I was not prepared for—if He came in the bustle of a marriage feast, or as a carpenter? That is how Jesus Christ appeared to the prejudices of the Pharisees, and they said He was mad. Today we are trying to work up a religious revival while God has visited the world in a moral revival, and the majority of us have not begun to recognize it. The characteristics that are manifested when God is at work are self-effacement, self-suppression, abandonment to something or someone other than myself.

BFB 22

## December 23

*The Son of man came eating and drinking, and they say, Behold a man gluttonous, and a winebibber, a friend of publicans and sinners.* Matthew 11:19

'The Son of man came eating and drinking.' One of the most staggering things in the New Testament is just this commonplace aspect. The curious difference between Jesus Christ's idea of holiness and that of other religions lies here. The one says holiness is not compatible with ordinary food and married life, but Jesus Christ represents a character lived straight down in the ordinary amalgam of human life, and His claim is that the character He manifested is possible for any man, if he will come in by the door provided for him.

SA 33

There is in our midst today a strong revival of pagan spirituality. Many are using the terms of Hinduism or Buddhism to expound Christianity, and they end not in expounding Christianity at all, but in expounding the very human experience of consecration, which is not peculiar to Christianity. The peculiar doctrine or Gospel of the Christian religion is Entire Sanctification, whereby God takes the most unpromising man and makes a saint of him.

DL 98

## December 24

*Mine eyes have seen thy salvation.* Luke 2:30

The apostle Paul speaks of 'the foolishness of God' as pitted against 'the wisdom of men', and the wisdom of men when it saw Jesus Christ said, 'That cannot be God.' When the Judaic ritualists saw Jesus Christ, they said, 'You are a blasphemer; you do not express God at all.' Anna and Simeon were the only two of the descendants of Abraham who recognized who Jesus was, hence the condemnation of the other crowd. If two who had lived a life of communion with God could detect Jehovah as the Babe of Bethlehem within the symbolism, the others who did not recognize Him are to be condemned. They did not see Him because they had become blinded on the line of absolute authority, the line of symbolism or creed, and when that which was symbolized appeared, they could not see Him.

BFB 92

*And the angel answered and said unto her, the Holy Ghost shall come upon thee, and the power of the Highest shall overshadow thee: therefore also that holy thing which shall be born of thee shall be called the Son of God.* Luke 1:35

Jesus Christ was born *into* this world, not *from* it. He came into history from the outside of history; He did not evolve out of history.

Our Lord's birth was an advent; He did not come from the human race, He came into it from above. Jesus Christ is not the best human being, He is a Being who cannot be accounted for by the human race at all. He is God Incarnate, not man becoming God, but God coming into human flesh, coming into it from the outside. His Life is the Highest and the Holiest entering in at the lowliest door. Our Lord entered history by the Virgin Mary.

Just as our Lord came into human history from the outside, so He must come into us from the outside. Have we allowed our personal human lives to become a 'Bethlehem' for the Son of God?... The conception of new birth in the New Testament is of something that enters into us, not of something that springs out of us.

PR 29–30

*The Word was made flesh.* John 1:14

In presenting Jesus Christ never present Him as a miraculous Being who came down from heaven and worked miracles and who was not related to life as we are; that is not the Gospel Christ. The Gospel Christ is the Being who came down to earth and lived our life and was possessed of a frame like ours. He became Man in order to show the relationship man was to hold to God, and by His death and resurrection He can put any man into that relationship. Jesus Christ is the last word in human nature.

AUG 44

The revelation given by Jesus Christ of God is not the revelation of Almighty God, but of the essential nature of Deity—unutterable humility and moral purity, utterly worthy in every detail of actual life. In the Incarnation God proves Himself worthy in the sphere in which we live, and this is the sphere of the revelation of the Self-giving of God.

BFB 98

*Not many wise...are called.* 1 Corinthians 1:26

What is as weak as one baby? Another! And so our Lord Himself taught that we must all become babes. No wonder Paul says: 'For ye see your calling, brethren, how that not many wise men after the flesh, not many mighty, not many noble, are called.'

It is the 'baby' weakness which is so misunderstood in the New Testament teaching, and the patience of our Lord with us until we learn the absolute necessity of being born from above is only equalled by His own patience with His Father's will.

DPA 145

Jesus Christ came to make the great laws of God incarnate in human life; that is the miracle of God's grace. We are to be written epistles, 'known and read of all men'. There is no allowance whatever in the New Testament for the man who says he is saved by grace but who does not produce the graceful goods. Jesus Christ by His Redemption can make our actual life in keeping with our religious profession.

SSM 90

*My little children, of whom I am again in travail until Christ be formed in you.* Galatians 4:19

What happened to Mary, the mother of our Lord, historically in the conception of the Son of God has its counterpart in what takes place in every born-again soul. Mary represents the natural individual life which must be sacrificed in order that it may be transfigured into an expression of the real life of the Son of God. The individual life is the husk of the personal life, and because of the forming of the Son of God in me, the sword must go through it. ('Yea, a sword shall pierce through thine own soul'—Luke 2:35.) It is the natural virtues that battle, not sin as we think of sin, but pride, egotism, my temperament, my affinities; all that has to have the sword run clean through it mercilessly by God, and if I stick to my natural inheritance the sword must go through me. The new creation is based on the new man in Christ (see Ephesians 4:24), not on the natural gifts of the first Adam. The natural life is not obliterated,

239

when I come to God in the abandon of faith He creates supernaturally on the basis of His own nature, and the Spirit of God makes me see to it that my natural life is lived in accordance with the new life formed in me. Our Lord can never be spoken of in terms of the natural virtues, they don't apply to Him, and they don't apply to the new man in Christ; all that is taken knowledge of in those possessed by Christ is that they have been with Jesus, the dominating personality that tells is that of the Son of God, it is His life that is being manifested.

GW 63

### December 29

*For what the law could not do, in that it was weak through the flesh, God sending his own Son in the likeness of sinful flesh, and for sin, condemned sin in the flesh: that the righteousness of the law might be fulfilled in us.* Romans 3:8–9

God does not expect us to *imitate* Jesus Christ: He expects us to allow the life of Jesus to be manifested in our mortal flesh. God engineers circumstances and brings us into difficult places where no one can help us, and we can either manifest the life of Jesus in those conditions, or else be cowards and say, 'I cannot exhibit the life of God there.' Then we deprive God of glory. If you will let the life of God be manifested in your particular human edition—where God cannot manifest it, that is why He called you, you will bring glory to God.

The spiritual life of a worker is literally, 'God manifest in the flesh'.

AUG 14

If Jesus Christ is not being manifested in my mortal flesh, I am to blame; it is because I am not eating His flesh and drinking His blood. Just as I take food into my body and assimilate it, so, says Jesus, I must take Him into my soul. 'He that eateth me, even he shall live by me.' Food is not health, and truth is not holiness. Food has to be assimilated by a properly organized system before the result is health, and truth must be assimilated by the child of God before it can be manifested as holiness. We may be looking at the right doctrines and yet not assimilating the truths which the doctrines reveal. Beware of making a doctrinal statement of truth *the* truth—'*I* am...the Truth,' said Jesus. Doctrinal statement is our expression of that vital

240

connection with Him. If we divorce what Jesus says from Himself, it leads to secret self-indulgence spiritually; the soul is swayed by a form of doctrine that has never been assimilated and the life is twisted away from the centre, Jesus Christ Himself.

GH 79

### December 30

*Unto an inheritance incorruptible, and undefiled, and that fadeth not away, reserved in heaven for you.* 1 Peter 1:4

'... reserved in heaven for you.' This is a great conception of the New Testament, but it is a conception lost in modern evangelism. We are so much taken up with what God wants us to be here that we have forgotten heaven. There are one or two conceptions about heaven that have to be traced back to their home to find out whether they have their root in our faith or whether they are foreign flowers. One of these is that heaven is a state and not a place; that is only a partial truth, for there cannot be a state without a place. The great New Testament conception of heaven is 'here-after' without the sin, 'new heavens and a new earth, wherein dwelleth righteousness'—a conception beyond us. Peter is reminding every Christian that there is an undefiled inheritance awaiting us which has never yet been realized, and that it has in it all we have ever hoped or dreamed or imagined, and a good deal more. It is always *better to come* in the Christian life until the *best of all* comes.

PH 201

### December 31

*Old things are passed away.* 2 Corinthians 5:17

By 'old things' Paul does not mean sin and the 'old man' only, he means everything that was our life as natural men before we were re-created in spirit by Christ. That means a great deal more than some of us mean. The 'old things' means not only things that are wrong, any fool will give up wrong things if he can, but things that are right. Watch the life of Jesus and you will get Paul's meaning. Our Lord lived a natural life as we do, it was not a sin for Him to eat, but it would have been a sin for Him to eat during those forty days in the wilderness, because during that time His Father's will for Him was otherwise, and He sacrificed His natural life to the will of God. That is the way the 'old things' pass away.

241

In his Second Epistle to the Corinthians Paul uses as an illustration of this the glory which came from Moses. It was a real glory, but it was a glory that was 'to be done away' (3:7); and the writer to the Hebrews writes of a covenant which was doomed 'to vanish away' (8:13). The natural life of man is a real creation of God, but it is meant to pass away into a spiritual life in Jesus Christ's way. Watch Paul's argument in the Epistle to the Romans—'But ye are not in the flesh, but in the Spirit...' (8:9). Paul was talking to flesh and blood men and women, not to disembodied spirits, and he means that the old order is passed. 'You used to look at things differently from Jesus Christ,' he says, 'but now that you have turned to the Lord' (God grant you may if you have not) 'the veil is taken away', and 'where the Spirit of the Lord is, there is liberty'.

OBH 28

# KEY TO REFERENCES

The letters at the end of each extract refer to titles of works by Oswald Chambers from which the extracts have been taken. Figures indicate page numbers.

# INDEX OF BIBLICAL REFERENCES

248

250